CareerView

CAREER & ACADEMIC READINESS SKILLS BOOK

Steven J. Molinsky
Bill Bliss

Contributing Author
Robert Walsh

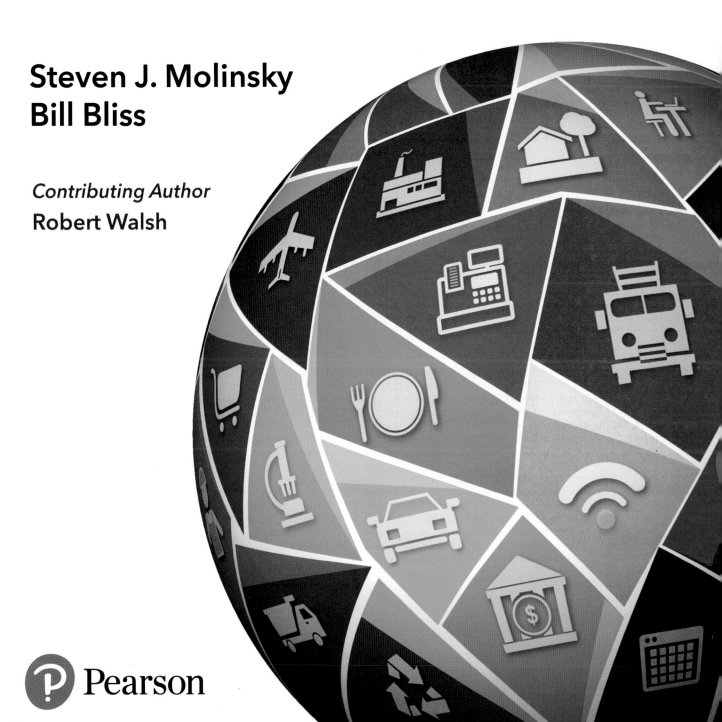

P Pearson

CareerView: Career & Academic Readiness Skills Book

Steven J. Molinsky and Bill Bliss

Pearson Education, 221 River Street, Hoboken, NJ 07030 USA

The O*NET Interest Profiler is part of the O*NET™ Career Exploration Tools.
My Next Move is developed by the National Center for O*NET Development.
O*NET™ is a trademark of the US Department of Labor/Employment and Training Administration (USDOL/ETA).

The characters appearing on pages 20, 45, 61, 79, 95, 113, 131, 173, and 194 are fictitious. No identification with actual persons, living or deceased, is intended or should be inferred.

Staff credits: The people who made up the *CareerView* team are Pietro Alongi, Elizabeth Barker, Jennifer Castro, Tracey Munz Cataldo, Dave Dickey, Gina DiLillo, Warren Fischbach, Pam Fishman, Nancy Flaggman, Lester Holmes, Gosia Jaros-White, Barry Katzen, Stuart Radcliffe, Alex Suarez, and Paula Van Ells.

Cover design: Wendy Wolf

Contributing Author: Robert Walsh

Editorial support: Christine Cervoni, Camelot Editorial Services, LLC

Project management: Jaime E. Lieber, JEL Collaborative, LLC

Text design and composition: Wendy Wolf

Photo Credits

Page 20: Emerald Raindrops/Shutterstock; **22:** Erik Isakson/Tetra Images/Alamy Stock Photo; **23:** Ariel Skelley/DigitalVision/Getty Images; **30:** Monika Wisniewska/123RF; **31 (left):** Serg_v/123RF; **31 (right):** Razor527/Shutterstock; **32:** Dan Kosmayer/Shutterstock; **37:** Bonezboyz/Shutterstock; **38:** Elena Elisseeva/Shutterstock; **39 (bottom, left):** Dmitry Kalinovsky/Shutterstock; **39 (top, right):** Alpa Prod/Shutterstock; **40:** Leonardo Ikeda/Shutterstock; **45:** PR Image Factory/Shutterstock; **46:** Anyaivanova/Shutterstock; **47:** Studio 72/Shutterstock; **48 (top):** RedFoxBrush/Shutterstock; **48 (bottom):** PhotoSky/Shutterstock; **54:** Everett Historical/Shutterstock; **55:** Everett Historical/Shutterstock; **56:** Microolga/123RF; **61:** Cineberg/Shutterstock; **62 (left):** Esbobeldijk/Shutterstock; **63 (bottom, left):** Africa Studio/Shutterstock; **63 (top, right):** Pearson Education Ltd; **62 (bottom right):** Dragon Images/Shutterstock; **64:** Rawpixel Ltd/Alamy Stock Photo; **71:** Michele Falzone/Alamy Stock Photo; **73 (top, left):** Education Images/Universal Images Group/Getty Images; **73 (bottom, left):** View Pictures/Edmund Sumner/VIEW/Newscom; **73 (right):** Michael Wheatley/Alamy Stock Photo; **74:** Hero Images Inc./Alamy Stock Photo; **79:** ESB Professional/Shutterstock; **80:** National Motor Museum/Heritage Image Partnership Ltd/Alamy Stock Photo; **81:** Miroslav110/123RF; **82:** Dolgachov/123RF; **88:** Morsa Images/DigitalVision/Getty Images; **89:** ABK/Corbis/Getty Images; **95:** Paula Solloway/Alamy Stock Photo; **96:** Elenabsl/Shutterstock; **97:** Hero Images Inc./Alamy Stock Photo; **98:** Monkey Business Images/Shutterstock; **104:** Deepadesigns/Shutterstock; **105 (top, left):** Maksbart/Shutterstock; **105 (bottom, right):** Andrea Danti/Shutterstock; **106:** Jackie Niam/Shutterstock; **107:** Aurielaki/Shutterstock; **113:** Nick White and Fiona Jackson Downes/Cultura Creative(RF)/Alamy Stock Photo; **114:** Rido/Shutterstock; **116:** Goodluz/Shutterstock; **124 (top):** Chronicle/Alamy Stock Photo; **124 (center):** Stock Folio 656/Alamy Stock Photo; **124 (bottom):** Monkey Business Images/Shutterstock; **125:** Monkey Business Images/Shutterstock; **126:** Bialasiewicz/123RF; **131:** Dmytro Zinkevych/Shutterstock; **132:** Panuwat phimpha/Shutterstock; **133:** Bloomua/Shutterstock; **134 (left):** Shutter_o/Shutterstock; **134 (right):** Redpixel.PL/Shutterstock; **135:** Baranq/Shutterstock; **142 (bottom, left):** Megan Maloy/Image Source/Shutterstock; **142 (top, right):** Peathegee Inc/Blend Images/Getty Images; **143 (bottom, left):** Wrangler/Shutterstock; **143 (top, right):** Diego Cervo/Shutterstock; **145:** Rawpixel.com/Shutterstock; **146:** Rawpixel.com/Shutterstock; **152:** Phil Coale/AP Images; **153:** Rawpixel.com/Shutterstock; **154 (bottom, left):** Zapp2Photo/Shutterstock; **154 (top, right):** Ssuaphotos/Shutterstock; **155 (center, left):** Metamorworks/Shutterstock; **155 (top, right):** Beros919/Shutterstock; **156:** Tzido Sun/Shutterstock; **164:** Andrey_Popov/Shutterstock; **165:** Andrey_Popov/Shutterstock; **166:** Golubovy/Shutterstock; **167 (top, left):** Serhii Bobyk/Shutterstock; **167 (bottom, right):** Maxim Grigoryev/TASS/Getty Images; **168:** Vectorfusionart/Shutterstock; **173:** Hongqi Zhang/123RF; **174 (top, right):** Akg images/Newscom; **174 (bottom, right):** Cristi180884/Shutterstock; **175 (top, left):** Akg images/Newscom; **175 (top, right):** Mikeledray/Shutterstock; **175 (bottom, right):** FPG/Retrofile RF/Getty Images; **176:** H. Armstrong Robert/Retrofile RF/Getty Images; **177:** Fine Art Images/Heritage Images/Newscom; **178:** Cristi Matei/Shutterstock; **184:** Auremar/Shutterstock; **185:** Luchschen/Shutterstock; **186 (top, left):** Studio 8/Pearson Education Ltd; **186 (bottom, right):** Redpixel.PL/Shutterstock; **187 (top, left):** Gorodenkoff/Shutterstock; **187 (bottom, right):** Arjuna Kodisinghe/Shutterstock; **188:** Redpixel.PL/Shutterstock; **194:** Asiseeit/E+/Getty Images; **195:** Goodluz/Shutterstock; **196:** Goodluz/123RF; **197 (top, left):** Tigergallery/Shutterstock; **197 (bottom, right):** Danil Roudenko/123RF; **198 (top, left):** Zstockphotos/123RF; **198 (bottom, right):** William Perugini/Shutterstock; **199 (top, left):** Charly Morlock/Shutterstock; **199 (bottom, right):** Sergei Primakov/Shutterstock.

Library of Congress Cataloging-in-Publication Data

A catalog record for the print edition is available from the Library of Congress.

ISBN-13: 978-0-13-516531-7

ISBN-10: 0-13-516531-8

Printed in the United States of America

1 18

www.pearsoneltusa.com/careerview

PART A:
SELF-EXPLORATION

PART B:
CAREER & ACADEMIC PREPARATION

CONTENTS

PART C: MY CAREER JOURNEY

SCOPE & SEQUENCE

	Readiness Skills		Standards

PART A
 	
Self-Exploration
	CAREER READINESS
	• Identify interests, skills, values, and personal qualities that influence career and education choices
	• Identify career clusters and related pathways that match career and education goals
	• Identify qualities of an effective employee
	• Identify employability/soft skills (personal qualities, leadership skills, customer care skills) necessary to succeed in post-secondary education, training, and employment (e.g., communication skills, responsibility, self-management, self-confidence, collaboration, negotiation, adaptability, ethical behavior)
	• Gain increasing command of work-related vocabulary
		CIVICS
		• Access and use government agency information
		
		DIGITAL LITERACY
		• Use basic keyboarding skills
		• Use Internet search engines to collect data and information
			CASAS: 4.1.9, 4.5.2, 7.2.8, 7.5.1, 7.7.2, 7.7.3
			CA IEL/CE: 23, 37, 52
			CCRS:
			  SL: 1, 4
			  L: 1-3
			ELCATE: CP.02, CP.03, DL.01, DL.03
			ELPS: 1, 2, 8-10
			TAELCS:
			  L5, III.2.8
			  L6, III.2.1,4

PART B
 	
Career & Academic Preparation
	CAREER READINESS
	• Locate, evaluate, and interpret career information
	• Identify career cluster and related pathways that match career and education goals
	• Research education/training/employment resources required to achieve goals
	• Locate, analyze, and describe job requirements, licenses, credentials, etc. needed for specific jobs
	• Identify educational opportunities
	• Demonstrate teamwork skills for working cooperatively
	• Identify and demonstrate qualities of an effective employee
	• Identify employability/soft skills (personal qualities, leadership skills, customer care skills) necessary to succeed in post-secondary education, training, and employment (e.g., communication skills, collaboration, negotiation, adaptability)
	• Identify work-related safety regulations, standards, and procedures*
	• Interpret information about employee legal rights, organizations, and benefits*
	• Gain increasing command of work-related vocabulary
	
	ACADEMIC READINESS
	• Gain increasing command of academic vocabulary
	• Interpret complex informational text and academic language
	• Comprehend STEAM academic subject matter: Science & Sustainability, Technology, Engineering, Arts & Architecture, Math
	• Identify main ideas and supporting details in informational text
	• Cite evidence from text
	• Use critical thinking skills
	• Use study skills for success in post-secondary education and training (e.g., note-taking, paraphrasing, summarizing)
	• Write about previously-discussed topics*
	• Follow basic steps of the writing process*
		CIVICS
		• Access and use community service and government agency information
		• Interpret information about civic organizations
		• Identify and describe volunteer agencies and opportunities in the community
		• Interact with educational institutions
		• Identify ways of conserving resources, including recycling and using energy efficiently
		
		DIGITAL LITERACY
		• Use basic keyboarding skills
		• Use Internet search engines to collect data and information
		• Use presentation software/apps
		• Effectively use online tools to communicate and collaborate with others
			CASAS: 2.5.8, 2.7.7, 4.1.6, 4.1.8. 4.2.2, 4.2.5, 4.2.6, 4.3.1, 4.3.2, 4.3.3, 4.3.4, 4.4.1, 4.4.2, 4.4.3, 4.4.4, 4.4.8, 4.5.1, 4.5.2, 4.6.1, 4.6.2, 4.6.3, 4.6.4, 4.8.1, 4.8.2, 4.8.3, 4.8.4, 4.8.5, 4.9.1, 5.6.2, 5.6.4, 5.6.5, 7.2.1, 7.2.4, 7.2.6, 7.4.2, 7.4.4, 7.7.1, 7.7.2, 7.7.3
			CA IEL/CE: 3, 13, 14, 23, 25, 32, 33, 35, 36, 37, 48, 50, 52
			CCRS:
			  R: 1-4, 7, 8, 10
			  W: 1, 2, 4-9
			  SL: 1, 4, 5
			  L: 1-6
			ELCATE: CP.01, CP.03, DL.01, DL.03
			ELPS: 1, 2, 3, 4, 5, 7, 8-10
			TAELCS:
			  L5, III.1.4,7,8
			  L5, III.2.1-4,8
			  L5, III.3.1-4
			  L5, III.4.1,2,4,6
			  L6, III.1.1-4
			  L6, III.2.1,2,3,4,5,8
			  L6, III.3.1,3-5,7
			  L6, III.4.1,3,4

PART C
 	
My Career Journey
	CAREER READINESS
	• Develop a career and education plan
	• Use job search skills, including completing an application, resume, cover letter, thank you letter
	• Identify and use effective interviewing techniques
	• Prepare and memorize an elevator speech
	• Research an organization to prepare for a job interview
	• Create a positive impression in a job interview regarding personal qualities, leadership skills, communication skills, responsibility, self-confidence
	• Work cooperatively in pairs and teams
	• Identify free or low cost employment-related services
	• Identify qualities of an effective employee
	
	CIVICS
	• Access and use government agency information
	• Access information for a successful transition to post-secondary education, training, or work
		DIGITAL LITERACY
		• Use basic keyboarding skills
		• Produce resumes and other documents using templates or software
		• Use Internet search engines to collect data and information
			CASAS: 2.7.7, 2.8.1, 2.8.7, 4.1.2, 4.1.3, 4.1.4, 4.1.5, 4.1.7, 4.4.1, 4.4.2, 4.4.5, 4.5.2, 4.9.2, 7.1.1, 7.7.2, 7.7.3
			CA IEL/CE: 14, 23, 32, 33, 34, 37, 49
			CCRS:
			  SL: 1, 4, 5
			  L: 1-3
			ELCATE: CP.04, DL.01, DL.02, DL.03
			ELPS: 1, 2, 5, 8-10
			TAELCS:
			  L5, III.2.1
			  L6, III.2.1-5,7,8

CASAS: Comprehensive Adult Student Assessment System
CA IEL/CE: California Integrated EL Civics Objectives
CCRS: College and Career Readiness Standards (R=Reading; W=Writing; SL=Speaking/Listening; L=Language)

ELCATE: English Literacy for Career and Technical Education (Florida Department of Education)
ELPS: English Language Proficiency Standards
TAELCS: Texas Adult Education and Literacy Content Standards

* Curricula provided in the **CareerView** *ToolSite* downloadable resources

The *CareerView* Career & Academic Readiness Skills **Book** is the companion reader and activity book for *CareerView: Exploring the World of Work*. Together, the core text and skills book offer integrated instruction in career and academic preparation that helps prepare high-intermediate and advanced English language learners for a successful transition to continuing education and job training. The course enables students to explore their work interests, the array of career opportunities across many employment sectors, and the pathways and education options for achieving short-term and long-term goals. Technology tasks in each unit develop learners' digital literacy skills as they research, prepare, and offer presentations on lesson topics. Through its integrated curriculum, **CareerView** promotes the employability and academic readiness goals of the new English Language Proficiency Standards (ELPS), the College and Career Readiness Skills (CCRS), and the Workforce Innovation & Opportunity Act (WIOA).

The skills book consists of three sections:

Part A focuses on the vocabulary and concepts of career exploration to help learners identify and describe their interests, likes and dislikes, personal characteristics, work styles and values, and how these dimensions relate to different employment sectors and jobs. Key objectives of this section are to enable learners to use the federal O*NET Career Exploration Tools at the mynextmove.org website to learn about jobs that may interest them, and to talk about their interests and career exploration with an employment counselor, career navigator, or other instructional support person. This section also orients students to the five *job zones* that describe the level of education, work experience, and job-specific training required for employment in particular occupations. It also introduces students to the concept of *soft skills*—the social and communication skills that are emphasized throughout the course and that are important for success in the 21st-century workplace.

Part B, the main section of the skills book, provides supplemental activities, readings, and academic lessons to support the 20 units in the core text.

- A **Career Vocabulary** cloze activity synthesizes the occupation names, worksite locations, job responsibilities, and equipment, tools, and objects that are introduced in the first three lessons of each unit. Students review key vocabulary as they complete a narrative description of the unit's opening scenes.

- A **Career Research** lesson offers a framework for students to research an occupation featured in the unit. The positions are listed by *job zone* so that students can choose an occupation that matches their current level of preparation or a higher level that they aspire to. Using the O*NET Career Exploration Tools as a resource, students write a description of the job they select: what a person does in the job; the tools, equipment, and technology used; the kind of person who would be interested in the job; the skills, abilities, education, training, and experience that are required; the job outlook; and even the average salary.

After students complete their research, they prepare and give a short presentation about the job. If classroom resources permit, it is strongly recommended that students use presentation software to create a slide show for the class. The website resources often include videos, which are useful and motivating for students to include in their presentations. (In addition to the federal web resources, many states have their own career exploration websites that can be used for this research task.)

- An **On-the-Job Instructions** activity in some units gives students practice reading workplace notices, safety procedures, or instructions for operating equipment and answering comprehension questions that focus on the close reading anchor skills described in current adult education standards.

As an additional activity, students use YouTube, WikiHow, or another source to search online for a demonstration of how to do a procedure, operate equipment, or follow safety instructions related to the unit's employment sector. They write out the instructions and, if resources permit, they prepare a media presentation. They might make screenshots of the steps and include them in a slide show, or they might video-record their demonstration on a smartphone and play the video. The goal is to give all students practice presenting instructional procedures to the class.

- A **Civics Connection Profile** in some units features a person who works in one of the unit's occupations. The profile usually focuses on the relationship between the employment sector and aspects of community life. Comprehension questions develop students' close reading skills. These lessons also suggest inviting classroom visitors from the sectors to talk with students about their jobs. Internet research tasks related to the civics or occupational contexts of the profiles are also suggested.

As an additional community-focused activity, the core text's Tech Task 3 suggests that students visit a workplace related to the unit, interview a worker there about the person's job, and report back to the class. If they have permission from the workplace and the worker, they might use a smartphone to video-record some or all of the interview and present it to the class.

(If students record interviews, encourage them to stand close to the interviewee for better video and audio quality, hold the smartphone horizontally instead of vertically in order to fill the screen, and hold it steady to avoid shaking or distortion. They should also record the video so that they can keep it or transfer it to a computer, rather than using one of the Stories apps in which videos disappear after 24 hours. Some students may have video editing skills through their use of social media. Encourage them to use these skills in their own presentations and to help other students as well.)

- An **Academic Lesson** in each unit gives students experience with the kind of lengthy subject-matter material they will encounter in mainstream classes as they continue their education. Each lesson relates to the employment sector of its unit and focuses on a STEAM topic (Science and Sustainability; Technology; Engineering; Arts and Architecture; or Math). Following the format of academic course materials, the lessons include questions that check students' understanding of lesson content and give them opportunities to apply their experiences or share opinions about the topic. The lessons also include academic vocabulary practice and comprehension questions that develop close reading skills and prepare students for standardized assessments.

Since the academic lessons are challenging, scaffolding activities are available as free reproducibles to support students' comprehension of the academic content. These activities include pre-teaching of key vocabulary and paired academic reading that develops students' speaking, listening, note-taking, paraphrasing, and summarizing skills.

- A **Listening** activity in each unit reinforces the core text's workplace communication practice and prepares students for the types of listening items that appear in standardized tests. Students listen to conversations between co-workers, between employees and supervisors, and between workers and customers, and then they answer multiple-choice questions about these interactions. (Audio for the Listening activities is included in the course's listening app.)

Part C helps learners synthesize their self-exploration of interests, characteristics, and work styles/values in Part A and their explorations of the employment sectors in Part B. They learn about career ladders and lattices, the different forms of education and training available including apprenticeships, the ways to approach a job search, how to use social media, and suggestions for creating resumes. As they work through the Part C lessons, students create a career lattice, a personal career pathway, an education plan, an elevator speech that briefly describes their skills and goals, a resume, and a LinkedIn profile. In a final set of lessons, students learn tips for successful job interviews, they create and rehearse answers to the most common interview questions, and they practice mock interviews in class.

The **CareerView** ToolSite provides downloadable resources to help with lesson planning and instruction. Reproducible materials include an interest survey ballot (for students to vote on employment sectors they would like to explore), teaching instructions for each type of lesson, and activity masters that provide additional lesson practice for both the core text and skill book, including a job application form, resume and cover letter templates, and other resources. To access the ToolSite go to pearsoneltusa.com/careerview and select *ToolSite Resources* from the menu.

We hope that the **CareerView** Career & Academic Readiness Skills Book helps you offer students an educational program that effectively integrates preparation for both employment and continuing education while advancing their English language proficiency. And we hope that the course enables your students to explore their work interests and options, develop their skills, and prepare for a successful journey on whatever pathway they choose to follow to achieve their goals.

Bill Bliss
Steven J. Molinsky

PART A: SELF-EXPLORATION

VOCATIONAL PERSONALITY TYPES

WORK STYLES

MY NEXT MOVE / JOB ZONES

SOFT SKILLS

* The O*NET Interest Profiler is part of the O*NET™ Career Exploration Tools.

My Next Move is developed by the National Center for O*NET Development.

O*NET™ is a trademark of the US Department of Labor/Employment and Training Administration (USDOL/ETA).

A SELF-ASSESSMENT QUESTIONNAIRE

One of the most valuable things to do when exploring career options is to think about your own interests and personality—what you like to do and the type of person you are. As you answer these questions, consider all aspects of your life, not just work. Think about how you like to spend your time, the things that interest you, and the way you interact with people. Whether you respond *Yes* or *No* to these questions, give examples to explain your answers.

1. Are you good at—or bad at—assembling, building, or repairing things?　　Yes ____ No ____

   Example: _____

   _____

2. Do you enjoy learning about things by browsing on the Internet, by reading　　Yes ____ No ____
   books, magazines, or newspapers, or by watching TV?

   What subjects interest you? How do you like to learn new things? _____

   _____

3. Do you enjoy writing, playing a musical instrument, singing, drawing, painting,　　Yes ____ No ____
   or performing?

   Explain: _____

   _____

4. Do you like to help people, give advice, teach people how to do things,　　Yes ____ No ____
   or do volunteer work?

   Explain: _____

   _____

5. Do you enjoy buying and selling things, or negotiating with people?　　Yes ____ No ____

   Have you ever thought about starting your own business?　　Yes ____ No ____

   Explain: _____

   _____

6. Are you a well-organized person? Do you keep track of documents, bills,　　Yes ____ No ____
   and your schedule or calendar? Are you good at managing your finances?

   Explain: _____

   _____

Now talk with another student. Share your answers to these questions. Then tell the class about the student you spoke with. (If you are in a new class, this is a great way for all the students to get to know each other.)

PERSONALITY EXPRESSIONS: How I See Myself, and How Others See Me

Many common expressions serve as short and effective ways to describe people. Can you match these expressions with their meanings?

_____ **1.** "I'm handy around the house."　　**a.** I like to make decisions for myself.

_____ **2.** "I have an inquiring mind."　　**b.** I like being in front of an audience.

_____ **3.** "I'm a natural-born performer."　　**c.** I think that being accurate and following the rules is important.

_____ **4.** "I'm a people person."　　**d.** I like to learn about things.

_____ **5.** "I'm my own boss."　　**e.** I have skills with tools and can fix things.

_____ **6.** "I'm a stickler for detail."　　**f.** I'm very social and get along well with everyone.

Which one of these expressions best describes you? Why?

_____

What other expressions (in your language) do family members and friends use to describe you? How would you translate these expressions into English? Write two of these expressions and the reasons why others use them to describe you. Then share with the class.

1. Expression: _____

   Reason: _____

2. Expression: _____

   Reason: _____

EXPLORING PREFERENCES

RANKING TASK 1

Here are some verbs that describe things people do at work. For each verb, write one or two nouns (direct objects) to name specific tasks.

☐ assemble _____　　☐ teach _____

☐ study _____　　☐ manage _____

☐ create _____　　☐ calculate _____

Now rank these tasks. Write a number in each box to indicate what would be your most favorite (1) to your least favorite (6). Then write the reason for your ranking. Share with the class.

_____

RANKING TASK 2

Here are some more verbs that describe things people do at work. For each verb, write one or two nouns (direct objects) to name specific tasks.

☐ build _____	☐ counsel _____
☐ research _____	☐ sell _____
☐ design _____	☐ keep records of _____

Now rank these tasks. Write a number in each box to indicate what would be your most favorite (1) to your least favorite (6). Then write the reason for your ranking. Share with the class.

RANKING TASK 3

For each worksite, write the occupation of a person who works there.

☐ a factory _____	☐ a school _____
☐ a science laboratory _____	☐ a telephone sales center _____
☐ a TV or movie studio _____	☐ an accounting department _____

Now rank these worksites. If you had to choose one of them as your place of work, which would be your most favorite (1) to your least favorite (6)? Then write the reason for your ranking. Share with the class.

USING THE O*NET INTEREST PROFILER

The **O*NET Interest Profiler** is a useful tool to help you identify your work-related interests. It is part of the O*NET™ Career Exploration Tools of the US Department of Labor/Employment and Training Administration (USDOL/ETA). This online questionnaire contains a list of 60 work activities that people do in various occupations. For each activity, you indicate how you would like doing that type of work on the following rating scale:

Strongly Dislike — Dislike — Unsure — Like — Strongly Like

Go to mynextmove.org/explore/ip and take the O*NET Interest Profiler. As you answer the questions, don't think about the skills or education needed to do each type of work or the salary for the occupation. Just think about whether you would enjoy the work. There are five question screens. You need to complete all twelve questions on a screen to move to the next one. When you finish, you will receive a Score Report. Print it out if you can, or write down the results, and bring it to class. We'll talk about the results in the next lesson.

(As you do the activity, make a list of any words that you didn't know and had to look up in a dictionary. As a class, discuss the meanings of the unfamiliar words on students' lists.)

INTERPRETING THE O*NET INTEREST PROFILER SCORE REPORT

The **O*NET Interest Profiler** is based on Dr. John L. Holland's theory of vocational personalities and work environments—one of the most important approaches used in career interest surveys. This theory describes six different vocational personality types. According to the theory, most people have one or more of these personality types, and the occupations and work environments they choose tend to match their personality descriptions. The six personality types are often summarized by their first letters as shown in the chart—R-I-A-S-E-C.

Vocational Personality Type	Likes work activities that involve . . .	Examples	LESS interested in . . .
Realistic (R)	Practical, hands-on problems and solutions	Working with tools, machinery, plants, animals, real-world materials; working outside; physical activity	Paperwork; working closely with other people
Investigative (I)	Ideas and thinking	Searching for facts; figuring out problems	Physical activity; leading people; persuading people
Artistic (A)	Creativity and self-expression	Acting, music, art, design	Following rules
Social (S)	Working with people to help them learn and grow	Teaching; giving advice; helping and serving others; communicating with people	Working with objects, machines, or information
Enterprising (E)	Starting up and carrying out projects (including businesses); taking action	Leading people; persuading people; making decisions; taking risks	Thinking about things
Conventional (C)	Following set procedures and routines; working with information; paying attention to details	Working with clear rules and standards; following a strong leader	Working with ideas; making own decisions

On your O*NET Interest Profiler Score Report, you will see a score for each personality type and a bar graph showing the results. The color-coding matches the color backgrounds of the questions you answered when you took the Interest Profiler.

Write the scores you received on the O*NET Interest Profiler.

Realistic _____   Social _____

Investigative _____   Enterprising _____

Artistic _____   Conventional _____

What are your top two vocational personality types?

Primary _____   Secondary _____

YOUR VOCATIONAL PERSONALITY

Let's see how your results on the O*NET Interest Profiler compare with your answers to the earlier activities in this lesson.

On pages 3 and 4, the six Self-Assessment questions and the six Personality Expressions relate to the vocational personality types. On both pages, put the letter for the personality type next to each number:

1: R   2: I   3: A   4: S   5: E   6: C

Do your Interest Profiler results match up with your answers?

On pages 4 and 5, the three Ranking Tasks also relate to the six types:

Vocational Personality Type	Ranking Task 1	Ranking Task 2	RANKING TASK 3
Realistic (R)	assemble	build	a factory
Investigative (I)	study	research	a science laboratory
Artistic (A)	create	design	a TV or movie studio
Social (S)	teach	counsel	a school
Enterprising (E)	manage	sell	a telephone sales center
Conventional (C)	calculate	keep records of	an accounting department

Do your Interest Profiler results match up with your answers?

Test Your Vocational Personality Knowledge

Choose the correct answer.

1. Alonso likes working in a nursing home. He enjoys taking care of the senior citizens who live there and talking with the family members who visit them. His vocational personality type is ___.
   A. conventional
   B. social
   C. investigative
   D. artistic

2. After working as a chef in a restaurant for several years, Bianca saved up enough money to start her own food truck business. It was risky, but her food truck is now the most popular one in town. Her vocational personality type is ___.
   A. realistic
   B. conventional
   C. social
   D. enterprising

3. Paul enjoys his work in a public health clinic's medical records department. He's responsible for making sure all patient records are filed correctly and that information is available quickly when needed. His vocational personality type is ___.
   A. conventional
   B. investigative
   C. social
   D. artistic

4. Rita really didn't like sitting at a desk all day at her previous office job. She's a dancer who loves to move around, so she's enjoying her new day job as a landscaper while she performs with a dance company on most weekends. Her vocational personality types are ___.
   A. conventional and social
   B. enterprising and investigative
   C. realistic and artistic
   D. investigative and artistic

YOUR PERSONAL QUALITIES

In addition to your work interests, your personal qualities are another important dimension of your vocational personality. They determine your work style. You're a stronger job candidate and employee when you demonstrate these positive personal characteristics. As you explore career options, you will see that occupations have different sets of qualities that are most important for success.

Choose the definition that best matches the meaning of the personal quality. Then write an example of how you demonstrate each quality in your life.

_____ 1. achievement-oriented

_____ 2. show concern for others

_____ 3. persistent

_____ 4. cooperative

_____ 5. adaptable

a. get along well with others

b. flexible

c. goal-oriented

d. untiring in the face of obstacles

e. sensitive to needs of others

1. _____

2. _____

3. _____

4. _____

5. _____

_____ 6. show initiative

_____ 7. dependable

_____ 8. independent

_____ 9. have integrity

_____ 10. tolerate stress

_____ 11. analytical

f. use information well and use logical thinking

g. not needing supervision

h. honest

i. reliable

j. deal calmly with difficult situations

k. take on responsibilities and challenges

6. _____

7. _____

8. _____

9. _____

10. _____

11. _____

_____ **12.** exercise self-control   **l.** able to take charge and give direction

_____ **13.** innovative   **m.** thorough and careful

_____ **14.** have leadership qualities   **n.** work well with others

_____ **15.** have a social orientation   **o.** keep emotions in check

_____ **16.** attentive to detail   **p.** develop new and creative ideas

12. _____

13. _____

14. _____

15. _____

16. _____

Now talk with other students in pairs, small groups, or as a class. Share your examples of how you demonstrate these qualities.

PERSONALITY EXPRESSIONS: Metaphors to Describe Personal Qualities

Sometimes we use metaphors to describe people's personal qualities related to work. Can you match these expressions with the personal qualities they refer to?

_____ **1.** "She thinks **outside the box**."   **a.** initiative

_____ **2.** "He has **a strong moral compass**."   **b.** persistence

_____ **3.** "She's **a self-starter**."   **c.** cooperation

_____ **4.** "He's **a team player**."   **d.** integrity

_____ **5.** "She has **dogged determination**."   **e.** innovative

Which one of these expressions best describes you? Why?

_____

What metaphors in your language do people use to describe personal qualities related to work? How would you translate these expressions into English? Write two expressions and their meanings. Then share with the class.

1. Expression: _____

    Meaning: _____

2. Expression: _____

    Meaning: _____

USING THE MY NEXT MOVE WEBSITE

Go to mynextmove.org to view the website's landing page as you read about this career exploration tool.

My Next Move is a website produced by the National Center for O*NET Development and sponsored by the US Department of Labor/Employment and Training Administration. The website is an interactive tool that provides information about more than 900 occupations, career exploration activities, and links to external sites such as the USDOL/ETA's CareerOneStop centers.

The website's landing page (the first page you reach) asks, "What do you want to do for a living?" You can search careers by typing in an occupation name, such as *electrician*, or you can type in key words such as *computer programming*. You can also browse careers by industry, using a pull-down menu to select an employment sector. If you click the *Start* button under "Tell us what you'd like to do," you will reach the O*NET Interest Profiler. The website is also available in a Spanish version.

To view the information that the website provides about each career, type in an occupation name in the box under "Search careers with key words" and click *Search*. This will bring you to a list of occupations. Click the one that is the closest match to what you're looking for, and you will then reach the website page for that occupation.

The website provides comprehensive information about each career. At the top of the web page for an occupation, you can read a description of what a person does in the career and the key tasks that person performs. You can also watch a video about the career and open a transcript so you can read along as the video plays. (The videos present a lot of information very quickly.)

Eight sections on the web page provide the following information for each career:

Knowledge: Relevant subject matter, such as Economics, Fine Arts, or Geography

Skills: Basic skills and social, technical, and other skills

Abilities: Physical strength, coordination, thinking, and other abilities

Personality: Personal qualities

Technology: Computer skills and other technology skills

Education: Training and credentials

Job Outlook: Forecast for future job opportunities and average salaries (state and local information may be available)

Explore More: Links to careers in the same employment sector or with similar skills

JOB ZONES

Go back to the mynextmove.org landing page and click on the *Job Prep* button in the bottom left corner. This will take you to a page that sorts all the careers into five Job Zones based on the amount of experience, training, and education required.

Zone 1: Little or no preparation needed

Zone 2: Some preparation needed

Zone 3: Medium job preparation needed

Zone 4: High preparation needed

Zone 5: Extensive preparation needed

Scroll through the "Careers Sorted by Job Preparation" page and complete this chart with general information to describe the experience, training, and level of education required for each Job Zone. Also, list five occupations for each zone.

	Experience	Training	Education	Occupations
Zone 1				
Zone 2				
Zone 3				
Zone 4				
Zone 5				

Each group of careers below has one occupation in each Job Zone. Work with another student or on your own. First, guess the Job Zones. Then use the mynextmove.org website to search for the correct answers.

1.

Occupation	Job Zone	
	Guess	**Actual**
accountant		
carpet installer		
dental assistant		
food preparation worker		
pharmacist		

2.

Occupation	Job Zone	
	Guess	**Actual**
computer programmer		
cosmetologist		
lawyer		
security guard		
waiter		

Answer these questions and discuss with other students.

What is your current Job Zone? _____   What Job Zone do you aspire to? _____

How do you plan to reach that goal? _____

_____

INTERPERSONAL SKILLS & PERSONAL QUALITIES FOR CAREER SUCCESS

When we think about the skills that are needed for a career, we often focus on the *hard skills*—the technical skills needed to use tools, equipment, and technology; the physical abilities that are required; and the skills to manage the resources and systems of a work setting. However, there is now a growing emphasis on *soft skills*—commonly called *people skills*—the social skills, communication skills, and personal qualities that enable us to work well with others and be successful in the 21st-century workplace.

Employers often consider soft skills to be more important than hard skills when they are hiring or promoting people, and many research studies indicate that a person's success in a job and long-term success in a career depend more on soft skills than technical skills. At a time when many workplaces are becoming more automated and more technical tasks are being done by computers and robots, the abilities to work well on a team, to have good social skills, and to offer a positive and enthusiastic attitude are increasing in importance.

Many of these soft skills relate to the personal qualities and work styles you explored on pages 8 and 9. They are about the person you *are* as much as the things you *do*. Good interpersonal skills include being friendly, patient, understanding, and honest. Having a positive attitude is also important and includes being enthusiastic, being confident about yourself, and encouraging others. Being flexible and adaptable to changing situations is essential. Having

a strong *work ethic* is another important personal quality that people demonstrate by showing up on time, working hard, managing their time well, and taking initiative.

You can think about other soft skills as belonging to the "Six Cs":

Conscientious—being responsible and reliable, someone people can count on;

Courteous—being polite and respectful of others;

Collaborative and Cooperative—working well as part of a team, and supporting and helping others;

Creative—being able to think of innovative solutions to problems and ways to improve things, and using one's imagination to brainstorm new ideas;

Committed—identifying with the mission of the workplace or job, and wanting to make the best effort possible for co-workers, clients, and customers;

Communicative—being a good listener, an effective speaker, and a skilled writer.

A final soft skill that combines many of the others is *leadership*. Personal qualities of a leader include having a positive attitude, self-confidence, and flexibility. Some of the defining skills of a strong leader include being able to communicate effectively, motivate people to do their best work, organize and support teams, think creatively, solve problems, and make decisions.

Writing And Sharing

Write about one or both of these topics. Then share with the class.

1. Think about people you know and the "Six Cs". Who is the most conscientious person you know? the most courteous? the most collaborative? the most creative? the most committed? the most communicative? Write an essay about these people and give examples to describe how they demonstrate these soft skills.

2. In your opinion, who is a strong leader? Write about a person you know, a person in the news, or someone else who demonstrates strong leadership skills.

MY SOFT SKILLS COMMUNICATION LOG

The way that we demonstrate strong soft skills is through the language we use and the interactions we have with the people around us. Through the conversation lessons in the *CareerView* Core Text, you will practice effective communication in a variety of workplaces: communication between co-workers, between employees and supervisors, and between workers and customers/clients. The communication skills are universal—they apply to all the employment sectors. As you go through the course, fill in this log with examples of the uses of language in the workplace. (Write the expression and its unit and page number.) Try to use these expressions so they become a regular part of your communication in English.

HELP/ASSISTANCE:

Offer help/assistance:

_____

_____

_____

Ask for help/assistance:

_____

_____

_____

Make and respond to requests:

_____

_____

Give advice:

_____

_____

Make a suggestion:

_____

_____

Report/Point out a problem:

_____

_____

FEEDBACK:

Ask a co-worker or supervisor for feedback:

_____

_____

_____

Give feedback:

_____

_____

_____

Respond to feedback:

_____

_____

_____

Give and respond to correction:

_____

_____

_____

COMMUNICATE WITH CUSTOMERS & CLIENTS:

Ask a customer for feedback:

_____

_____

Handle customer complaints:

_____

_____

Help a customer with a problem:

_____

_____

PART B: CAREER & ACADEMIC PREPARATION

The *CareerView* *ToolSite* at pearsoneltusa.com/careerview provides downloadable resources for lessons in this section.

Look at pages 2–3 of the core text. Write the correct words to complete the description.

assisting	carton	display case	information	shelves	warehouse
associate	department	hand truck	merchandise	stock	

It's a typical busy day at the department store. A sales _____associate_____ 1 in the electronics

_____2 is giving _____3 to a customer about flat-screen TVs. Another is

_____4 a customer with a camera she has taken out from the _____5.

The _____6 clerks are also busy. One is bringing out a large _____7 on a

_____8 from the _____9 area. Two of them are working in the toy department.

One is stocking the _____10 and the other is arranging _____11.

delivery	manager	rack	signing	trucker
inventory	operator	scanning	stocking	unpacked
ladder	pallet	shipping carton	support	workers

In the warehouse area, one of the warehouse _____12 is _____13 merchandise

onto shelves. She's standing on a _____14 and wearing a safety back brace _____15.

Another is putting heavy boxes onto a _____16. A _____17 has just arrived with some

merchandise and the warehouse _____18 is _____19 for the _____20.

A forklift _____21 is moving heavy items on a forklift. A stock clerk has _____22

clothing items from a _____23 and is putting the items on a clothing _____24.

Another is _____25 merchandise into store _____26.

bags	checkout	manager	return	setting up	table
cart	clothing	processing	sale sign	straightening	till
cashiers	customer service	receipt	scanner	swipe	unit
checked	inventory	representative	security		

There are three _____27 in the _____28 area. One of them is carrying

the _____29 for the cash register. One is scanning items on the _____30 and

_____31 a customer's transaction. And another has _____32 a customer's ID

and is going to _____33 the customer's credit card. A _____34 person is checking

a customer's _____35 as she is leaving the store with several shopping _____36

in a shopping _____37. At the _____38 counter, a customer service

_____39 is processing a _____40 of some merchandise.

In the _____41 department, a stock clerk is taking _____42 with a handheld

inventory _____43 and is speaking with the department _____44. Two

salespeople are _____45 a display. One is putting up a _____46, and the other is

_____47 up a display _____48.

CAREER RESEARCH

Using the O*NET Career Exploration Tools at mynextmove.org, search for information about one of the retail sector jobs in Unit 1. Write the information in the job profile below. Then prepare and give a presentation about the job.

Job Zone 1 (little or no job preparation)
cashier

Job Zone 2 (some job preparation)
customer service representative, department manager, forklift operator, salesperson, security person (loss prevention specialist), stock clerk, trucker, warehouse worker

Job Zone 4 (high job preparation)
store manager, warehouse manager

Job name: _____

What does a person do in this job?

_____

_____

_____

What tools and equipment does a person use in this job?

_____

What skills and abilities are important?

_____

_____

What technology might a person use in this job?

_____

What kind of person will be interested in this work?

_____

What level of education, job training, and experience is required?

_____

_____

What is the job outlook?   What is the average salary?

_____   _____

Read the department store safety memo and answer the questions.

1 To: All Store Employees
2 From: The Store Manager
3 Subject: Workplace Safety

4 Please remember to always follow these safety guidelines. Let's ensure a safe workplace for
5 our customers and our employees.

6 ✓ Check your work area daily to make sure the floor is not cluttered.

7 ✓ Clean up any spills on the floor immediately to prevent someone from slipping and falling.

8 ✓ Be careful when moving large items through the store aisles on a handtruck to prevent
9   injury to a customer.

10 ✓ You have all received first-aid training. Be prepared to help a customer or co-worker in an
11   emergency. First-aid kits are at the customer service counter and in the warehouse area.
12   Notify your department manager about the emergency and we will call 911 for assistance
13   if necessary.

14 ✓ In the event of a fire, there are fire extinguishers in the warehouse area and in each
15   department.

16 ✓ If you observe shoplifting by a customer, report this to the security officer. Do not confront
17   the shoplifter yourself. Our security person handles all loss control in the store.

18 Our store has been accident-free for the past three months. Keep up the good work!

1. What would be another good subject line for this memo instead of "Workplace Safety"?
A. Be Careful
B. What to Do in an Emergency
C. Assuring a Safe Workplace
D. Preventing Injury

2. What is the store manager's purpose for writing this memo?
A. to describe accidents at the store
B. to remind employees about safety guidelines
C. to give safety information to customers
D. to notify department managers about safety problems

3. In Line 17, what does *loss control* refer to?
A. when a customer gets lost in the store
B. when a customer gets very angry
C. when a fire occurs
D. when a customer takes something without paying for it

4. Which sentence suggests that the store manager is happy about safety in the store?
A. Keep up the good work!
B. You have all received first-aid training.
C. Please remember to always follow these safety guidelines.
D. Let's assure a safe workplace for our customers and our employees.

DEMONSTRATING A PROCEDURE

Using YouTube, WikiHow, or another source, search online for a demonstration of how to do a procedure, operate equipment, or follow safety instructions in the retail sector. Write out the instructions. Then prepare a media presentation. Make screenshots of the steps or video-record your demonstration. Present the procedure to the class.

Suggestions: how to fold shirts for a retail display; how to lift a heavy object correctly; how to take inventory

A Retail Community Relations Manager

1 My name is Isabella Rojas, and I'm a regional community relations manager for my department store company. I like to say that I'm part of our company's mission to give back to the communities where we operate.

2 Our company makes major grants to local schools to support the use of technology, we contribute several million dollars each year to local museums and arts organizations, and we provide funding for public health programs, shelters for the homeless, and college scholarships for youth in our communities.

3 Our employees are another major part of our company's effort to be a good corporate citizen. They make donations to the United Way and other charities through our payroll deduction program, and we match their personal contributions dollar-for-dollar. They also volunteer in many schools and community organizations. They read to children in elementary schools, they serve meals in nutrition programs, they offer leadership training to teens in after-school programs at community centers, and they perform countless other volunteer activities.

4 In my position, I supervise the employee donation and volunteer programs for several stores in our region. I also meet with leaders of community organizations to learn how we can support them and to see if our donations and volunteerism are having a positive impact. There are opportunities to speak at community events, and I occasionally appear on radio and television to share about our company's community-supportive activities.

5 I've worked my way up to this job over several years. I started as a stock clerk at the store near my home, speaking very little English at the time. As my language skills improved, I became a sales associate at that location, then a customer service representative, and then the customer service manager. During those years as a manager, I completed college part-time and earned a degree in public relations. With my retail experience, strong customer relations and communication skills, and my media training, the company promoted me to this position last year. I love the job, and I'm very proud of the work we do.

1. In the context of this reading, what does *giving back* in paragraph 1 refer to?
   A. receiving a product a customer returns
   B. refunding an amount paid
   C. getting a promotion
   D. helping the community

2. Which phrase in paragraphs 2 or 3 DOESN'T refer to money?
   A. provide funding
   B. volunteer
   C. make donations
   D. make major grants

3. Select the paragraph that indicates this manager's job responsibilities.
   A. Paragraph 1
   B. Paragraph 3
   C. Paragraph 4
   D. Paragraph 5

4. Which word has the same meaning as the word *earned* in paragraph 5?
   A. received
   B. improved
   C. promoted
   D. started

CLASSROOM VISITOR

Invite a manager of a local department store to visit your class. Prepare questions in advance about the retail jobs at the store, the job requirements, and the ways that the store or its parent company gives back to the community. Or, do an Internet search for information about a local department store and its community relations activities.

Technology and the Changing Retail Industry

1   Whether purchasing life's daily needs or buying things we like, shopping is a regular activity for almost everyone. It is not surprising that the retail industry—the business of selling goods and services to customers—is one of the largest sectors of the economy. Businesses are constantly trying to attract consumers to their products and to increase their sales, and advances in technology are giving them new ways to do that.

The retail business is changing

2   The retail business has been experiencing significant changes in the past decades. One big change is the rise of "big box" retailers that sell many different kinds of products and operate a network of large stores. These companies have put many small community stores out of business by offering lower prices. This has been good for consumers, but bad for local businesses and the people who work in them.

3   Another big change is the trend toward online shopping. With the rise of the Internet, retailers have set up websites to show and sell their products to consumers, and online sales have become an essential component of retail operations for most companies. Customers like the convenience of making purchases at home on their computers without needing to go to a physical location (a "brick-and-mortar" store). One effect of this trend is that new businesses have been created that don't have stores and sell only online. These online retailers, or "e-tailers," have put pressure on traditional businesses that must maintain costly buildings, a large supply of merchandise, and a large staff. Competition from online retailers has caused some traditional retailers to close stores in order to reduce their expenses.

4   The latest development in online shopping is the use of apps on smartphones. Many traditional retail companies have created their own apps that make accessing product information and processing sales easy. Online retailers have shopping apps that present products in a range of categories from many different manufacturers, with a conveniently arranged system for payment and shipment. Another type of app lists coupons or discounts offered by retailers for their products and services. The use of mobile phones to make payments in stores quickly and easily has also been increasing.

5   The Internet is now part of the business plan for all large retailers, and one of its main uses is for advertising. Companies have traditionally advertised in newspapers and magazines and on television and radio, but advertising on the Internet is growing rapidly. Businesses pay websites to show their ads, and search engines and social media sites, such as Google and Facebook, are widely used by companies to put their products in front of consumers' eyes. Advertisers also connect with potential customers through their smartphones. These developments play a part in the "omni-channel" retailing used by many big businesses—a powerful combination of stores, websites, social messaging, and e-mail and phone communication.

6   New technologies are also allowing businesses to gather detailed information about customers and their buying habits. Retailers collect information about their customers by following their purchases on company websites, on credit cards, and with store club cards. Other companies collect data about people's Internet searches and responses to advertising on their computers and smartphones. Through "data mining" of this information on individuals' interests and buying history, companies can determine what kinds of products consumers like. They can then send them individually targeted ads on the Internet and social media to try to get them to buy things. The information can also help the company make decisions about what to sell, how to set prices, and what the best market is for their products.

Working in retail

7   Millions of people work in retail businesses, performing a variety of functions. On the sales floor there are sales associates, cashiers, stock clerks, customer service representatives, managers, and security personnel. Companies that maintain large

quantities of stock and supplies to store and deliver employ warehouse workers, distribution managers, and drivers. Staff in company offices decide what products or goods to sell, how to set prices, how to improve sales and business operations, and how to get information to customers through marketing and advertising. Other employees manage staff and set company policies.

8   Many common retail functions involve the use of technology. Cashiers use scanners and computerized stock systems. Many stores have self-checkout lanes where customers scan and pay for their purchases themselves. Stock clerks use a portable scanner to check supplies and take inventory. Computerized systems using UPC (universal product code) labeling keep track of inventory and product information as well as the location and movement of goods.

Technology and retail jobs in the future

9   In the future, there will still be stores with salespeople and stock clerks, as well as warehouse workers and distribution managers, but their duties and the skills they need will be different. Sales associates will have to find product information quickly on computer systems, and communicate with customers who are using their smartphones to research information about products and prices. Cashiers must be able to use smart cash registers that can print coupons, calculate discounts, and receive store communications. And supply staff will use computers and devices to get and record information about stock and products and to keep track of merchandise.

10   However, some jobs may be lost to technological developments. New systems using sensors and personal identification technology are being used to scan shoppers' purchases and process payments as customers walk out of a store—without the need for a cashier. Robots are now being used in large warehouses to move merchandise and perform tasks in the shipping process, replacing human workers. Drones are being tested for delivering packages by air, and could reduce the need for vehicle delivery drivers.

11   With strong competition in the retail industry, some companies will reduce costs by closing stores, and some will go out of business. But with the rise of "e-commerce," jobs will be created in other areas of the retail industry, jobs that may require a higher level of skills. More customer service workers with computer skills will be needed to assist in online sales functions. Warehousing and distribution jobs will involve the use of new technologies. Companies will need workers with information technology (IT) and software development skills to design websites, create Internet sales systems, and manage online retailing.

LIFE IN THE INFORMATION AGE

Retailers, social media companies, search engines, and phone apps collect not only information about consumers' spending, but also their personal data, and information about their friends, their interests, their habits, and their communications. They can use this information for whatever they want and sometimes they can sell it to other companies. This has created a growing concern about personal privacy in this new technological time.

12   Technical skills will also be important for other functions:

- Companies will need data management specialists, software developers, and computer and IT technicians to create and manage information systems that will collect, process, and analyze data about sales, business operations, and customers.

- As retailers try to reach out to consumers on their mobile devices, advertising and messaging through phone apps will increase. Online shopping and payment on smartphones will become routine. Companies will need staff who can develop new mobile marketing strategies and sales plans.

- Ordering, transport, storage, and delivery systems for retail products will need to be efficient and economical. Software developers and system managers will play an important part in keeping retail businesses competitive and profitable.

13   Most retail workers will need to have basic math and computer literacy skills, and they should also know how to use spreadsheets and databases. Schools and job training programs are good places to learn these skills. Workers will need to be good at using the Internet, social media, and mobile devices. For higher-level jobs, computer programming, software development, web development, and data management will be important skills to have. Retail business is changing, and people looking for jobs in the industry need to have the right skills.

DID YOU UNDERSTAND?

1. What do retail businesses do?
2. What are "big box" retailers?
3. What is *online shopping*?
4. What advantage do "e-tailers" have over businesses with stores?
5. What are some of the types of shopping apps for smartphones?
6. How do businesses advertise on the Internet?
7. How do businesses collect information about their customers?
8. How do businesses use information about consumers?
9. What are some of the jobs in retail businesses? List five jobs.
10. What are some of the positions that might lose jobs due to new technology?
11. What effect does the rise of online shopping have on retail jobs?
12. What kinds of skills will be important in the future for people who want to work in retail businesses?

WHAT'S YOUR EXPERIENCE?

1. Have you ever worked in a retail job? If you did, what was your experience?
2. Do you use self-checkout lanes in stores? If you use them, is it easy or difficult? If you don't use them, why not?
3. What experience have you had with buying things online?
4. How do you use your mobile phone for shopping?
5. Do you see ads when you use the Internet or on your mobile phone? Do these ads seem be targeting you?

WHAT'S YOUR OPINION?

1. Is it important to you to have small stores and shops in your community? Do you buy things from them to support them, or do you always shop at big stores with lower prices?
2. What do you think about the advertising you see on the Internet?
3. Are you concerned about privacy on the Internet? Is it a problem if companies sell people's personal information?

READING COMPREHENSION

1. According to the reading, many companies have closed their stores because of _____.
   A. online shopping and "big box" retailers
   B. marketing and advertising
   C. television and radio
   D. computerized supply systems

2. The word *staff* in paragraph 3 refers to _____.
   A. a company's location
   B. a company's employees
   C. a company's budget
   D. a company's inventory of goods

3. How have companies been changing their approach to advertising?
   A. They are using more traditional kinds of ads.
   B. They are changing from advertising in newspapers and magazines to television and radio.
   C. They are advertising more on the Internet.
   D. They are charging websites to show their ads.

4. Which of the following is NOT part of omni-channel retailing?
   A. the use of social media sites
   B. e-mailing
   C. the use of portable scanners
   D. smartphone communications

5. In paragraph 6, *data mining* refers to _____.
   A. searching for product information on the Internet
   B. researching data on new technologies that would appeal to customers
   C. finding information about new products
   D. looking through data to find useful customer information

6. Which paragraph suggests that the skills of today's workers will not be sufficient in the future?
   A. Paragraph 7
   B. Paragraph 8
   C. Paragraph 9
   D. Paragraph 10

7. The main idea of the reading is that _____.
   A. more retail industry workers will be needed in the future
   B. technical skills are essential in today's workplace
   C. new technology is changing the retail industry
   D. the retail industry is an important employment sector

8. Which of the following can be concluded from information in the reading?
   A. It is difficult for small businesses to compete with large retail stores.
   B. Advertising is no longer as important as it once was.
   C. More jobs have been lost to online retailing than are being gained from e-commerce.
   D. Consumers prefer using smartphone apps over home computers for online shopping.

9. According to the reading, what challenge will applicants for retail work face in the future?
   A. There will be a lot of competition for few jobs.
   B. Many retail jobs will require technical skills.
   C. It may be hard to get training.
   D. There will be fewer permanent jobs available in retail.

10. The purpose of the sidebar about "Life in the Information Age" is to _____.
    A. warn readers about personal privacy concerns in the retail industry
    B. explain why search engines can be helpful
    C. explain how information about consumers is collected
    D. describe the information age

ACADEMIC VOCABULARY

1. Retail is one of the most important _____ of a country's economy.
   - A. items
   - B. sectors
   - C. processes
   - D. purchases

2. A "brick-and-mortar" store is an example of _____.
   - A. a media site
   - B. distribution
   - C. technology
   - D. a physical location

3. It is expensive to _____ a supply of merchandise and a large company staff.
   - A. maintain
   - B. design
   - C. distribute
   - D. register

4. A _____ ad is one that is specifically directed toward particular individuals.
   - A. traditional
   - B. technical
   - C. technological
   - D. targeted

5. Each of our employees performs a very important _____ for our company.
   - A. response
   - B. function
   - C. location
   - D. design

6. The _____ personnel at our company protect people, records, and merchandise.
   - A. security
   - B. promotion
   - C. distribution
   - D. monitor

7. It is essential to have company _____ that protect the rights of workers.
   - A. economies
   - B. credits
   - C. policies
   - D. employment

8. We keep track of inventory in our store through _____.
   - A. data mining
   - B. marketing
   - C. development
   - D. UPC labeling

9. IT technicians create information systems that are able to _____ data about a company's customers.
   - A. require
   - B. analyze
   - C. design
   - D. establish

10. A tablet is an electronic _____.
    - A. device
    - B. location
    - C. process
    - D. function

11. Companies are always exploring new _____ for marketing their products.
    - A. experiences
    - B. codes
    - C. strategies
    - D. operations

12. Online sales have become an essential _____ of retail operations.
    - A. component
    - B. site
    - C. research
    - D. outcome

13. In the future, retail workers will need to have basic _____ literacy skills.
    - A. programming
    - B. media
    - C. company
    - D. computer

14. Consumers use apps on their smartphones to _____ information about products.
    - A. require
    - B. research
    - C. create
    - D. inspect

UNIT 1 LISTENING

PART A

Practice:	A	B	C		3.	A	B	C
1.	A	B	C		4.	A	B	C
2.	A	B	C		5.	A	B	C

PART B

Practice:	A	B	C		3.	A	B	C
1.	A	B	C		4.	A	B	C
2.	A	B	C		5.	A	B	C

Look at pages 16–17 of the core text. Write the correct words to complete the description.

baking	counters	dietician	oven	roasting	supervisor
board	cutting	icing bag	pastry	scale	tasting
boiling	decorate	manager	rack	service	weighing
broiling	delivery	mitt	receiving	spoon	workers

It's a typical busy day at this hospital kitchen. The kitchen _____manager_____ [1] is verifying a food

_____ [2] in the _____ [3] area. The chef and the hospital _____ [4] are

planning a menu in the chef's office. The food prep _____ [5] is supervising the busy food prep

_____ [6]. One of them is _____ [7] food portions on a portion _____ [8],

another is preparing salad, and another is _____ [9] vegetables on a cutting _____ [10].

There are several cooks. One is _____ [11] pasta, another is _____ [12] fish, and another

is _____ [13] chicken in the roasting _____ [14]. A food service worker is cleaning the

_____ [15]. The kitchen supervisor is speaking to a food _____ [16] worker. The head

cook is _____ [17] tomato sauce with a wooden _____ [18]. The _____ [19]

chef is using an _____ [20] to _____ [21] cakes. The baker is taking rolls from a

baking _____ [22] and putting them in the _____ [23] oven. He's using an oven

_____ [24] so he won't burn himself.

attendant	checking out	greeting	manager	resolving	steam table
basket	cooking	grill	order	scoop	taking
calling	dishing out	grilling	replenishing	serving	tongs
checking	frying	line	reservations	short-order	

In the restaurant, the head cook is holding an _____ [25] ticket and is _____ [26]

out orders. There are three _____ [27] cooks. One is _____ [28] steaks on the grill using

_____ [29], another is _____ [30] chicken in a deep fryer _____ [31],

and another is _____ [32] vegetables. A food service worker is _____ [33] the salad

bar. A waiter is _____ [34] a food order and a waitress is _____ [35] a meal. The

hostess is _____ [36] customers and taking _____ [37], and the restaurant manager is

_____ [38] a customer's complaint.

In the cafeteria, a _____ [39] cook is grilling hot dogs and hamburgers and a

_____ [40] cook is making sandwiches. The food service _____ [41] is

_____ [42] food supplies. One food service worker is bringing food to the _____ [43]

and another is _____ [44] food for a customer with a serving _____ [45]. The cashier is

_____ [46] a customer and a cafeteria _____ [47] is bussing a table.

CAREER RESEARCH

Using the O*NET Career Exploration Tools at mynextmove.org, search for information about one of the jobs in Unit 2. Write the information in the job profile below. Then prepare and give a presentation about the job.

Job Zone 1 (little or no job preparation)
busperson, cafeteria attendant, cashier, dishwasher, food prep worker, food service worker, host, hostess, line cook, server, short-order cook, waiter, waitress

Job Zone 2 (some job preparation)
baker, cook, food prep supervisor, food service manager, grill cook, kitchen manager, kitchen supervisor, pastry chef, restaurant manager

Job Zone 3 (medium job preparation)
chef, head cook

Job Zone 5 (extensive job preparation)
hospital dietician

Job name: _____

What does a person do in this job?

_____
_____
_____

What tools and equipment does a person use in this job?

_____

What skills and abilities are important?

_____
_____

What technology might a person use in this job?

_____

What kind of person will be interested in this work?

_____

What level of education, job training, and experience is required?

_____
_____

What is the job outlook?   What is the average salary?

_____   _____

Read the memo to restaurant employees and answer the questions.

1 To: All Kitchen Ranch Hands

2 From: Chelsea Chase

3 Subject: Grease Removal

4 I'm happy to announce that Chelsea's Chicken Ranch has contracted with
5 Yellow Gold Solutions to be the service provider for our new used cooking
6 oil collection and pickup program. As the most popular fried chicken restaurant in the
7 region, we generate an extraordinary amount of yellow grease. With this new initiative,
8 we will simultaneously solve a disposal problem and help the environment by recycling
9 our oil for a variety of reuses, including animal feed and biofuel. Starting next Monday,
10 everyone must follow these procedures:

11 Never pour grease down the drains. It clogs the pipes, and repairs are costly. We have
12 never allowed this, and some ranch hands have gotten the boot for breaking this rule.

13 Stop throwing away oil in the garbage. This is no longer necessary. Oil will now go to the
14 interior tank that Yellow Gold has installed in the rear of the building.

15 We receive a higher payment for our oil if it isn't contaminated, so make sure the oil is
16 free of any garbage or food debris.

17 Keep track of the grease tank's volume. There will be a regular pickup schedule, but if
18 we have a very busy weekend or holiday crowd, we'll probably need an earlier pickup.

19 Watch out for thieves! Only Yellow Gold trucks are allowed to pump out our oil. It's a valuable
20 resource, and many restaurants in the area have been robbed. If you see a suspicious truck
21 out back, get the license number, take a photo, tell me right away, and I'll call the police.

1. What would be another good subject line for this memo instead of "Grease Removal"?
   A. New Procedures to Help the Environment
   B. We're the Most Popular Restaurant in the Region!
   C. Watch Out for Thieves
   D. Cooking with Biofuel

2. Which line in the memo indicates the economic arrangement in the contract between the restaurant and the oil collection company?
   A. Line 3
   B. Line 4
   C. Line 15
   D. Line 17

3. In Line 12, what does *have gotten the boot* refer to?
   A. employees who had to wear special footwear after doing something wrong
   B. employees who have been warned
   C. employees whose pay has been lowered
   D. employees who have been terminated

4. What is the purpose of the final instruction in the memo?
   A. to help the environment
   B. to protect the restaurant
   C. to solve the used oil disposal problem
   D. to avoid costly repairs

DEMONSTRATING A PROCEDURE

Using YouTube, WikiHow, or another source, search online for a demonstration of how to do a procedure, operate equipment, or follow safety instructions in a restaurant or food service setting. Write out the instructions. Then prepare a media presentation. Make screenshots of the steps or video-record your demonstration. Present the procedure to the class.

Suggestions: how to cut vegetables into flower shapes; how to make a grilled cheese sandwich; how to clean a griddle

The Science of Culinary Arts

1 Cooking is a basic task of daily life. Some people are better cooks than others, but we can all recognize and appreciate good cooking. We know from personal experience that cooking requires skill, but we also know that cooking can be an art.

2 The term "culinary arts" refers to preparing, cooking, and presenting food. Culinary arts is also a course of study offered by cooking schools, vocational programs, colleges, and universities. Most graduates of culinary arts training programs work as cooks in restaurants, cafeterias, health facilities, hotels, and many other places where meals are prepared. Some specialize in baking breads, pastries, and cakes. Some culinary professionals find jobs as research chefs in test kitchens. Others follow a more scientific path.

Food Science

3 When we think of science, we don't usually think about food and cooking. But the sciences of biology, chemistry, and physics help us understand the nature of food, what happens to food when it is cooked, how conditions affect food, and how food can be processed and manufactured for the food industry.

4 Advanced culinary arts courses include the study of food science. Food science examines the physical, chemical, and biological makeup of food and the concepts of food processing. Food scientists usually work for companies that process and produce food in large quantities. Some of the different areas of food science include:

Food chemistry – the study of the biological components of food, the chemical processes that create foods, the interaction of foods, and how foods change in cooking;

Food microbiology – the study of microorganisms in food, including those that might cause food to spoil or that might cause food poisoning;

Food preservation – the study of how to keep food from losing its quality, including the use of chemical additives;

Food substitution – the replacement of elements such as fat and sugar in natural foods;

Food engineering and manufacturing – the science of processing food and developing and producing food products for the food industry;

Food packaging – packaging food to preserve it from production to distribution.

5 Food engineering is an important science for the fast-food industry, which needs food products with an appealing taste and appearance that can be produced cheaply and in very large quantities. The food also needs to be easy to cook quickly and conveniently with consistent results.

6 One of the products of food engineering is food that contains GMOs—genetically modified organisms. GMOs have special characteristics, such as increased nutrients or the ability to resist plant diseases. Many American food manufacturers have been using genetically modified corn, soybeans, and other foods in their food products. The use of these foods is controversial because many people think they are not safe to eat.

Nutrition and Dietetics

7 Two other scientific areas related to the culinary arts are nutrition and dietetics, which examine the nutritional value of food and how the food we eat affects our body and our health.

8　　The field of nutrition studies the content of foods and how food relates to health, growth, and disease. It looks at nutrients such as carbohydrates, protein, fats, fiber, and vitamins and minerals, and examines their biological and physiological effects. Dietetics is the science of human nutrition and the regulation of diet—what people regularly eat—to achieve beneficial effects on health. A healthy diet contributes to proper growth, maintaining strength, and avoiding illness.

9　　Cooks and culinary specialists who work in school cafeterias, health-care facilities, or other situations where they may be planning meals should understand basic nutrition as well as the components of a healthy diet. They need to know proper cooking practices and techniques to ensure that the nutritional value of foods is retained in cooking—for example, the fact that vegetables can lose nutrients when they are boiled. They need to be aware that people who have certain health conditions may require a special diet, and that it is unhealthy for food to contain high levels of salt, fat, and sugar.

10　　Many people follow a vegetarian or vegan diet. Vegetarians don't eat meat, and may or may not eat fish, eggs, or dairy products. A vegan diet consists only of plant-based foods. Understanding the science of food substitution is important for culinary specialists in planning vegetarian and vegan diets and meals since important nutrients found in meat must be included in some other way.

11　　Diets differ from one region to another, but not all are equally healthy. Many traditional diets, such as the Mediterranean diet and the Asian diet, include nutritious foods cooked in a healthy way. The typical American diet contains a lot of fried foods, meat, sugary drinks, and processed food products, and lacks sufficient fresh fruits and vegetables. It has led to health problems such as obesity in millions of Americans. Because of American influence and marketing, many of these foods are becoming increasingly popular in developing countries, where similar health effects are appearing. Public information campaigns to promote healthy eating are important. For their part, cooks and menu planners need to try to follow the principles of nutrition and proper food preparation.

MOLECULAR GASTRONOMY

Developed by a chemist and a physicist, molecular gastronomy, or experimental cuisine, is an extreme application of science to cooking. It makes use of chemical and physical principles and special processes and ingredients to create foods in unusual forms, such as small spheres or beads of juices, and desserts prepared with liquid nitrogen.

Sustainability

12　　Sustainability involves the conservation and responsible use of natural resources and concern for the environment. Environmental awareness is growing across our society, including in the culinary arts. The farm-to-table movement has become popular in recent years. Restaurants buy fresh vegetables and other products from farms in their area rather than from large producers that are far away. This supports small local businesses that use "green" (environmentally friendly), organic, and sustainable growing and production practices. It also reduces the amount of pollution caused by transporting products long distances.

13　　Reducing food waste also contributes to sustainability. Restaurant managers, research chefs, and food manufacturers can plan for better use of food products and develop more efficient production and manufacturing processes to reduce the amount of food that is wasted in cooking, in production, and by food consumers.

The Science of Taste

14 The main thing that culinary professionals are concerned with is taste—the foods they prepare need to taste good. We all know what tastes good to us, but science can be applied in understanding taste. Sensory evaluation is an area of science that analyzes human reactions to products through the senses (sight, hearing, touch, smell, taste). It is especially relevant to food engineers and manufacturers because the effects of processed food on the senses are vital factors in creating products people will like and buy. For example, tests can evaluate the point when ingredient levels make foods taste sweeter or saltier. In addition to taste and smell, sensory evaluation labs examine characteristics such as appearance and texture. They also measure the reactions and preferences of consumers in tasting various food products.

15 Whether working in a restaurant or any other facility where food is being served, cooks always need to know not only what foods to serve, but ways of preparing food to make it appealing to the people who will be eating it. To do this successfully, the skill and the art of culinary science must come together in preparation and presentation to create a meal that customers will enjoy. As the French say, Bon appétit!

DID YOU UNDERSTAND?

1. What are the culinary arts?

2. What are some possible career paths for culinary specialists?

3. Where do food scientists usually work?

4. Why do food scientists study microbiology?

5. Why would food scientists want to find substitutes for certain food elements in a food product?

6. How are nutrition and dietetics related to the culinary arts?

7. Why is a healthy diet important?

8. Describe the typical American diet.

9. How can culinary professionals contribute to sustainability?

10. What is the science of sensory evaluation?

WHAT'S YOUR EXPERIENCE?

1. Who cooks at your home? How do you decide what you are going to cook and eat? Is nutrition part of your decision?

2. What kind of food do you usually eat? Do you eat traditional food from your country?

3. Do you like fast food? How often do you eat it?

4. Do you look at the list of ingredients when you buy packaged food? Are there certain ingredients you look for? Why?

WHAT'S YOUR OPINION?

1. When you eat at a restaurant, what factors do you consider in deciding where to eat and what to eat? (For example: type of food, taste, price, location, quantity of food, nutritional value, quality or source of food ingredients)

2. What do you think influences most people to eat what they eat, even if it is not healthy?

3. What do you think about eating food that has been engineered and manufactured and packaged? Are you concerned about chemical additives? Are you concerned about genetically modified food?

READING COMPREHENSION

1. Science helps us to understand _____.
   A. why some people are good cooks
   B. why cooking is considered to be an art
   C. how the process of cooking affects food
   D. how food is prepared in different cultures

2. Which of the following areas of food science explains why people can get sick from eating certain foods?
   A. food preservation
   B. food microbiology
   C. food engineering
   D. food substitution

3. Foods that can be produced cheaply and in large quantities are especially important for _____.
   A. culinary arts courses
   B. people with health problems
   C. the fast-food industry
   D. vegans and vegetarians

4. Why are genetically modified foods controversial?
   A. They have too many nutrients.
   B. They may contain plant diseases.
   C. Many consumers dislike their taste.
   D. Some people are worried about their effect on health.

5. The term *dietetics* in paragraph 7 refers to _____.
   A. ways to lose weight
   B. ways that food affects people's health
   C. food safety regulations
   D. food scientists

6. The word *retained* in paragraph 9 means _____.
   A. kept
   B. changed
   C. received
   D. reduced

7. Which of the following is a response to concerns about the environment?
   A. food substitution
   B. the farm-to-table movement
   C. the typical American diet
   D. special diets for people with certain health problems

8. The purpose of the sidebar is to show that _____.
   A. chemists and physicists are able to work together creatively on experiments with food
   B. scientists are able to produce food in the shape of spheres and beads
   C. liquid nitrogen is an important component of molecular gastronomy
   D. scientific applications to food preparation can yield extremely nonconventional results

9. What is the main idea of the reading?
   A. Cooking requires skill, but it can also be an art.
   B. Culinary arts is the preparation, cooking, and presentation of food.
   C. The science of culinary arts plays an important role in today's food industry.
   D. A healthy diet contributes to good health and proper growth.

10. Which of the following supports the main idea of the reading?
    A. The study of food science is included in culinary arts programs.
    B. Understanding the science of food substitution is important for culinary specialists.
    C. The field of nutrition studies the content of foods.
    D. Cooks and menu planners try to follow principles of good nutrition.

ACADEMIC VOCABULARY

1. Menu planners need to follow the _____ of good nutrition.
   A. reactions
   B. principles
   C. chemicals
   D. methods

2. The area of food _____ studies the replacement of elements such as fat and sugar.
   A. regulation
   B. sustainability
   C. substitution
   D. evaluation

3. Eating the right foods will help you _____ strength and avoid illness.
   A. maintain
   B. contribute
   C. create
   D. appreciate

4. There is a growing focus on environmental _____ in the area of culinary arts.
   A. distribution
   B. facility
   C. reaction
   D. awareness

5. The science of _____ food is important for the food industry.
   A. processing
   B. consisting
   C. ensuring
   D. involving

6. It is important to understand the _____ of a healthy diet.
   A. facilities
   B. techniques
   C. components
   D. resources

7. Many research studies have examined the _____ of different foods with each other.
   A. instructions
   B. interactions
   C. processes
   D. factors

8. A goal of the fast food industry is to prepare food conveniently with _____ results.
   A. physical
   B. considerable
   C. various
   D. consistent

9. Scientists examine how different conditions can _____ the food we eat.
   A. affect
   B. achieve
   C. analyze
   D. react

10. Doctors hope that the regulation of patients' diets will have a _____ effect on their health.
    A. controversial
    B. beneficial
    C. modified
    D. necessary

11. There are many _____ diets based on a healthy combination of nutritious foods.
    A. environmental
    B. professional
    C. traditional
    D. physical

12. Unfortunately, some diets lack a _____ amount of fruits and vegetables.
    A. sustainable
    B. sufficient
    C. positive
    D. responsible

13. Pollution is increased when food products are _____ long distances.
    A. transported
    B. transmitted
    C. provided
    D. processed

14. Many people follow a vegan diet, which _____ only of plant-based foods.
    A. requires
    B. contributes
    C. contains
    D. consists

UNIT 2 LISTENING

PART A

Practice: A B C	**3.** A B C
1. A B C	**4.** A B C
2. A B C	**5.** A B C

PART B

Practice: A B C	**3.** A B C
1. A B C	**4.** A B C
2. A B C	**5.** A B C

Look at pages 30–31 of the core text. Write the correct words to complete the description.

cherry	landscape	mowing	respirator	sod	trimmer
edger	lawnmower	office	safety	spreader	trimming
edges	light bulbs	picking	scaffold	squeegee	walkways
equipment	maintaining	power	shovel	stick	washer
fertilize	maintenance	prune	shrubbery	supervisor	
handler	mechanic	pruner			

There are several workers at this _____office_____ ¹ park. A tree _____ ² is using a pole

_____ ³ to _____ ⁴ trees. A pesticide _____ ⁵ is wearing a spray

_____ ⁶ while spraying pesticides. An HVAC _____ ⁷ is _____ ⁸

the HVAC _____ ⁹. There are several _____ ¹⁰ workers. One is using a broadcast

_____ ¹¹ to _____ ¹² the lawn. Another is _____ ¹³ the lawn while

sitting on a ride-on _____ ¹⁴. One of the workers is _____ ¹⁵ hedges. Another is using

a round point _____ ¹⁶ to plant _____ ¹⁷. Another is trimming the

_____ ¹⁸ of the lawn with a power _____ ¹⁹. The landscape _____ ²⁰

is speaking to a worker who is laying _____ ²¹. There are several grounds _____ ²²

workers. One is _____ ²³ up litter from the sidewalk with a litter _____ ²⁴.

Another is cleaning _____ ²⁵ with a _____ ²⁶ washer. Another is standing on a

_____ ²⁷ picker and changing _____ ²⁸. There is also a window _____ ²⁹

who is standing on a hanging _____ ³⁰, wearing a _____ ³¹ harness, and cleaning

windows with a _____ ³².

boiler	changing	custodians	lights	polishing	shampoo	vacuum
broom	cleaner	extractor	mopping	removing	step ladder	wiping
carpeted	cleaning	filters	moving	repairs	storage	

It's evening, and there are several _____ ³³ and office _____ ³⁴ workers

in this office building. One office _____ ³⁵ is using a carpet _____ ³⁶ to

_____ ³⁷ a _____ ³⁸ floor. Another is wet _____ ³⁹ a tiled floor, another

is _____ ⁴⁰ down walls, and another is _____ ⁴¹ trash. The workers are using

many different pieces of equipment. One is using an upright _____ ⁴², another is using a floor

_____ ⁴³ machine, and another is using a push _____ ⁴⁴. The custodians are also

very busy. One custodian is standing on a _____ ⁴⁵ and _____ ⁴⁶ fluorescent ceiling

_____ ⁴⁷. Another is doing _____ ⁴⁸ in the bathroom. Another is changing furnace

_____ ⁴⁹ in the _____ ⁵⁰ room. Another is _____ ⁵¹ furniture in the

_____ ⁵² room.

CAREER RESEARCH

Using the O*NET Career Exploration Tools at mynextmove.org, search for information about one of the jobs in Unit 3. Write the information in the job profile below. Then prepare and give a presentation about the job.

Job Zone 1 (little or no job preparation)
grounds maintenance worker, landscape worker

Job Zone 2 (some job preparation)
cleaning supervisor, cleaning worker, custodian, head custodian, office cleaner/office cleaning worker, pesticide handler, security person, tree trimmer, window washer

Job Zone 3 (medium job preparation)
grounds maintenance supervisor, heating & air conditioning (HVAC) mechanic/technician, landscape supervisor

Job name: _____

What does a person do in this job?

_____

_____

_____

What tools and equipment does a person use in this job?

_____

What skills and abilities are important?

_____

_____

What technology might a person use in this job?

_____

What kind of person will be interested in this work?

_____

What level of education, job training, and experience is required?

_____

_____

What is the job outlook?   What is the average salary?

_____   _____

Read the safety poster and answer the questions.

GROUNDS WORKERS: USE YOUR PPE!

Don't forget to use your Personal Protective Equipment!

1 **Protect your hands!** Avoid scrapes, cuts, burns,
2 and nerve damage from vibrating equipment. Wear the
3 correct gloves for the task at hand.

4 **Protect your feet!** Make sure you have the correct work
5 shoes or boots for adequate support and protection of
6 ankles, feet, and toes.

7 **Protect your hearing!** Ear muffs and ear plugs are essential for hearing protection when
8 using noise-producing equipment.

9 **Protect your eyes!** Wear goggles or face shields to protect eyes from dust and flying
10 debris. Wear sunglasses that provide protection from UVA and UVB exposure.

11 **Protect yourself from chemical exposure and airborne contaminants!** Use gloves
12 and a mask or respirator when handling pesticides. Use a respirator to avoid harmful vapors
13 and contaminants.

14 **Make sure your PPE fits properly!** If you wear it incorrectly, you aren't protected.

15 **Use common sense to avoid injuries that Personal Protective Equipment can't prevent!**
16 Avoid working during lightning storms, weather emergencies, and times of extreme heat or
17 cold.

---

1. Which line of this safety poster gives general (not specific) advice about using PPE?
- A. Line 1
- B. Line 4
- C. Line 14
- D. Line 15

2. The terms *UVA* and *UVB* aren't explained in the poster, but they probably refer to _____.
- A. parts of the eye
- B. airborne contaminants
- C. chemical exposure
- D. sun exposure

3. In Line 3, what does *the task at hand* mean?
- A. an activity a worker is currently doing
- B. an unsafe work activity
- C. a safety work glove
- D. an activity that requires the use of one's hands

4. The writer of this safety poster would probably agree that _____.
- A. grounds workers aren't careful at work
- B. grounds work can be dangerous
- C. common sense is more important than PPE
- D. hands and feet are more difficult to protect than ears and eyes

DEMONSTRATING A PROCEDURE

Using YouTube, WikiHow, or another source, search online for a demonstration of how to do a procedure, operate equipment, or follow safety instructions in a buildings and grounds occupation. Write out the instructions. Then prepare a media presentation. Make screenshots of the steps or video-record your demonstration. Present the procedure to the class.

Suggestions: how to clean a window like a pro; how to mop a floor; how to break down a cardboard box for recycling

Making Buildings Greener

1   As pollution and global warming increase, concern for the future of the environment is growing. More and more energy is needed as the world's population grows and as poor countries develop their economies. Unfortunately, burning fossil fuels for energy such as oil, coal, and natural gas to generate electricity produces harmful gases that pollute the atmosphere.

2   Governments, businesses, and individuals want to help, and they look for ways to reduce their use of energy. Currently, commercial and residential buildings use 40% of the total energy consumed in the United States and around the world. One way for communities to help the environment is to reduce the amount of energy that buildings use. Not only is it good for the environment, it is also good for building owners financially, since they would be spending less on electricity and gas.

Green Building Strategies

3   New methods and technologies for conserving energy are constantly being developed. When new buildings are constructed, energy-saving features can be built into them. Modifying—or "retrofitting"—existing buildings can be more challenging, but there are many ways to make older buildings more energy-efficient. Companies specializing in this work prepare plans with different options for the various elements involved in the "green" retrofitting of buildings. Local governments, environmental agencies, and utility companies offer programs in many communities that advise on ways to make buildings and homes more energy-efficient. Many of these programs also offer financial incentives.

4   Green retrofitting an existing building has several goals. The main goal is to reduce the amount of energy—electricity and gas—that the building uses. Two important ways of doing this are to increase the efficiency of equipment and systems in the building that use energy, and to decrease heat loss and heat transfer. Another way to reduce the use of electricity and gas from power companies is for a building to generate its own electricity with

solar panels. Conserving water can also reduce a building's environmental impact.

5   This checklist shows steps that a green retrofit might follow.

Increase the efficiency of equipment and systems that use energy

Install energy-efficient equipment

☑ **Replace heating, ventilation, and air conditioning (HVAC) equipment with modern, energy-efficient systems.**

The furnaces in new systems use less energy to deliver the same amount of heat as older systems that use more gas or electricity. Improving and sealing air ducts can help move air faster through a building and can reduce loss of hot or cold air through leaks. Keeping air intakes and filters clean maintains maximum air flow. In buildings that use hot water for heating, more efficient boilers can reduce energy consumption.

☑ **Replace incandescent light bulbs with CFL or LED lights.**

Compact fluorescent lamps (CFLs) are small curled versions of long fluorescent tubes. Light-emitting diodes (LEDs) contain semiconductors that convert electricity into light. These new types of bulbs cost more than incandescent bulbs, but they last much longer and use only 10% to 25% of the amount of electricity.

Use "smart" building-control systems

 Equip the HVAC system with a smart control system.

The HVAC system is the largest user of energy in a building, and closely controlling heating and cooling can greatly reduce overall energy consumption. Programmable thermostats on HVAC systems can be set to turn heating and cooling on and off at precise times and to maintain set temperatures. In smart control systems, sensors placed throughout a building transmit information to the HVAC system about conditions in specific areas, and heat and cooling can be sent to or excluded from particular places. Sensors also monitor room occupancy and external weather conditions.

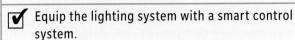 **Equip the lighting system with a smart control system.**

Lighting systems can have automatic controls that turn lights on and off according to a programmed schedule or based on room occupancy, or that adjust to levels of sunlight.

 Integrate all building controls into a comprehensive smart technology system.

A comprehensive smart technology system controls multiple building operations in an integrated way, including HVAC, lights, and other systems.

Decrease heat loss and heat transfer

 Replace windows.

 Installing modern double-pane windows greatly reduces temperature transfer and maintains indoor temperature with much less additional heating or cooling. Efficiency can be greater when either tinting or a low-emittance coating is added to the glass. One simpler improvement is to add a reflective film on the outside of the glass in existing windows.

 Seal leaks.

Installing weather-stripping around building entrances helps prevent interior heat from escaping and cold from entering.

 Install adequate insulation in ceilings and walls.

 Adding adequate insulation material will block heat from escaping through outside walls and up into the attic of homes. Insulation can be added inside a wall or on the outside of a building when new siding is installed. A thick layer of insulation in the attic of a home helps to maintain heat in the rooms below.

 Improve roofs.

Heat can enter a building when intense sun strikes the roof. Painting roofs with a light-colored reflective coating reduces the thermal effect of strong sunlight.

Rooftop gardens have become popular in many cities in Europe and the United States. They decrease heat transfer into the building on hot summer days, keeping it cool and reducing the need for air conditioning. In addition, plants improve local air quality by taking in harmful carbon dioxide and creating oxygen. Gardens also have a cooling effect on the nearby area.

Use alternative energy sources

 Install a solar energy system.

Building owners can install solar panels that use photovoltaic cells to generate electricity. Large-scale solar energy systems can greatly reduce the need for additional commercial power.

 Contract with alternative or "green" energy suppliers.

In some areas, utility companies sell electricity that is generated from renewable sources, such as solar, wind, and hydroelectric power.

Conserve water

 Install water-conserving plumbing fixtures.

These include low-flow water fixtures, improved flush valves, and flow control systems that use sensors. Sensor controls on retrofits are usually battery-powered rather than wired in.

✓ **Use alternative water sources for irrigation and toilet flushing.**

In commercial buildings where bath and laundry water is available, reuse of "grey water" is possible. However, it can be expensive since it requires processing and a separate piping system. Harvesting rainwater for these uses is another option.

✓ **Equip irrigation systems with smart control systems.**

Smart systems monitor moisture in the ground and regulate the amount of water used for irrigating plants. Another method for conserving water is to install a rain sensor that shuts off irrigation when it is raining.

✓ **Use electronic monitoring of overall water consumption.**

A comprehensive water usage monitoring system receives information on water flow from sensors placed at every water outlet across a building or facility. Points with excessive use can be identified, and overall water usage can be monitored.

6 Policies and guidelines promoted by government agencies, building associations, and construction companies are helping to promote environmentally conscious practices in building construction. Buildings account for a major portion of the world's energy use, and the more efficient we can make them, the more we will be contributing to the health of the planet.

DID YOU UNDERSTAND?

1. Why is the world using more energy?

2. How much of the world's energy do buildings use?

3. What is the goal of green retrofitting a building?

4. What are two important ways to reduce the amount of energy a building uses?

5. What is the advantage of modern, energy-efficient HVAC systems over older systems?

6. How does the energy consumption of new-style light bulbs compare with older bulbs?

7. How does a smart building-control system monitor conditions inside a building?

8. Why would an automatic lighting system adjust the lights because of the amount of sunlight?

9. Why are heat loss and heat transfer problems for buildings?

10. What are two sources of alternative or renewable energy? What advantage do they have?

11. What are some types of plumbing fixtures that conserve water?

12. How does a smart irrigation system conserve water?

WHAT'S YOUR OPINION?

1. Some developing countries say they should not have to reduce their energy use because they are growing, and that rich countries like the United States should cut back more. What do you think?

2. Elena runs a small business in a building she owns. The building doesn't use much energy, and the utility bill is low. Elena knows that if she makes improvements in the building, it will use a little less energy. The changes would cost $12,000 to make, but her bill would be lowered by only about $30 a month. Do you think Elena should make these changes to conserve energy? Why or why not?

3. Would you get electricity from a company that provided energy from renewable sources, even if it cost more than electricity from the regular power supplier?

READING COMPREHENSION

1. Burning fossil fuels _____.
   A. reduces the use of energy
   B. conserves water
   C. causes pollution
   D. helps the environment

2. Older buildings can be made more energy-efficient through _____.
   A. global warming
   B. retrofitting
   C. heat transfer
   D. environmental impact

3. Which of the following does NOT increase the energy efficiency of equipment?
   A. adding reflective film on the outside of glass windows
   B. updating heating systems
   C. switching from CFL to LED lights
   D. installing "smart" building control systems

4. Which of the following will do the most to lower electricity costs?
   A. replacing windows
   B. replacing refrigerators and freezers
   C. sealing leaks
   D. installing adequate insulation

5. Buildings can generate their own electricity by _____.
   A. conserving water
   B. decreasing heat loss
   C. installing double-pane windows
   D. using solar panels

6. A thermostat that is programmable _____.
   A. adjusts to levels of sunlight
   B. is based on room occupancy
   C. turns heat and cooling on and off at precise times
   D. requires a lot of electricity

7. Which section of the checklist in paragraph 5 suggests contracting with green suppliers of electricity?
   A. Increase the efficiency of equipment and systems that use energy
   B. Use "smart" building-control systems
   C. Decrease heat loss and heat transfer
   D. Use alternative energy sources

8. In paragraph 3, a synonym for the word *incentive* is _____.
   A. motivation
   B. investment
   C. award
   D. contract

9. The main focus of the reading is to _____.
   A. explain the benefits of conserving water and electricity
   B. explore ways in which buildings can be made more energy-efficient
   C. compare and evaluate alternative energy sources
   D. promote the construction of new energy-efficient buildings

10. Which of the following supports the rationale for the main focus of the reading?
    A. Currently buildings use 40% of the total energy consumed in the United States.
    B. Renewable energy is becoming more affordable.
    C. Modern buildings should incorporate modern technologies.
    D. Burning fossil fuels causes harm to the environment.

ACADEMIC VOCABULARY

1. The use of fossil fuels to _____ energy produces harmful gases that pollute the atmosphere.
   A. integrate
   B. generate
   C. send
   D. contribute

2. There are many ways to _____ existing buildings to make them more energy-efficient.
   A. maintain
   B. create
   C. modify
   D. identify

3. Conserving water can reduce a building's _____ on the environment.
   A. impact
   B. goal
   C. policy
   D. strategy

4. New heating and cooling equipment _____ much less electricity than older models.
   A. converts
   B. transmits
   C. integrates
   D. requires

5. Controlled heating and cooling reduces a building's energy _____.
   A. construction
   B. consumption
   C. sources
   D. features

6. It is essential to install _____ insulation in ceilings and walls.
   A. adequate
   B. available
   C. integrated
   D. overall

7. Many building owners install solar _____ that use photovoltaic cells to generate electricity.
   A. layers
   B. panels
   C. foundations
   D. sources

8. Efficient irrigation systems _____ the amount of water used for irrigating plants.
   A. process
   B. equip
   C. require
   D. regulate

9. Many government agencies are working to _____ environmentally conscious practices.
   A. replace
   B. consume
   C. promote
   D. provide

10. There are many _____ benefits to reducing energy usage.
    A. financial
    B. flexible
    C. integrated
    D. alternative

11. New technologies for conserving energy are _____ being developed.
    A. significantly
    B. constantly
    C. excessively
    D. functionally

12. Our company is planning to install new energy-efficient _____.
    A. construction
    B. features
    C. methods
    D. equipment

13. HVAC systems with smart controls are able to either send or _____ cooling from different areas.
    A. consume
    B. schedule
    C. exclude
    D. construct

14. Lighting systems with automatic controls can turn lights on and off based on room _____.
    A. occupancy
    B. environment
    C. guidelines
    D. technologies

UNIT 3 LISTENING

PART A

Practice: A B C

1. A B C
2. A B C
3. A B C
4. A B C
5. A B C

PART B

Practice: A B C

1. A B C
2. A B C
3. A B C
4. A B C
5. A B C

Look at pages 44–45 of the core text. Write the correct words to complete the description.

applying	client	counter	manager	shampooist	stations
apron	color	cut	salon	shears	stylists
area	colorist	dryer	sample	smocks	towels
bin	comb	hair	selecting	standing	
capes	consulting	hairpiece	shampooing		

The salon _____manager_____ ¹ is greeting a _____ ² at the check-in

_____ ³ of this hair _____ ⁴. The hair _____ ⁵ are busy at their

stylist _____ ⁶. The stylists are wearing _____ ⁷ and the clients are wearing

_____ ⁸. One stylist is using _____ ⁹ to _____ ¹⁰ a client's

hair. Another is braiding a client's _____ ¹¹. Another is _____ ¹² with a client

who is _____ ¹³ a hair _____ ¹⁴ from a _____ ¹⁵ book. One of

the stylists is using a wig _____ ¹⁶ to style a _____ ¹⁷. A _____ ¹⁸

is _____ ¹⁹ a client's hair in the shampooing _____ ²⁰. There are many fresh

_____ ²¹ on the shelf in that area and there are used towels in the towel _____ ²².

A _____ ²³, who is wearing a colorist _____ ²⁴, is _____ ²⁵ color to a

client's hair. One of the salon customers is talking to a stylist while she's sitting under a _____ ²⁶

hair _____ ²⁷.

applying	blending	esthetician	mirror	polish	stool
apron	brush	makeup	nail	pushing back	therapist
artist	chair	massage	pedicurist	spa	
bib	cleansing	massaging	plucked	stations	

Manicurists in the _____ ²⁸ salon are very busy at their manicurist _____ ²⁹.

One is _____ ³⁰ a client's hands and another is _____ ³¹ a client's cuticles.

A makeup _____ ³², who is wearing a _____ ³³ and tool _____ ³⁴,

is with a client who is wearing a makeup _____ ³⁵ and sitting in a _____ ³⁶ chair

in front of a large makeup _____ ³⁷. The makeup artist is _____ ³⁸ eye shadow

to a client and _____ ³⁹ her makeup. A _____ ⁴⁰ is sitting on a pedicurist

_____ ⁴¹ and is applying _____ ⁴² to the toenails of a client who is sitting in a

pedicure spa _____ ⁴³. In the _____ ⁴⁴ area, an _____ ⁴⁵ has

_____ ⁴⁶ a client's eyebrows and is now _____ ⁴⁷ her skin. Another client is lying

on a _____ ⁴⁸ table. A massage _____ ⁴⁹ is massaging his neck.

CAREER RESEARCH

Using the O*NET Career Exploration Tools at mynextmove.org, search for information about one of the jobs in Unit 4. Write the information in the job profile below. Then prepare and give a presentation about the job.

Job Zone 2 (some job preparation)
assistant/shampooist, manicurist, pedicurist, receptionist

Job Zone 3 (medium job preparation)
colorist, esthetician, hair stylist, makeup artist, masseur/masseuse/massage therapist, salon manager

Job name: _____

What does a person do in this job?

_____

_____

_____

What tools and equipment does a person use in this job?

_____

What skills and abilities are important?

_____

_____

What technology might a person use in this job?

_____

What kind of person will be interested in this work?

_____

What level of education, job training, and experience is required?

_____

_____

What is the job outlook?   What is the average salary?

_____   _____

A Nail Salon Owner

1   I'm Tina Tran—the proud owner of Tina's Nail Garden, a nail salon that I opened last year. I've worked at a few different nail salons over the past few years, but I always dreamed of having my own business and being my own boss. The reason is that I wanted to create a salon that would be safer for both customers and workers.

2   Salons can be hazardous places. We have on-the-job exposure to lots of chemicals that give us headaches and rashes and make us sick. We call three of these chemicals the *toxic trio*—dibutyl phthalate, toluene, and formaldehyde. (They're hard to pronounce, and hard to get out of your system.)

3   I'm a supporter of an association of nail salons in our area, and my new salon is part of our Healthy Salon Initiative, which certifies salons that employ safe workplace practices. We don't use nail polishes that contain the toxic trio, we avoid using nail polish thinners with acetone, we require staff to wear the correct type of gloves to protect their skin, and we have special ventilation units to assure the air we breathe is safe.

4   I love this work, and I love my customers. Many have been loyal customers for many years. They

share about both good and bad things in their lives, and many of them treat me like a close friend.

5   My daughter and my son would like to join me in this business in the future, but I won't let them. They're teenagers now, and I would be concerned for their health. Too many of the women I have worked with over the years have developed asthma and other breathing problems, skin disorders, and cancer. Some have also had miscarriages or had babies born with low birthweights or birth defects.

6   I hope that someday all nail salons will be safer places for workers and customers. In the meantime, my personal goal is to offer my customers a "green" salon experience by using more organic products, and to be a voice for healthier products and safer working conditions in this industry.

---

1. What is the meaning of *certifies* as used in paragraph 3?
   A. owns
   B. supports
   C. approves
   D. operates

2. Select the paragraph that gives the most details about how to improve working conditions in this industry.
   A. Paragraph 3
   B. Paragraph 4
   C. Paragraph 5
   D. Paragraph 6

3. Select the paragraph that indicates the person's job satisfaction.
   A. Paragraph 2
   B. Paragraph 3
   C. Paragraph 4
   D. Paragraph 5

4. Which word has the same meaning as the phrase *to be a voice for* in paragraph 6?
   A. to dream about
   B. to complain about
   C. to purchase
   D. to advocate for

CLASSROOM VISITOR

Invite the owner of a local hair or nail salon to visit your class. Ask about the types of jobs at the salon, the working conditions, and any issues regarding the safety of the products used. Also, ask about the visitor's career and the process of starting one's own business.

(Or, do an Internet search for information about an association of businesses or workers that acts to promote healthier conditions in the workplace.)

The Chemistry of Cosmetology

1   Beauty salons are common businesses in most countries around the world. They offer customers services such as hair styling, application of cosmetics, skin care, and manicures. The application of beauty treatments is called cosmetology, and specialists in this field are called cosmetologists. Professional cosmetologists usually need to complete a specialized educational program and obtain a license from their state government.

2   Cosmetologists use a variety of products in their work. Common products for hair treatments include shampoos, rinses, conditioners, straighteners, relaxers, perm solutions, hair coloring, and sprays. For skin, there are lotions, cleansers, creams, and many other products. Manicures involve nail polish, nail polish remover, artificial nails, creams, and lotions. Makeup for the face includes products such as lipstick, eyeliners, powders, and face creams. All of these cosmetic products, as well as perfumes, are created in scientific laboratories by cosmetic chemists.

Cosmetic Science

3   Cosmetic chemists work in the field of cosmetic science. They study the materials and chemicals used in cosmetic products, how these ingredients interact with each other, and their effect on the human body. Cosmetics are made of natural substances such as oils, waxes, and minerals, as well as various types of chemicals, which are often derived from petroleum. Common components of cosmetic products are colorants, softeners, binders, mixing agents, and preservatives. These ingredients are combined to create cosmetics that have a particular effect or produce a certain look. Chemists also make products that cosmetologists use in salons for hair treatments to straighten, smooth, or curl hair, and for nail treatments.

4   Cosmetic chemists test the safety of cosmetics for the people who use them—for example, to see if they cause skin irritation or allergic reactions. Cosmetics do not cause health problems for most people. However, some salon products contain chemicals that can have a harmful effect not only on customers but on the cosmetologists who work with the products regularly. Some cosmetologists have had serious health problems and left the profession.

Salon Chemicals

5   A variety of chemical products are used in hair treatments, and many of them can be harmful to one's health, especially after long or regular exposure. The most common dangerous chemical is formaldehyde, an ingredient in many products that smooth or straighten hair. It is a colorless liquid with a strong smell. It evaporates easily, and clients and salon staff can breathe it in as a gas or vapor. Formaldehyde can also be released as a gas from other chemicals in certain conditioners and shampoos. It is released at room temperature, and especially when the chemical is heated, for example, during blow drying. It gets into the nose and lungs and can irritate the eyes, throat, and skin. It can cause breathing difficulties, chest

ANIMAL TESTING

It has been common for laboratories developing cosmetics to test ingredients and products on animals such as rats, mice, and rabbits to assess their safety for use on humans. The chemicals used in this testing can have painful and even fatal effects on the animals. After protests by animal rights groups, animal testing has become very controversial, and many countries have prohibited it.

pain, and headaches. Formaldehyde is classified by government agencies as a carcinogen (a substance that can cause cancer) and is connected to nasal and lung cancer and possibly other types of cancer.

6   The U.S. Department of Labor Occupational Safety and Health Administration (OSHA) has identified chemicals that contain formaldehyde or methylene glycol (which is formaldehyde dissolved in water). Formalin, methanal, methanediol, or formaldehyde monohydrate are other names for formaldehyde or methylene glycol. Timonacic acid and dimethoxymethane are chemicals in salon products that can release formaldehyde when they are heated. OSHA requires manufacturers to list these chemicals on the label of the product's bottle or box and also on a safety data sheet (SDS) for the product. However, some manufacturers do not accurately list product ingredients. Also, the U.S. Food and Drug Administration does not inspect and approve these kinds of products.

7   Cosmetologists who work in nail salons are exposed to a variety of hazardous chemicals. They often work long hours and are in close contact with these chemicals. Formaldehyde is sometimes used as an ingredient in nail polish. Other dangerous ingredients include toluene, dibutyl phthalate, and ethyl acetate. These chemicals and others used in nail polish, nail polish remover, and artificial nail products can cause headaches and dizziness, and irritate eyes, skin, nose, throat, and lungs. They can cause difficulty in breathing, asthma, and damage to the liver and kidneys. Exposure to these chemicals during pregnancy may be harmful to unborn children.

Workplace Safety

8   The most important way for shop owners to avoid serious health risks for salon workers and salon customers is to use products that contain the least hazardous chemicals. The owner and the employees should know the health effects of the products they use and should follow instructions on using them safely.

9   Good ventilation is very important. Doors and windows should be open to let in fresh air. The salon should have an exhaust system to pull out

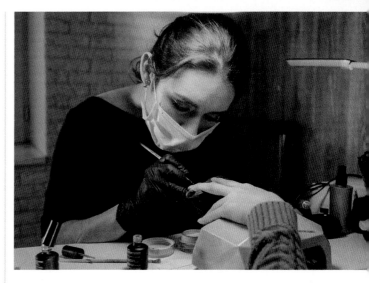

the vapors from the work area, and it should always be kept running. If there is no exhaust system, the heating, ventilation, and air conditioning system should be running. The work area should have exhaust fans to pull air in one end of the salon and push it out the other.

10   When storing chemical products, bottles should be tightly closed. Workers should immediately put used materials that are soaked in chemicals into a trash container that has a tight lid. Used chemicals should be disposed of according to safety instructions. Workers should not eat or drink in work areas and should keep their food and drinks covered.

11   To keep products off their skin, salon workers may need to wear long-sleeved shirts. They should use the correct kind of gloves when handling chemical products and replace them when there are cuts or holes in them. If they notice that a product is irritating their skin, they should stop using it. They should wash their hands after working on clients, and before they eat or drink. Dust masks can protect nail workers from dust, but not from chemical vapors.

12   OSHA and state governments have regulations that require hair salons to follow safe practices. Salons need to test the air inside the salon to determine formaldehyde levels and install ventilation systems if the level is too high. They need to provide workers with gloves and other protective equipment, and there needs to be eye and skin washing equipment in the salon. Workers

must be informed about the health effects of formaldehyde and be trained in using it, handling it, and storing it. There are also regulations about the use of dangerous products in nail salons. Many states have produced information sheets about working safely in nail salons in English as well as in languages such as Vietnamese, Korean, and Spanish, since most of the workers are immigrants.

13 Beauty salons are popular businesses, and the technicians who work in them are skilled professionals who try hard to please their customers. We assume that salons and the products they use are safe, but we may not think about the people who work all day in environments that could be endangering their health. Even though there are regulations, it is essential that cosmetologists and

other workers in hair and nail salons learn about the possible hazards of their workplace, and that businesses take proper precautions to lessen the risks for their employees.

DID YOU UNDERSTAND?

1. What services do beauty salons offer?
2. Where are beauty salon products created?
3. What do cosmetic chemists study?
4. Are cosmetics and salon products harmful?
5. What is formaldehyde, and where is it used?
6. What are the harmful effects of formaldehyde?
7. What is OSHA?
8. How can salon staff know what chemicals are in the products they use?
9. What are some of the dangerous chemical ingredients in nail polish?
10. Why is good ventilation important in nail salons?
11. What are some of the safety practices salon workers should follow?
12. How can salon workers learn about salon safety?

WHAT'S YOUR EXPERIENCE?

1. Have you been in or walked past a hair salon or nail salon? Did you notice a chemical smell?
2. Have you worked in a workplace that was dangerous or had health risks? If you have, did the company take steps to make sure workers were safe?

WHAT'S YOUR OPINION?

1. What do you think workers should do if they feel they are working in unsafe conditions?
2. What is your opinion about testing cosmetics on animals? Would you consider this when you select cosmetics and other products you buy?

READING COMPREHENSION

1. Conditioners, straighteners, and relaxers are _____.
   A. types of makeup
   B. hair treatment products
   C. natural substances
   D. used for cleansing

2. Workers might breathe in formaldehyde because _____.
   A. it has a strong smell
   B. it is colorless
   C. it evaporates easily
   D. it is a dangerous chemical

3. Which of the following is NOT true about cosmetic chemists?
   A. They work in scientific laboratories.
   B. They study the materials and chemicals used in cosmetic products.
   C. They offer services in hair and nail salons.
   D. They make the products that are used in beauty salons.

4. Which paragraph describes the particular dangers for manicurists?
   A. Paragraph 3
   B. Paragraph 4
   C. Paragraph 6
   D. Paragraph 7

5. Having an exhaust system to pull out vapors is important for proper _____.
   A. storage
   B. ventilation
   C. temperature control
   D. safety instructions

6. What is the meaning of *derived from* in paragraph 3?
   A. based on
   B. consisting of
   C. similar to
   D. different from

7. Which of the following would the author of this reading probably consider the most problematic?
   A. OSHA has identified chemicals that contain harmful ingredients.
   B. Formaldehyde is sometimes listed on a product label by other names.
   C. Not all manufacturers accurately list product ingredients.
   D. Products are required to have a safety data sheet.

8. What is the main topic of the reading?
   A. Cosmetic chemists test the safety of cosmetics for the individuals using them.
   B. Some cosmetic products contain harmful ingredients.
   C. Cosmetologists are exposed to a variety of hazardous chemicals.
   D. It is essential to know the dangers of cosmetic products and how to take necessary precautions.

9. Which of the following supports the main idea of the reading?
   A. Professional cosmetologists must complete a specialized training program.
   B. Salons and their employees need to follow safety instructions carefully.
   C. Formaldehyde is a dangerous chemical that is used in many salon products.
   D. Shop owners should use products that contain the least hazardous chemicals.

10. Many states have prepared bilingual information sheets because of the large number of _____.
    A. immigrant workers
    B. shop owners
    C. government regulations
    D. hair and nail salon clients

ACADEMIC VOCABULARY

1. Professional cosmetologists need to complete a training program and then _____ a license.
   A. retain
   B. contain
   C. obtain
   D. register

2. Cosmetic products are _____ in scientific laboratories.
   A. displayed
   B. distributed
   C. maintained
   D. created

3. Scientists study how the chemical ingredients in cosmetic products _____ with each other.
   A. interact
   B. involve
   C. participate
   D. relate

4. Many chemical products are _____ from petroleum.
   A. received
   B. derived
   C. contacted
   D. found

5. Mixing agents and preservatives are common _____ of cosmetic products.
   A. formulas
   B. features
   C. components
   D. sources

6. It is possible to have an allergic _____ to certain cosmetic chemicals.
   A. reaction
   B. relation
   C. result
   D. effect

7. Some chemical products can be harmful after long _____ to them.
   A. examination
   B. exposure
   C. administration
   D. distribution

8. Several chemicals containing formaldehyde have been _____.
   A. contained
   B. contacted
   C. assumed
   D. identified

9. Many chemicals in beauty salon products _____ formaldehyde when they are heated.
   A. dispose
   B. release
   C. allow
   D. identify

10. OSHA _____ manufacturers to list chemicals on the label of a product.
    A. requires
    B. inspects
    C. reports
    D. restricts

11. Cosmetologists who work in nail salons are _____ to a variety of hazardous chemicals.
    A. available
    B. involved
    C. exposed
    D. examined

12. Used chemicals must be _____ of according to safety instructions.
    A. displayed
    B. consumed
    C. assessed
    D. disposed

13. There are many government _____ about the use of dangerous chemicals in nail salons.
    A. responsibilities
    B. regulations
    C. responses
    D. inspections

14. Testing cosmetic products on animals has been _____ in many countries.
    A. instructed
    B. released
    C. contacted
    D. prohibited

UNIT 4 LISTENING

PART A

Practice: A B C   3. A B C
       1. A B C   4. A B C
       2. A B C   5. A B C

PART B

Practice: A B C   3. A B C
       1. A B C   4. A B C
       2. A B C   5. A B C

Look at pages 58–59 of the core text. Write the correct words to complete the description.

assemblers	conveyor	floor	machine	parts	robot	tester
assembly	crates	grinding	move	pinstripe	safety	tightening
assistant	distribution	hoist	moving	quality	sealing	unloading
attaching	fabrication	imperfections	packing	rack	shipping	welder
bending	fabricator	inspector	paint	receiving	supervisor	welding

The workers at the motorcycle factory are busy doing their jobs. A _____receiving_____ [1] clerk is

_____ [2] crates from a truck. A _____ [3] clerk is using a parts _____ [4]

to _____ [5] parts to different areas of the factory. Two bench _____ [6] are

in the engine _____ [7] area. One is _____ [8] an engine part and the other

is _____ [9] a gasket. In the _____ [10] area, a _____ [11] is

_____ [12] frame pieces and a _____ [13] is _____ [14] tubing. In

the _____ [15] shop, an articulated paint _____ [16] is painting gas tanks and

two _____ [17] artists are pinstriping them. There are several factory line assemblers in the

bike assembly area. One is _____ [18] a front wheel, another is _____ [19] a rear

assembly using a hydraulic assist _____ [20], another is _____ [21] handlebars, and

another is talking to the factory line _____ [22]. A shop floor _____ [23] is bringing

finished _____ [24] to the production _____ [25]. In the _____ [26]

control area, a quality control _____ [27] is feeling for _____ [28] and a quality

control _____ [29] is testing a motorcycle. There are several _____ [30] clerks in the

_____ [31] area. Some are using a _____ [32] to lift a motorcycle. Others are putting

motorcycles into shipping _____ [33] on the rolling _____ [34] belt.

assemblers	box	clean	drawings	manual	samplers	testing
assembly	carton	defective	electronics	packers	snapping	trays
attaching	checkpoint	department	engineer	production	soldering	wires

There are many workers at the electronics _____ [35] plant. A technical _____ [36]

is doing technical _____ [37]. One of the _____ [38] assemblers in the

_____ [39] room is trimming _____ [40] on a component and another is

_____ [41] a component to a PCB. The _____ [42] on the _____ [43] line

are doing different tasks. They are _____ [44] LCDs to casing tops and _____ [45]

covers onto the bottoms. Quality control _____ [46] at the quality control _____ [47]

are _____ [48] the units. If they find a _____ [49] unit, they put it in a bin. Hand

_____ [50] at the packing area are placing units in plastic packing _____ [51]. They put

an owner's _____ [52] into each tray, slide the tray into a product _____ [53], put it into a

shipping _____ [54], and finally bring the shipping cartons to the shipping _____ [55].

CAREER RESEARCH

Using the O*NET Career Exploration Tools at mynextmove.org, search for information about one of the jobs in Unit 5. Write the information in the job profile below. Then prepare and give a presentation about the job.

Job Zone 2 (some job preparation)
assembler, bench assembler, distribution clerk, electronics assembler, factory helper, factory line assembler, factory line supervisor, hand packer, packing clerk, receiving clerk, shipping clerk, shop floor assistant

Job Zone 3 (medium job preparation)
fabricator, pinstripe artist, quality control sampler, quality control tester, paint robot operator, technical engineer, welder

Job Zone 4 (high job preparation)
quality control inspector

Job name: _____

What does a person do in this job?

_____

_____

_____

What tools and equipment does a person use in this job?

_____

What skills and abilities are important?

_____

_____

What technology might a person use in this job?

_____

What kind of person will be interested in this work?

_____

What level of education, job training, and experience is required?

_____

_____

What is the job outlook?   What is the average salary?

_____   _____

Read the safety bulletin and answer the questions.

LOCKOUT/TAGOUT PROCEDURES TO PREVENT INJURIES & FATALITIES

1 According to OSHA*, failure to follow lockout/tagout procedures is the most common violation of
2 manufacturing safety standards and is the leading cause of machine-related severe injuries and
3 death. Incidents occur when machinery starts up unexpectedly while it is being set up, maintained,
4 serviced, or repaired. Remember to follow these hazardous energy control procedures:

5 **Lockout:**
6 Lock any parts of a system that must be shut down. Switches, valves, and levers must be
7 locked in the Off position. Only use the lock, block, or chain that is identified as your personal
8 and exclusive authorized lockout device. Do not use the device for any other purpose.

9 De-energize. Locate and shut down all power sources:
10 • Disconnect electrical power.
11 • Block gas or liquid flowing in hydraulic or pneumatic systems.
12 • Block or release stored energy in springs, pressure tanks, or other systems.
13   (Do not release flammable, toxic, or explosive substances into the work area.)
14 • Block moveable machine parts. Lower any suspended parts to their resting positions.

15 After shutting down all power, test controls to assure that power doesn't go on.
16 Remember to turn controls back to their Off position after testing.

17 **Tagout:**
18 Machinery that cannot be locked out must be tagged out. A tag must be placed
19 on any switch, button, valve, lever, or other device that energizes the equipment.
20 Only authorized tags indicating your identity may be used.

21 **Restarting Machinery:**
22 When maintenance or repairs are completed, the only worker authorized to remove the lock or tag is
23 the person who installed it. Before restarting the equipment, inspect the repair work. Make sure all
24 maintenance and repair tools have been removed and any machine guards that were removed have
25 been reinstalled. Before re-energizing the system, make sure that you and other workers are a safe
26 distance from any dangerous areas. When the equipment is operational again, notify all workers.

* Occupational Health and Safety Administration

1. What is the main purpose of the first paragraph of this bulletin?
   A. to explain lockout procedures
   B. to explain tagout procedures
   C. to list hazardous energy control procedures
   D. to explain the reason for the bulletin

2. In Line 3, what does the term *incidents* refer to?
   A. safety standards
   B. procedures
   C. violations
   D. injuries and accidents

3. In Line 8, what does *exclusive* refer to?
   A. a device for any purpose
   B. a device for a specific worker
   C. a device that is authorized by OSHA
   D. a device that locks in the *Off* position

4. How does the final paragraph relate to the rest of the bulletin?
   A. It gives the reason for hazardous energy control procedures.
   B. It assures that power is turned off correctly.
   C. It explains what to do after lockout/tagout procedures aren't needed.
   D. It summarizes the lockout/tagout procedures.

DEMONSTRATING A PROCEDURE

Using YouTube, WikiHow, or another source, search online for a demonstration of how to assemble something, do a procedure, operate equipment, or follow safety instructions in a factory. Write out the instructions. Then prepare a media presentation. Make screenshots of the steps or video-record your demonstration. Present the procedure to the class.
Suggestions: how to assemble a bicycle; how to work safely with a conveyor belt; how to work safely on an assembly line

Revolutions in Manufacturing: From Assembly Lines to Robotics

1   We live in a world where there are manufactured goods of every imaginable kind—from clothing and cookware to cars and computers. In the past, most of these items were produced in thousands of factories across the United States. Factory work was a lifelong occupation for millions of people. But times have changed. Many factories have closed, many factories have moved out of the United States, and products that are manufactured in the remaining factories are often made with different processes. We are living through a time of historical change.

The Industrial Revolution

2   One of the greatest historical changes in the world occurred during the period 1760 to 1830, beginning in Great Britain. It is called the Industrial Revolution. Prior to this time, goods were produced by hand. Artisans worked in small workshops and used their hands and hand tools to make individual products. Around the year 1770, simple machinery was invented for spinning yarn and weaving cloth. Textiles could be produced quickly and easily in large quantities.

3   The first machines used horses to turn the wheels of the machinery. Then machines were set up in factories on rivers that used moving water to power the machinery. Inventors constantly improved the machinery, which soon could produce 40 times the output of a single worker working by hand. A little later, steam engines provided power for all kinds of machinery. This important invention allowed factories to be set up in cities, where many people were available to work. Steam engines were later used to power trains and boats. Other developments in these years included improvements in manufacturing iron and machine tools, and in producing chemicals, cement, glass, paper, and gas for lighting. These grew into large industries with factories across Europe and in the United States.

4   The development of machinery led to the beginning of the factory system of manufacturing. This new system changed how goods were

produced. It also changed how people worked and where they lived. Individuals working in traditional professions could not compete with factories that produced large quantities of goods very quickly. New farming machinery put many agricultural workers out of work. As a result, many people went to live in cities and work in factories. Traditional skills were less important in factory work, where most workers were either low-skilled laborers who operated machinery, or unskilled laborers who moved materials and goods.

The Second Industrial Revolution

5   Another era of change took place from about 1860 to 1914. With more advances in technology, industries in Europe and the United States continued to expand. New processes for making iron and steel were developed, transcontinental railroads were built, the petroleum industry grew, the use of electric power began, and the automobile was invented. Better machines and tools enabled industries to operate on a large scale.

6   The invention of the sewing machine made it much easier to make clothing, and garment-making grew into a large industry, especially in New York City. At first, most of the work was done by women working for a contractor at home. Later the work was done in small "sweatshops" and in factories that exploited the workers.

7   Factories needed workers, and immigrants provided the labor. Most of the workers in the garment industry and in many other factories were new immigrants. Between 1880 and 1920, more than 20 million immigrants, the majority from Eastern and Southern Europe, entered the United States. They contributed to the growth of business and industry, as well as to the growth of the nation.

8   In manufacturing, the two biggest developments were electrification and the production line. Electricity was used to light factories and to power electric motors to run machinery. Electric power enabled machinery to move large quantities of products through the manufacturing process. The Ford Motor Company was famous for creating an assembly line to manufacture automobiles, where workers attached parts as cars moved along past their workstations. Many of the basic manufacturing processes developed in this period have continued to the present time.

Manufacturing in the Twenty-first Century

9   Manufacturing and factory work remained much the same through most of the twentieth century. But since the 1980s, the development of new technologies, scientific advancements in electronics, and the invention of computers have brought a third industrial revolution, sometimes called the Digital Revolution—a change from mechanical technology to electronic technology. The primary element of this revolution is the computer. Computers can process information with great speed and accuracy. Another major development is the Internet, which is now the primary place to store and share information. A third important development is the cellular phone, which has become a universal means of communication as well as a tool capable of multiple other functions.

10   New technologies have had a significant impact on manufacturing as well as many other areas of production. The biggest development may be automation. Going beyond the mechanization brought about by the industrial revolution in which motorized machines did the work, automation involves the automatic control of machinery, systems, and operations with reduced involvement by human workers. Controlled by electrical, electronic, or computerized control systems, automated machinery increases production and lowers companies' labor costs. Systems such as computer-aided manufacturing (CAM) improve both the accuracy of production processes and the quality and consistency of products. Automation has been transforming manufacturing. However, it has also led to the loss of thousands of jobs.

11   Computer technology is now used for many functions and work tasks that were previously done manually. These include writing (word processing), publishing, photography (imaging), cataloguing information, data analysis, computer-aided design (CAD), and medical diagnosis. A recent development is the creation of models of new products through computerized 3-D printing. Computers, electronic devices, and communications technology continue to change, and information technology is progressing to the point that our current era is often referred to as "The Information Age."

12   A field of technology that is growing rapidly and has limitless possibilities in the future is robotics. Robots are widely used in automobile manufacturing processes to perform tasks such as welding, painting, and handling materials. In industries such as steel production and plastics, robots do jobs that are dangerous for humans. Future innovations will include household, agricultural, and medical robots.

Skills for the Workers of the Future

13 It is predicted that in the next twenty years, millions more jobs could be lost to automation and the advancement of artificial intelligence, primarily through robots and other machines doing the work humans now do. This phenomenon is moving beyond manufacturing and will be affecting food service jobs, office support jobs, truck and taxi drivers, and other low-paying occupations. Some researchers think this trend will seriously affect the availability of jobs in the future for the population as a whole. Others think technological development will bring economic growth and more jobs. But in any case, there will be a greater need for skilled workers rather than low-skilled workers, whose jobs may be replaced by machines. For example, workers with high-level technical skills will be needed to operate computerized systems that control machines, and fewer workers will be needed to operate the machines themselves.

14 As we look ahead, it is clear that skills in using technology and computers are becoming more important not only for workers in production industries but across the entire employment spectrum. Educational programs that emphasize the subject areas of science, technology, engineering, art and design, and math—or STEAM—can help prepare the students of today to become the workforce of tomorrow.

15 Continued growth of automation and international competition are creating a major challenge for industry and labor. One thing is certain: The future is coming. Will we be ready for it?

DID YOU UNDERSTAND?

1. What did the Industrial Revolution change about how products were made?

2. What was used at that time to provide power to run machinery?

3. What effect did the factory system have on people's lives?

4. How was clothing produced for the garment businesses in New York City?

5. How did factories get the workers they needed?

6. What were the two biggest developments of the Second Industrial Revolution?

7. What is the third industrial revolution?

8. What are three major developments in the Digital Revolution?

9. What is automation?

10. How does automation lower companies' labor costs?

11. What are some of the current and future uses of robots?

12. What kinds of skills are needed for the jobs of the future?

READING COMPREHENSION

1. The Industrial Revolution began with the invention of _____.
   A. hand tools
   B. manufacturing
   C. simple machinery
   D. workshops

2. As a result of the invention of the steam engine, _____.
   A. moving water was able to power machinery
   B. artisans were able to work in small workshops
   C. textiles were able to be produced quickly and easily
   D. factories were able to be set up in cities

3. The reason workers began moving to cities is explained in _____.
   A. Paragraph 3
   B. Paragraph 4
   C. Paragraph 5
   D. Paragraph 6

4. Which of the following did NOT take place during the Second Industrial Revolution?
   A. the development of new farming equipment
   B. the invention of the sewing machine
   C. the use of electric power
   D. the arrival of several million immigrants

5. According to the author, which of the following is most responsible for the emergence of the Digital Revolution?
   A. mechanical technology
   B. the invention of the computer
   C. assembly lines
   D. the invention of cell phones

6. In recent times, the loss of production jobs has been the result of _____.
   A. greater accuracy in production
   B. better quality and consistency of products
   C. automation
   D. the development of the Internet

7. Which of the following is an effect of automation on production?
   A. The quality of manufactured goods has declined.
   B. Machines are no longer involved in the manufacturing process.
   C. More functions and work tasks are being done manually.
   D. Fewer workers are needed to manufacture products.

8. Models of new products can be created through _____.
   A. computerized 3-D printing
   B. mechanization
   C. robotics
   D. word processing

9. The author predicts that in the future, there will be a greater need for _____.
   A. food service and office support workers
   B. machine operators
   C. workers with artificial intelligence
   D. workers with technical skills

10. Which of the following statements would the author most likely disagree with?
    A. The workplace has always been affected by new innovations and advances.
    B. Technological developments always result in more jobs.
    C. Educational changes will be needed to prepare the workers of tomorrow.
    D. Low-skilled workers will be in less demand in the future.

ACADEMIC VOCABULARY

1. Working in factories has been a lifelong _____ for millions of people.
   A. demonstration
   B. occupation
   C. assignment
   D. employment

2. Many significant changes _____ during the Industrial Revolution.
   A. occurred
   B. occupied
   C. proceeded
   D. transmitted

3. The _____ of a single worker cannot be compared to what a machine is capable of producing.
   A. tasks
   B. profession
   C. output
   D. outcome

4. New manufacturing _____ have resulted in greater productivity.
   A. structures
   B. factors
   C. projects
   D. processes

5. Sweatshops were factories where workers were _____.
   A. discriminated
   B. exploited
   C. enabled
   D. submitted

6. Immigrants have always _____ to the growth of business and industry.
   A. achieved
   B. generated
   C. contributed
   D. cooperated

7. The digital revolution took place as a result of a change from mechanical to electronic _____.
   A. technology
   B. automation
   C. invention
   D. development

8. Computers are capable of _____ information with great speed.
   A. affecting
   B. processing
   C. expanding
   D. enabling

9. Cellular phones are able to perform multiple _____.
   A. abilities
   B. skills
   C. devices
   D. functions

10. New technological developments have had a significant _____ on manufacturing.
    A. impact
    B. emphasis
    C. revolution
    D. involvement

11. It is essential that today's education programs _____ the subject areas of science and technology.
    A. define
    B. create
    C. emphasize
    D. prepare

12. Robots are capable of performing many manufacturing _____.
    A. items
    B. tasks
    C. trends
    D. themes

13. It is almost impossible to predict what some of the future _____ in manufacturing might be.
    A. innovations
    B. communications
    C. elements
    D. services

14. Many researchers think that automation will affect the _____ of jobs in the future.
    A. contribution
    B. demonstration
    C. capability
    D. availability

UNIT 5 LISTENING

PART A

Practice: A B C   3. A B C
       1. A B C   4. A B C
       2. A B C   5. A B C

PART B

Practice: A B C   3. A B C
       1. A B C   4. A B C
       2. A B C   5. A B C

Look at pages 72–74 of the core text. Write the correct words to complete the description.

attaching	caulking	glazier	installing	mixing	shimming
blockmason	cutting	helpers	mark	roofers	square
buttering	duct	installers	measuring	setting	stapling

Many workers are involved in the early stage of construction of this home. Two _____roofers_____ [1] are working on the roof. One is _____ [2] tar paper and the other is _____ [3] shingles. There are also two skylight _____ [4]. One is _____ [5] a skylight opening and the other is _____ [6] a skylight. Brickmasons are _____ [7] bricks and then _____ [8] them, and an HVAC technician is installing _____ [9] work. There are several carpenters and carpenter's _____ [10]. One is using a carpenter's _____ [11] to _____ [12] dimensions on OSB. Another is _____ [13] a wall with a tape measure and another is _____ [14] a door frame. A _____ [15] is _____ [16] a window. A _____ [17] is cutting cement blocks and his apprentice is _____ [18] mortar.

charging	installers	saw	screwing	stapling	testing
contractor	plastering	sawing	sheathing	taper	tightening
cutting	positioning	scoring	soldering	taping	wiring

Several plumbers are working at the next stage of construction. One is _____ [19] the water heater. Others are _____ [20] pipes, _____ [21] fittings, and _____ [22] connections. An electrician is _____ [23] the electrical panel and an assistant is _____ [24] voltage. An insulation _____ [25] is installing insulation. A drywall plasterer is _____ [26] the walls and a drywall _____ [27] is _____ [28] seams. There are two drywall _____ [29]. One is _____ [30] it and the other is _____ [31] it in. An HVAC technician is _____ [32] the HVAC unit. A carpenter is _____ [33] clapboard with a radial arm _____ [34]. A carpenter's helper is nailing clapboard to the _____ [35] on the garage wall and another is _____ [36] house wrap.

brush	grouting	installers	laying	spray gun	tile
flooring	hanging	installing	roller	spray paint	trim

At the final stage of construction, a _____ [37] installer is _____ [38] tile. Carpet _____ [39] are _____ [40] and trimming carpet. A _____ [41] installer is installing floors. Also, there are several painters. One is using a paint _____ [42] to paint interior walls. Another is standing on a ladder and using a paint _____ [43] to paint the _____ [44]. Another is using a _____ [45] to _____ [46] the exterior walls. Paperhangers are _____ [47] wallpaper and a finish carpenter is _____ [48] cabinet doors.

CAREER RESEARCH

Using the O*NET Career Exploration Tools at mynextmove.org, search for information about one of the jobs in Unit 6. Write the information in the job profile below. Then prepare and give a presentation about the job.

Job Zone 2 (some job preparation)

blockmason, blockmason apprentice, brickmason, carpenter, carpenter's helper, carpet installer, construction laborer, drywall installer, drywall plasterer, drywall taper, electrician's assistant, finish carpenter, flooring installer, glazier, insulation contractor, painter, paperhanger, roofer, skylight installer, tile installer

Job Zone 3 (medium job preparation)

electrician, HVAC technician, plumber

Job name: _____

What does a person do in this job?

_____

_____

_____

What tools and equipment does a person use in this job?

_____

What skills and abilities are important?

_____

_____

What technology might a person use in this job?

_____

What kind of person will be interested in this work?

_____

What level of education, job training, and experience is required?

_____

_____

What is the job outlook?   What is the average salary?

_____   _____

A Home Construction Professional and Volunteer

1   My name is Daniel Vargas. I'm a home builder—owner of Vargas Home Construction. It's a small business. We build just one or two homes a year. We could do more, but instead I prefer to donate a lot of time to volunteering with a very special organization—Building to Care.

2   BTC plays an important role in our local community and around the world. We renovate and repair existing homes and build new ones to provide families with safe, decent, and affordable housing. The homes we build in the U.S. and Canada aren't too large. They're a decent size to house a family—typically three bedrooms. The homes usually have wood frame construction, vinyl siding, and asphalt shingle roofs.

3   Costs are lower than for usual home construction since we rely on the labor of volunteers who work under the supervision of experienced construction professionals. That's my role. I'm a team leader. I oversee all aspects of the building process, from framing, roofing, and siding to painting, finish work, and cleanup. I provide instruction to our volunteers, who are mostly inexperienced. I enjoy that part of my role. I'm pretty sure if I weren't in construction, I'd be in education. I love teaching.

4   As an Army veteran, one of the aspects of our work that means the most to me is our veterans' assistance program. It helps veterans who need some help with home repairs or, in some cases, with building safe and affordable new housing.

5   My world has definitely expanded through volunteer work I've done with BTC overseas. First, I volunteered in Haiti after the 2010 earthquake. I was in the Philippines in 2013 doing reconstruction after Typhoon Haiyan. Most recently, I was in Puerto Rico in 2017 to help after the devastation of Hurricane Maria. As a result, I've learned how to employ cement blocks, metal roof panels, and other materials in ways that work best for local conditions. But more important, I've learned a lot about different people and cultures.

6   Whether you've got some experience in construction or not, I encourage you to look for an opportunity to volunteer with an organization such as Building to Care—locally or globally. Everyone deserves a decent place to live. It's great work.

1. Which paragraph has the most information about this volunteer's responsibilities?
   A. Paragraph 1
   B. Paragraph 2
   C. Paragraph 3
   D. Paragraph 4

2. Which occupation or role probably wouldn't appear on his resume?
   A. builder
   B. teacher
   C. veteran
   D. volunteer

3. Select the two paragraphs that show differences in home construction techniques.
   A. Paragraphs 1 and 3
   B. Paragraphs 2 and 4
   C. Paragraphs 3 and 5
   D. Paragraphs 2 and 5

4. Which word has the same meaning as the word *employ* as used in paragraph 5?
   A. hire
   B. donate
   C. use
   D. give work to

CLASSROOM VISITOR

Invite a local home builder to visit your class. Ask about home construction in your area, the types of jobs available, and the process of starting and managing a residential construction business. Or, invite an official of your local government's housing department to visit your class. Ask about what type of housing assistance is available for low-income residents, the elderly, and the homeless in your area. (Or, do an Internet search for information about a local or global volunteer organization.)

Designing a Green Home

1   With society's increasing awareness of the changing world climate, green homes are becoming more and more popular. A green home is environmentally friendly and sustainable, which means that it has a low and *eco-friendly* impact on the environment.

2   Green building practices have developed over time and in different parts of the world, particularly in Europe, the United States, and Australia. Many of the developments have come from scientific studies in the field of sustainable architecture, which focuses on energy and ecological conservation in building design. Architects and construction companies that specialize in green building construction strive to have their projects certified as meeting rigorous green building standards.

3   In addition to seeing that a home meets the client's living needs, is well constructed, and has an aesthetic appearance, the architect must keep in mind the aim of limiting the impact on the environment. The most important aspect of a green home is its energy efficiency, and a primary concern for the architect in the building design is keeping its energy consumption as low as possible. The more the house can use natural sources of heating and cooling, and the more efficiently the home uses energy and manages the interior air, the less energy the home will use.

Design Considerations Related to Energy Efficiency

Site and orientation

4   A thorough analysis of the building site is essential. The location, size, and natural features of the property need to be considered in the design of the home and its landscaping. Factors include views from the property, the slope of the land, the lot's exposure to the sun at various times of the day and year, the direction of breezes, and the location of trees and vegetation. The way a house is positioned on a lot can help it make use of these natural features.

Size

5   A smaller house is more energy-efficient than a larger one, since it takes less energy to heat and cool a smaller structure. This means it will be more environmentally friendly and also will cost less to maintain over time. In addition, a smaller house is cheaper to build. It uses less construction material, and construction charges are usually figured by the number of square feet or square meters in the overall structure.

Layout

6   In consultation with the client, the architect designs the overall layout of the building and the location of the various rooms. In general, a compact structure is more energy-efficient than one that is spread out over a larger area. Most green homes have an open floor plan, which improves lighting and ventilation. A factor in the placement of rooms is how much natural light and air can enter them. The design of the ventilation system, including the placement of ducts for the home's heating and cooling system, is also part of the building plan.

Passive solar design

7   An important technology applied in many green homes is *passive solar design*. Through this technology, windows, walls, and floors collect warmth from the sun, and this warmth is distributed to heat the home. This is accomplished without the use of mechanical heating systems. In one type of passive solar system, cement or brick walls absorb heat from sunlight, store it, and then use this heat to warm the building at night. An effective passive solar design includes strategically placed windows and vents that can direct airflow inside the home and allow for cross ventilation that aids air movement.

Windows

8   The placement, number, and size of windows are important elements of the building design. Windows should be placed on the sides of the house that receive morning and early afternoon sun. To avoid overheating in hot summer months, the roof should be designed with overhangs that block direct sunlight from entering the windows. Some parts of the structure may require fewer windows. For example, west-facing windows may get too much direct sunlight in the summer. The windows should be double- or triple-glazed and well-sealed to achieve maximum insulation and minimize temperature transfer.

Insulation and sealing

9   Placing the proper amount of insulation inside walls and ceilings is essential for keeping heat in during the cold season and cool air in during the hot season. The effectiveness of the insulation is indicated by its R-value—a measure of thermal resistance. Insulation is made from a variety of substances, including environmentally friendly materials such as recycled newspaper, sheep's wool, and shredded denim. Openings around windows, doors, and vents need to be well-sealed. Eliminating air leakage reduces energy needs.

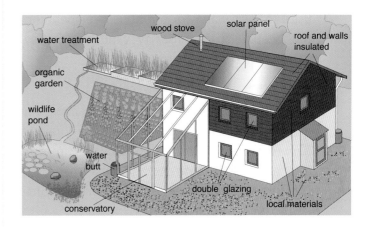

Other Features of Green Homes

Materials

10   The choice of building materials and construction methods is important to consider in terms of their effect on the environment—for example, the use of nonsynthetic and nontoxic paints, finishes, and glues; the use of wood products for kitchen cabinets that do not contain air contaminants; and the use of renewable resources such as bamboo and wood for flooring. It is also worth noting that an efficient home design and proper building techniques can reduce the quantity of materials used in construction.

Equipment

11   Energy-efficient appliances such as refrigerators, freezers, and water heaters will keep energy consumption low, as will the use of LED light bulbs. The heating, ventilation, and air conditioning (HVAC) system in a house usually accounts for at least 50% of the home's total energy consumption. A highly energy-efficient system can greatly reduce the amount of gas and electricity a home would otherwise use.

12   Some builders prefer a geothermal or ground source heat pump, an alternative heating and cooling system that makes use of the natural temperature of the earth. A heat pump moves heat

to and from the house through an underground heat exchanger filled with a chemical refrigerant.

Alternative energy sources

13   Solar photovoltaic panels can be incorporated into the design so that the building can generate its own electricity, and solar thermal panels can be used to heat water for the house. Depending on the location of the property, wind power may be another alternative energy option.

Water use

14   Plumbing fixtures such as low-flow toilets and shower heads conserve water. A rainwater harvesting system can drain rainwater from roofs into an underground storage tank that delivers the water to the house to use in toilets, or to the landscaping irrigation system.

The Design Process

15   An effective way of achieving the maximum benefit from green building strategies is through a process called *integrated design*, or *whole-building design*. In this approach, the architect collaborates with specialists in sustainable design in areas such as HVAC, plumbing, and lighting, as well as with the builder who will construct the home. The architect

gets input from this team during the design process, and often one element of the design can affect another. For example, room layout could be influenced by the desire for efficient placement of HVAC ducts or plumbing lines.

16   There are many elements architects have to take into account in designing green homes. A good design brings them all together to create a successful result—a home that is not only a comfortable fit for the owner's needs but is truly eco-friendly.

DID YOU UNDERSTAND?

1. What makes a green home *eco-friendly*?

2. What is the focus of sustainable architecture?

3. What is the most important aspect of a green home?

4. Why is a site analysis important?

5. How does the size of a house relate to its energy efficiency?

6. What is a passive solar design system?

7. How should windows be placed in a green home design?

8. What is the function of insulation?

9. What are some examples of environmentally friendly materials that could be used in home construction?

10. What is a geothermal heat pump?

11. What is the advantage for a home in generating its own electricity from solar energy?

12. What is the integrated design approach?

WHAT'S YOUR OPINION?

1. What do you think governments could do to encourage the construction of green homes, even if they are more expensive to build?

2. What do you think would be effective ways to get people to conserve electricity, gas, and water at home?

READING COMPREHENSION

1. Which of the following does the author consider to be the most important aspect of green home design?
   A. following the latest scientific trends
   B. using energy efficiently
   C. having an aesthetic appearance
   D. being well constructed

2. According to the reading, which of the following is true?
   A. A large home is more energy-efficient than a small home.
   B. A small home doesn't use as much energy as a large home.
   C. A large home isn't as expensive to build as a small home.
   D. A small home isn't as easy to maintain as a large home.

3. Which paragraph explains why the positioning of a house is important?
   A. Paragraph 4
   B. Paragraph 5
   C. Paragraph 6
   D. Paragraph 8

4. According to the reading, an open floor plan _____.
   A. collects warmth from the sun
   B. is expensive to build
   C. is better insulated than a structure that is spread out
   D. improves lighting and ventilation in a home

5. In a house with _____, windows, walls, and floors collect warmth from the sun.
   A. passive solar design
   B. insulation
   C. non-synthetic paints
   D. trees and vegetation

6. In paragraph 9, the term *thermal* refers to _____.
   A. light
   B. heat
   C. water
   D. electricity

7. The use of _____ can be harmful to the environment.
   A. products without air contaminants
   B. bamboo for flooring
   C. non-toxic glues
   D. synthetic paints

8. Solar voltaic panels and solar thermal panels are _____.
   A. effective types of insulation
   B. renewable resources
   C. alternative energy sources
   D. lighting and plumbing fixtures

9. Which of the following best describes the type of design and construction process the author would consider to be most important in building a green home?
   A. creative
   B. collaborative
   C. efficient
   D. friendly

10. The purpose of the reading is to _____.
    A. explain why green homes are becoming more and more popular
    B. compare traditional and green home construction
    C. present design considerations for constructing energy-efficient homes
    D. inform the reader about problems associated with green construction

ACADEMIC VOCABULARY

1. The popularity of green homes is a result of an increased _____ of the changing world climate.
   A. opinion
   B. awareness
   C. knowledge
   D. focus

2. A _____ home is one that has an eco-friendly impact on the environment.
   A. primary
   B. comprehensive
   C. strategic
   D. sustainable

3. The goal of green home design is to keep energy _____ as low as possible.
   A. outcome
   B. storage
   C. consumption
   D. integration

4. Before designing a home, there must be a thorough _____ of the building site.
   A. analysis
   B. example
   C. impact
   D. location

5. When planning a home, ongoing _____ between the architect and various specialists is essential.
   A. exposure
   B. structure
   C. construction
   D. consultation

6. A smaller house is more efficient than a larger one since it requires less _____ to heat and cool it.
   A. design
   B. energy
   C. ability
   D. aid

7. If windows are _____ placed, it is possible to achieve maximum airflow.
   A. directly
   B. strategically
   C. passively
   D. minimally

8. One of the goals of effective home design is to _____ as much as possible the leakage of air.
   A. eliminate
   B. encounter
   C. maintain
   D. include

9. Home designers should try to maximize the use of renewable _____.
   A. functions
   B. structures
   C. resources
   D. investments

10. Wind power is worth exploring as a good _____ energy option.
    A. minimal
    B. capable
    C. conservative
    D. alternative

11. Close cooperation and communication are essential during every stage of the _____ process.
    A. project
    B. design
    C. structure
    D. concept

12. In a passive solar home, warmth is collected from the sun and then _____ to heat the home.
    A. achieved
    B. constructed
    C. distributed
    D. transformed

13. Through the use of solar photovoltaic panels, a building is able to _____ its own electricity.
    A. prepare
    B. receive
    C. transmit
    D. generate

14. Careful planning is needed in order to _____ the maximum benefit of green building strategies.
    A. require
    B. achieve
    C. influence
    D. replace

UNIT 6 LISTENING

PART A

Practice: A B C

1. A B C
2. A B C
3. A B C
4. A B C
5. A B C

PART B

Practice: A B C

1. A B C
2. A B C
3. A B C
4. A B C
5. A B C

Look at pages 88–89 of the core text. Write the correct words to complete the description.

backhoe	dirt	flagger	installers	safety
bill	dump	flatbed	jobsite	stakes
bulldozer	electrician	foreman	laying	taking
cutting	fencing	hats	officer	vests

Construction is beginning. There is safety barrier _____ _fencing_ _____ [1] around the construction site. The construction _____ [2] is reading site plans. An excavator is loading _____ [3] into a _____ [4] truck. A _____ [5] is grading the foundation floor. Surveyors are _____ [6] measurements and pounding survey _____ [7] into the ground. Concrete workers are _____ [8] and tying rebar. They're all wearing hard _____ [9] and safety _____ [10]. Formwork _____ [11] are connecting concrete forms with pins. Plumbers are _____ [12] PVC pipe. An equipment operator is using a _____ [13] to dig a trench for utilities. An _____ [14] is laying utility pipes. A _____ [15] truck driver has arrived with a large supply of pipes and the _____ [16] foreman is reading the _____ [17] of lading. A construction safety _____ [18] is pointing out a _____ [19] issue to an equipment operator, and a _____ [20] is controlling traffic.

basket	driving	guide	leveling	releasing	torch
cement	forms	hoisting	mixer	shield	trowels
controlling	foundation	installers	out	signals	truck
crane truck	front-end	laying	picker	steelworker	welder

Construction is continuing. A _____ [21] truck operator is pulling cement from the cement _____ [22] truck. Concrete pump truck operators are _____ [23] the boom and cement flow and are filling foundation _____ [24]. Formwork _____ [25] are removing concrete panels. A _____ [26] operator is _____ [27] a steel beam, and a _____ [28] is using crane hand _____ [29] to _____ [30] the beam. A flatbed truck operator is _____ [31] the tie-down straps on a large supply of beams on his flatbed _____ [32]. Concrete workers are doing many tasks. Some are _____ [33] down support decking and others are spreading _____ [34] concrete. Construction workers are _____ [35] bolts to attach the decking to beams. Two concrete finishers are _____ [36] the concrete floor with a screed. Cement masons are using power _____ [37]. An equipment operator in a _____ [38] loader is filling in around the _____ [39]. A _____ [40], who is wearing a welding safety _____ [41], is using a metal cutting oxy-fuel _____ [42] to cut a beam to size. Another welder is working while standing in the _____ [43] of a cherry _____ [44] truck.

(continued)

CAREER VOCABULARY

Look at pages 90–91 of the core text. Write the correct words to complete the description.

bending	cutting	laborers	pipe	rolling out	technician
blockmason	driving	laying	pipefitter	roofers	tile
bucket	dumping	leveling	plumber	securing	walkway
construction	erecting	manager	pouring	spreading	welding
cutter	glazier	mopping			

At the next stage of construction, an HVAC _____ 45 is installing a roof HVAC unit. Several _____ 46 are also working on the roof. One is _____ 47 tar into a service _____ 48. Another is _____ 49 tar with a tar mop. Other roofers are _____ 50 cap sheets. A solar panel installer is also working on the roof. He's _____ 51 metal mounts. On the second floor, a _____ 52 is _____ 53 PVC pipe. A _____ 54 is _____ 55 conduit pipe with a conduit hand bender. The project _____ 56 is speaking with the _____ 57 supervisor. On the side of the building, a construction laborer is _____ 58 scaffolding. On the first floor, a plumber is threading a _____ 59. A _____ 60 is using a glass _____ 61 to cut glass. A _____ 62 setter is unloading boxes of tile. In the front of the building, a _____ 63 is _____ 64 rows of cement blocks and a welder is _____ 65 a stair rail. Several concrete _____ 66 are building a _____ 67. One is _____ 68 a stake into the ground. One is _____ 69 gravel. Another is _____ 70 down mesh wire. Another is _____ 71 cement.

applying	cable	contractor	installer	plasterer	stonemason
apprentice	ceiling	cutting	laying	sanding	trimming
automatic	channel	electrician	panels	smoothing	wall
brickmasons	clipping	finisher	panes	spacing	

Near the final stage of construction, a solar panel _____ 72 is installing solar panels on the roof. He's _____ 73 PVC panels to the rails. On the second floor, one carpenter is _____ 74 a stud and another is putting a stud into a track _____ 75. An _____ 76 is pulling an electrical _____ 77 through the studs. A _____ 78 tile installer is putting ceiling _____ 79 on a suspended ceiling track. On the first floor, a _____ 80 is _____ 81 a plastered wall, a tile setter is _____ 82 tile, and a glazier is _____ 83 glazier's putty to a window. Outside the building, _____ 84 are _____ 85 brick. An insulation _____ 86 is attaching rigid insulation. An _____ 87 door installer is installing a door. A glass processor _____ 88 is moving glass _____ 89. A cement _____ 90 is _____ 91 in control joints and _____ 92 the surface of the walkway. A _____ 93 is building a decorative stone _____ 94.

Using the O*NET Career Exploration Tools at mynextmove.org, search for information about one of the jobs in Unit 7. Write the information in the job profile below. Then prepare and give a presentation about the job.

Job Zone 1 (little or no job preparation)

plasterer

Job Zone 2 (some job preparation)

automatic door installer, blockmason, brickmason, bulldozer operator, carpenter, ceiling tile installer, cement finisher, cement mason, cement truck operator, concrete finisher, concrete laborer, concrete pump truck operator, concrete worker, construction laborer, construction worker, crane truck operator, dump truck operator, equipment operator, excavator operator, flagger, flatbed truck driver, flatbed truck operator, formwork installer, glass processor apprentice, glazier, insulation contractor, roofer, solar panel installer, stonemason, tile setter

Job Zone 3 (medium job preparation)

construction foreman, construction safety officer, construction supervisor, electrician, HVAC technician, jobsite foreman, pipefitter, plumber, steelworker, welder

Job Zone 4 (high job preparation)

project manager, structural engineer, surveyor

Job name: _____

What does a person do in this job?

_____

_____

What tools and equipment does a person use in this job?

_____

What skills and abilities are important?

_____

_____

What technology might a person use in this job?

_____

What kind of person will be interested in this work?

_____

What level of education, job training, and experience is required?

_____

_____

What is the job outlook?   What is the average salary?

_____   _____

Read the safety poster and answer the questions.

PREVENT CONSTRUCTION SITE FALLS!
Falls are the leading cause of construction worker injuries and death.
These deaths are preventable!

Prevent Falls from Ladders:
24% of all construction deaths from falls occur due to falls from ladders.
Choose the correct ladder for the task.
Put the base of the ladder on a firm, solid surface.
For every 4 feet of height, the ladder should be 1 foot away from the surface it is resting on.
Fasten the top of an extension ladder to an upper support.
Always face the ladder and grip its rungs, not the side rails.
Use three points of contact with the ladder— 2 hands + 1 foot, or 2 feet + 1 hand.
Use a tool belt. Don't carry tools in your hands.
Wear slip-resistant shoes.

Prevent Falls from Roofs:
Wear a full body harness or other Personal Fall Arrest System (PFAS).
Don't sit or step on or lean against a skylight.
Securely cover or guard a roof opening or hole with railings or guardrails.

Prevent Falls from Scaffolding:
Use fully planked scaffolds.
Make sure scaffolds are level.
Complete all guardrails, and don't stand on them.
Don't use a ladder on scaffolding.

Prevent Falls from Equipment:
Set the parking brake so equipment doesn't move.
Use hand and step holds. Make sure they are clean—no mud, grease, or other fluids.
Use three points of contact with hand and step holds—2 hands + 1 foot, or 2 feet + 1 hand.
Wear shoes that provide support and traction.
Don't carry materials or tools when getting on or off equipment.
Don't jump off equipment.

Learn more at your worksite's Safety Stand-Down on <u>May 8 – Noon – Extended Lunch Break</u> .

1. What does *three points of contact* relate to?
   - A. correct use of scaffolding
   - B. preventing falls from roofs
   - C. ladder and equipment safety
   - D. a Personal Fall Arrest System

2. In how many of the fall hazards described does the carrying of tools play a role?
   - A. one
   - B. two
   - C. three
   - D. four

3. If a ladder is 12 feet in height, what should its correct distance be from the surface it rests on?
   - A. one foot
   - B. two feet
   - C. three feet
   - D. four feet

4. What does a *Safety Stand-Down* refer to?
   - A. an injury that occurred at the worksite
   - B. workers refusing to work because of safety hazards
   - C. stopping work because of an accident
   - D. a meeting about worksite safety

DEMONSTRATING A PROCEDURE

Using YouTube, WikiHow, or another source, search online for a demonstration of how to build something or follow safety instructions related to home projects or construction. Write out the instructions. Then prepare a media presentation. Make screenshots of the steps or video-record your demonstration. Present the procedure to the class.

Or, go to www.osha.gov/dts/vtools/construction.html or use the search term *construction hazards prevention videos* to learn how to identify common construction hazards. (The videos describe injuries and deaths at construction sites and might therefore be disturbing for some students.) Share what you learn with the class.

LEED Certification in Commercial Building Construction

1   In the United States, Canada, and Europe, buildings account for about 40% of overall energy consumption. The green building movement is a response to growing concern about the impact of buildings on the environment. A program known as LEED—Leadership in Energy and Environmental Design—is part of that response. Since it was initiated in 1994 by the U.S. Green Building Council, this green building certification program has become popular around the world as a means of promoting the construction of environmentally responsible buildings. The program expanded to Canada in 2003 upon the creation of the Canada Green Building Council. LEED-certified buildings conserve energy and water and reduce greenhouse gas emissions.

2   LEED certification is awarded to buildings that meet the program's high standards for design, construction, operation, and maintenance. Certification is available for three broad categories of projects: commercial buildings, homes, and neighborhood development. The program can be applied to all types of buildings, including office buildings, retail buildings, warehouses, hospitals, schools, community buildings, and residences. When awarding construction contracts, many government agencies now require builders to meet LEED standards and obtain LEED certification.

3   In addition to new construction, the LEED program is widely followed when renovating existing buildings. One example of a major retrofit project is New York City's famous skyscraper, the Empire State Building. Originally completed in 1931, the renovated building was awarded LEED Gold Certification in 2011.

The Certification Procedure

4   A project registers with the U.S. Green Building Council to notify its intent to seek certification, usually early in the project's design phase. During design and construction, project engineers follow LEED guidelines in a number of design categories. The guidelines specify standards that projects are required to meet. The categories address sustainability issues and include location and

New York City's famous landmark, the Empire State Building, has saved millions of dollars on its energy costs since its LEED retrofit.

transportation, sustainable sites, water efficiency, energy and atmosphere, materials and resources, indoor environmental quality, innovation in design, and regional priority. When the project is completed, the builder submits detailed documentation indicating how the building meets LEED standards, including calculations and analysis, which the building council then reviews. The project earns points for meeting standards and goals in each of the categories according to a rating system for the particular type of building. Certification is awarded at various levels according to the point total.

> **LEED CERTIFICATION LEVELS**
> (100 total points possible)
> Certified: 40 to 49 Points
> Silver: 50 to 59 Points
> Gold: 60 to 79 Points
> Platinum: 80 points and above

LEED Requirements for Certifying Buildings

5   For a building to meet the kinds of sustainability goals and performance specifications that LEED certification requires, engineering, design, and construction must come together in an effective way. The following are some examples of LEED requirements.

MATERIALS AND RESOURCES

Goals	Requirements
Reduce the waste that is generated by building occupants and deposited in landfills	Provide areas for separating recyclable materials
Optimize the environmental performance of products and materials	Use software tools and data sets to conduct a life-cycle assessment of the new construction (built to last at least 60 years) and take steps to reduce by 10% its carbon dioxide impact, its acidification of land and water resources, and its depletion of nonrenewable energy sources
(For healthcare facilities) Design for flexibility of the building and ease of future adaptation	Allow for 5% extra space in the building design for general use and 30% for medical use

ENERGY AND ATMOSPHERE

Goals	Requirements
Achieve a minimum acceptable level of energy efficiency for the building and its systems	Comply with design recommendations for HVAC and water heating requirements, including equipment efficiency, economizers, ventilation, and ducts
Support energy management by tracking the building's energy use	Install advanced energy metering that transmits data to a central monitoring system
Reduce the use of fuel generated by fossil fuels	Use renewable energy systems to contribute to the building's energy needs

INDOOR ENVIRONMENTAL QUALITY

Goals	Requirements
Improve indoor air quality	Comply with design strategies for mechanically ventilated and naturally ventilated spaces
Provide for the thermal comfort and well-being of building occupants	Design heating, ventilating, and air-conditioning (HVAC) systems and the building's interior perimeters to meet the specified standards
Provide high-quality lighting to promote occupants' productivity and comfort	In at least 90% of individual occupant spaces, allow for individual adjustment of lighting

WATER EFFICIENCY

Goals	Requirements
Reduce outdoor water consumption	Reduce the project's landscaping water requirement by at least 30% from the site's calculated maximum monthly rate
Reduce indoor water consumption	Install water-saving plumbing fixtures that will reduce water use by 20% from the calculated base amount
Support water management by tracking water consumption	Install permanent water meters for irrigation, indoor plumbing, or other system

INNOVATION IN DESIGN

Goals	Requirements
Encourage projects to achieve exceptional or innovative performance	Achieve significant, measurable environmental performance using a strategy *not* addressed in the LEED green building rating system
Encourage team integration	Include a LEED Accredited Professional on the project team

Examples of LEED-Certified Projects

6   In South Central Los Angeles, the Council District 9 Neighborhood City Hall is a LEED-certified building with many sustainable features. Its courtyard contains eight solar arrays that move during the day to follow the sun and provide shade to the space below. An 8,000 square-foot public rooftop garden reduces the "heat island effect" of the building, which occupies an entire block. The garden also absorbs some rainwater during storms. A 7,000-gallon underground cistern collects rainwater so it can be reused for irrigation.

7   In London, a magnificent building called the Crystal is the location of the Siemens Urban Sustainability Centre. It has Platinum LEED certification—the highest level of the rating system—and is considered the world's most sustainable venue for meetings and events. The building is all-electric. It uses solar power and ground source heat pumps to generate all the energy it requires for power, heating, and cooling. An energy management system controls all electrical and mechanical systems, including heat, ventilation, air-conditioning, and hot water systems, lighting, and fire alarms. The system uses 3,500 indoor sensors and an outdoor weather station to monitor conditions and automatically control everything from the brightness of lighting to the opening and closing of windows. Rainwater is collected from the roof and stored in an underground storage tank, and the irrigation system and toilets use only recycled water. Tours of the building are available and include the largest world exhibition on the future of cities.

8   The Vancouver Convention Centre has double LEED Platinum certification. It was awarded LEED certification by the Canada Green Building Council in 2010 for New Construction, and in 2017 for Existing Buildings Operations and Maintenance. It earned these certifications for excellence in energy efficiency, reduction of indoor water use, waste management, and other aspects of its sustainability program. The building complex is located on the city's downtown waterfront. Its West building has a six-acre living roof with over 400,000 plants and grasses and four beehives. (The bees pollinate the plants and provide honey for a restaurant kitchen onsite.) It also includes a marine habitat that is built into the building's foundation and supports a variety of sea life. The building's heating and cooling

system uses seawater. Recent improvements to its onsite water treatment plant and plumbing fixtures have significantly reduced water usage, and an expanded recycling program now diverts over 75% of the waste produced by the complex into recycling.

A Third "E": Energy, Environment—and Engineering

9   Designing buildings on a large scale involves the work of many kinds of engineers who play a big role in achieving LEED certification. Architectural engineers are responsible for creating the overall design and layout of a building and its many components, taking into account needs, standards, and the local environment. Specialists in mechanical, electrical, and plumbing systems focus on the LEED standards in those aspects of design and construction, including equipment performance, energy-efficiency, and documentation. Structural engineers, with their expertise in materials and in designing a building's physical structure, can help decrease material use, identify local material sources, and design rainwater runoff systems. With an integrated design process that brings these specialists together in a collaborative team, projects can achieve maximum efficiency and lower costs.

10   Architects and engineers have earned university degrees in their fields. They then take a licensing examination to become licensed engineering professionals. Passing the LEED accreditation exam qualifies them further as a LEED Accredited Professional and opens up wider employment possibilities. It enables them to serve as an important resource for building design and construction companies, where they join teams to create the green buildings of the future.

DID YOU UNDERSTAND?

1. Why did the green building movement begin?

2. What does *LEED* stand for?

3. How can buildings qualify for LEED certification?

4. What is the highest level of LEED certification?

5. What is one way recommended by LEED for reducing landfill waste?

6. What is the purpose of allowing extra space in the building design?

7. What can be achieved by complying with LEED design strategies for mechanically ventilated and naturally ventilated spaces?

8. What is a LEED specification for providing high-quality lighting for individual building occupants?

9. From reading the LEED requirements, what is meant by *innovation* in design?

10. What areas of engineering are involved in building design?

11. How can a structural engineer help projects achieve LEED certification?

12. How can engineers become a LEED Accredited Professional?

READING COMPREHENSION

1. Environmentally responsible buildings _____.
   A. are responsible for many environmental problems
   B. increase greenhouse gas emissions
   C. account for 40% of overall energy consumption
   D. conserve water and energy

2. The purpose of the LEED program is to _____.
   A. require builders to meet its standards
   B. promote the construction of buildings that don't harm the environment
   C. grant certification to builders who meet LEED standards
   D. give awards to successful builders

3. According to the reading, which of the following statements is true?
   A. The Empire State Building was the first LEED-approved building in New York.
   B. Renovations are not eligible for LEED certification.
   C. The Empire State Building's retrofit was awarded LEED certification.
   D. The Empire State Building's renovation was completed in 1931.

4. Water efficiency, energy and atmosphere, and materials and resources are LEED _____.
   A. design categories
   B. certificates
   C. awards
   D. innovations

5. In the Materials and Resources Goals section of paragraph 5, what is the meaning of *optimize*?
   A. provide options for
   B. express optimism about
   C. examine
   D. make as effective as possible

6. Which section would additional information regarding airflow be added to?
   A. Materials and Resources
   B. Energy and Atmosphere
   C. Indoor Environmental Quality
   D. Innovation in Design

7. Reducing a building's landscape requirement will help to reduce _____.
   A. indoor water consumption
   B. outdoor water consumption
   C. problems with ventilation
   D. dependence on water meters

8. A unique feature of _____ is the seawater heating and cooling system.
   A. the South Central Los Angeles Neighborhood City Hall
   B. the Crystal building in London
   C. the Vancouver Convention Centre
   D. most LEED-certified buildings

9. Which paragraph describes the advantages of collaboration?
   A. Paragraph 1
   B. Paragraph 4
   C. Paragraph 9
   D. Paragraph 10

10. According to the reading, which of the following is a way of encouraging innovation?
    A. Use strategies that are not part of the LEED framework.
    B. Carefully follow all of the LEED certification guidelines.
    C. Consult with teams of engineers and architects.
    D. Join teams of LEED accredited professionals.

ACADEMIC VOCABULARY

1. A building project must notify its intention to _____ LEED certification.
   A. identify
   B. seek
   C. require
   D. adapt

2. It is necessary to submit detailed _____ to show a building meets required standards.
   A. indication
   B. recommendations
   C. documentation
   D. innovation

3. There are various performance _____ that must be met in order to quality for project approval.
   A. specifications
   B. sources
   C. systems
   D. resources

4. Data about energy use is transmitted to a central _____ system.
   A. examination
   B. structural
   C. licensing
   D. monitoring

5. It is essential to reduce the use of fuel that is _____ by fossil fuels.
   A. promoted
   B. generated
   C. contributed
   D. conducted

6. The indoor _____ quality of a building relates to the comfort of the occupants.
   A. environmental
   B. strategic
   C. space
   D. integrated

7. One of the LEED requirements is to allow individual _____ of lighting.
   A. performance
   B. adjustment
   C. application
   D. integration

8. The designers are attempting to reduce the project's landscaping water _____.
   A. resources
   B. construction
   C. requirements
   D. energy

9. Most of the project's construction materials _____ recycled content.
   A. consist
   B. contain
   C. compose
   D. compile

10. Designing large-scale projects _____ the work of many kinds of professionals.
    A. initiates
    B. contributes
    C. derives
    D. involves

11. We are searching for individuals with _____ in effective building design.
    A. focus
    B. analysis
    C. expertise
    D. knowledge

12. Our project goal is not only to lower construction costs, but to achieve _____ efficiency.
    A. maximum
    B. minimum
    C. responsible
    D. available

13. Passing the accreditation exam will _____ you to join many different construction teams.
    A. achieve
    B. establish
    C. engage
    D. allow

14. Guidelines _____ construction standards that must be met.
    A. register
    B. transmit
    C. specify
    D. modify

UNIT 7 LISTENING

PART A

Practice: A B C

1. A B C
2. A B C
3. A B C
4. A B C
5. A B C

PART B

Practice: A B C

1. A B C
2. A B C
3. A B C
4. A B C
5. A B C

Look at pages 108–109 of the core text. Write the correct words to complete the description.

absorber	balance	diagnosing	leaks	oil	suspension	undercarriage
advisor	bay	draining	lube	pad	system	waiting
analyzer	brake	exchange	mounting	scanner	technicians	work order
auto lift	charging	exchanging	muffler	service	tuning up	

It's a busy day at the auto _____service_____ [1] department. A service _____ [2] is preparing a _____ [3] for a customer in the _____ [4] room. An auto technician is _____ [5] a problem on a car in the service _____ [6] using a diagnostic _____ [7]. Another is using a charging system _____ [8] and is _____ [9] a battery. Another is _____ [10] radiator coolant using a fluid _____ [11] machine. Another is checking a car's restraint _____ [12]. One of the tire specialists is balancing a tire using the tire _____ [13] machine. Another is _____ [14] a tire. A tune-up and electronics specialist is _____ [15] a car. A _____ [16] specialist is changing a brake _____ [17]. Automotive exhaust emissions _____ [18] are inspecting the _____ [19] of a car on a two-post _____ [20] and replacing the _____ [21]. An automotive _____ [22] technician is installing a new shock _____ [23]. Also, _____ [24] technicians are _____ [25] the oil, changing an _____ [26] filter, and examining a hose for _____ [27].

driver	grinder	mixing	sanding	stapler	tow truck
filler	grinding	removal	seat	straighten	upholsterer
filling	hammer	roof	smooth	sunroof	windshield
frame	lowering	sander	spray gun	tint film	

In the auto body repair facility, a tow truck _____ [28] is _____ [29] a car from a flatbed _____ [30]. A _____ [31] repairperson is working with another on a frame pull machine to pull a car frame to _____ [32] it. A collision repair technician is using a door panel _____ [33] tool to take off a door panel. An auto glass technician is replacing a _____ [34]. A window tint specialist is adhering _____ [35] to a window. Other auto body repair workers are doing a variety of tasks. One is _____ [36] in a crack with plastic body _____ [37]. Another is _____ [38] paint off a dented area with an auto _____ [39]. One is _____ [40] down welded draw pins with a power _____ [41], another is shaping an area of a car with a _____ [42] and dollies, and another is sanding by hand to _____ [43] out an area. A _____ [44] installer is cutting a hole in the _____ [45] of a car. An auto _____ [46] is using an upholstery _____ [47] to reupholster a ripped _____ [48]. And auto painters are _____ [49] paint and spraying a car panel with an auto body _____ [50].

Using the O*NET Career Exploration Tools at mynextmove.org, search for information about one of the jobs in Unit 8. Write the information in the job profile below. Then prepare and give a presentation about the job.

Job Zone 2 (some job preparation)
auto body repairperson, auto paint helper, auto painter, auto upholsterer, service advisor, tire specialist, tow truck driver, window tint specialist, windshield/auto glass technician

Job Zone 3 (medium job preparation)
auto technician, automotive exhaust emissions technician, automotive suspension technician, brake specialist, collision repair technician, frame repairperson, lubrication/lube technician, shop foreman, sunroof installer, tune-up and electronics specialist

Job Zone 4 (high job preparation)
estimator

Job name: _____

What does a person do in this job?

_____

_____

_____

What tools and equipment does a person use in this job?

_____

What skills and abilities are important?

_____

_____

What technology might a person use in this job?

_____

What kind of person will be interested in this work?

_____

What level of education, job training, and experience is required?

_____

_____

What is the job outlook?   What is the average salary?

_____   _____

An Auto Repair Shop Owner

1 I'm Alejandro Lopez—the owner of A1 Auto Repair. I've worked here for many years. My father started the business a few decades ago, and after he retired, I took it over. (He was a great auto mechanic—one of the best. These days we call ourselves auto repair technicians—too fancy a job title for my Dad.)

2 My repair shop is a small operation. One other auto repair tech works with me, and we have one helper. About a quarter of our business comes from customers who bring their vehicles in for regular preventive maintenance such as oil changes, fluid level checks, basic tune-ups, and tire rotation. We're also an inspection station for our state's required vehicle and emissions inspections.

3 Most of our business involves diagnosing, repairing, and replacing mufflers, brakes, suspension systems, transmissions, and other mechanical items. We can't do everything, though, since as a small shop we don't have some of the latest electronic equipment for diagnosing and repairing problems with cars' computer and electronic systems.

4 I'm proud to be keeping in place a tradition that my Dad started many years ago. We try to hire felons as helpers in order to offer them some job training, a salary, and an opportunity to move forward in life after incarceration. A small auto repair shop like mine is actually considered a good place for someone to get back into the workforce after prison. A person willing to start as a helper doesn't need certification, can learn on the job, and can attend a technical school or training program in order to eventually get certified.

5 Our current helper has been with us for more than a year. He's a hard worker and very ambitious. He's currently studying to take the Auto Maintenance and Light Repair test—one of the Automotive Service Excellence exams. He goes to a training program, and since the ASE practice tests are online, he often arrives at the shop when I do an hour before we open so he can use the computer and our Internet access to prepare for the test. I'm confident he's going to do well.

6 Although my business receives a small government Work Opportunity Tax Credit for hiring someone in a target group that has barriers to employment, that isn't the reason for doing it. My Dad believed that everyone deserved a second chance to succeed in life, and I'm proud to be following in his footsteps.

1. Select the two paragraphs that best describe the services provided by the repair shop.
   A. Paragraphs 2 and 3
   B. Paragraphs 3 and 4
   C. Paragraphs 3 and 5
   D. Paragraphs 4 and 5

2. What is the meaning of *latest* as used in paragraph 3?
   A. not on time
   B. most valuable
   C. most recent
   D. most expensive

3. Which paragraph describes a certification requirement for auto repair technicians?
   A. Paragraph 2
   B. Paragraph 3
   C. Paragraph 4
   D. Paragraph 5

4. Which word in this article DOESN'T refer to a barrier to employment?
   A. incarceration
   B. inspection
   C. prison
   D. felon

CLASSROOM VISITOR

Invite the owner of a local auto repair shop to visit your class. Ask about the types of jobs at the shop, opportunities for work in automotive repair, how technology is changing these jobs and the training required, and the process of starting and managing an auto repair business.

(Or, do an Internet search for information about the Automotive Service Excellence ASE certification exams.)

Innovations in Automotive Technology

1   Since its modest beginnings in the 1880s, the automobile has undergone enormous changes through advances in automotive technology. In the first seventy years, many improvements were made to gasoline engines and to the automobile's mechanical systems. Automatic transmissions became common, as did power-assisted steering and brakes. But in the 1970s, the introduction of electronic technology began to have a significant impact on the way vehicles operated, especially the engine. Other changes came about due to growing concerns about passenger safety and fuel economy. From that time until the present, most developments have been in these areas.

Engines

2   Today's automobiles have a computerized engine control unit (ECU) or engine management system that controls functions such as fuel injection, spark timing, and valve operation. This is designed to help an automobile achieve maximum engine performance and efficiency. Automotive engineers are constantly striving to make mechanical improvements to existing engine components and work on devising newer approaches to engine design that will enable future automobiles to achieve even higher power output and greater fuel efficiency. In addition, automobile manufacturers are working on producing engines that can use varieties or grades of fuel that have less of an impact on the environment.

Safety

3   Many of the latest innovations focus on safety. One strategy for keeping vehicle occupants safe is to protect them inside the car through the use of airbags, which have been used for many years. New "smart" airbag systems receive information from sensors about the size and position of the occupant of the seat, and as a result can vary the level of force with which the bag opens. Another safety strategy that engineers are constantly working to improve is modification to the design of a vehicle's structure so it can withstand the force of a collision in a way that lessens the impact on passengers.

4   Since most car accidents are caused by human error, a major new strategy is to try to prevent collisions from happening in the first place! Electronics play a significant role in systems that either monitor a vehicle's position and inform the driver, or that actively take control of a vehicle's operation. One such innovation is a lane-departure system that signals the driver with a warning sound when the car starts to move out of its lane in the presence of other vehicles. With active lane-keeping assist, the system can intervene in the steering and actually move the car back into a safe position. This function is sometimes part of a blind-spot detection system, which uses sensors to detect vehicles at the side and rear of the vehicle that may not be visible in the car's mirrors, and alerts the driver by means of a light or sound.

5   A collision avoidance or pre-crash system uses radar to detect when a vehicle is about to collide with another vehicle in front of it. The system warns the driver and can take control of the braking and steering systems in order to try to prevent a collision. Another braking feature is automatic emergency braking. This technology detects hard braking by a driver and fully applies the vehicle's brakes to slow the vehicle more effectively.

6   An electronic stability control system goes further than anti-lock brakes, which most cars already have. In certain driving situations, such as in wet or icy conditions or when a driver is swerving or making unusually sharp, fast turns, a car may begin to slide or skid on the roadway. Electronic stability control sensors detect this unusual movement, and the

> **EARLY TECHNOLOGY TRANSFER!**
> The first practical automobile was built by Carl Benz in Germany in 1885. The wire-spoked wheels, pneumatic rubber tires, chain drive, and ball bearings used on the first automobiles were originally developed for bicycles.

system applies the brakes to each wheel in such a way that brings the vehicle back in line with the intended direction. The computerized controls may also reduce the engine power in order to slow down the vehicle.

7   Many new cars are equipped with a rear-facing back-up camera and a monitor. This enables the driver to see what is behind the car in order to avoid hitting vehicles or people when moving in reverse.

8   Because so many car accidents are caused by drivers that fall asleep, many automobile manufacturers have developed electronic monitoring systems to look for signs of driver fatigue and alert drivers who become drowsy. These include systems that monitor the driver's steering, the position and movement of the vehicle in the lane, and a camera that views the driver's face and eyes. The computerized system analyzes the data and produces audible and visual signals to alert a drowsy driver.

9   The ultimate in computer control is the self-driving car, or *autonomous* vehicle. Sensors read the environment surrounding the vehicle and allow it to navigate the streets without human control. The goal of collision avoidance technology is to ensure safe travel. Semi-autonomous cars are now in operation; fully autonomous vehicles may be on the streets in the near future.

10   Other recent safety innovations include vehicle-to-vehicle (V2V) communication that can share information about weather, speed, and accidents to extend drivers' awareness of road conditions; digital instrument panels that can display the navigation system in front of a driver's line of sight; active-cornering headlights that turn in the direction the vehicle turns to improve visibility at night; a smart front axle that can improve handling and maneuverability; and "run-flat tires" that will support the car even when the tires are flat.

Fuel Economy

11   The other major area of technological innovation is fuel economy. Though consumer demand for fuel-efficient vehicles tends to vary depending on the price of gasoline, reducing fuel consumption is a continuing goal of automobile technology and design. One approach is to achieve greater fuel efficiency through advances in engine computer control systems. Through turbocharging, engine power and fuel efficiency are increased.

12   Another strategy is to use lightweight materials to construct car parts, since lower vehicle weight means lower fuel consumption. Many car manufacturers are using aluminum and magnesium instead of iron and steel in engines and in car bodies to save weight. Carbon fiber and new composite materials are other types of lightweight materials also being used in car bodies.

Alternative Power Sources for Vehicles

13   Electric vehicles do not use any gasoline and produce no emissions from burning fuels, although energy is consumed in generating the electricity used to charge the car's battery. Electric-powered cars were present in the earliest days of the automobile, but then—as now—the main drawback was the limited driving range due to battery life, as well as the lack of charging stations. Hybrid vehicles, which have both an electric motor and a gasoline engine, are a popular alternative. They have greater fuel economy than a car that has only a gasoline engine, and they avoid worries over battery charge. Battery technology is constantly being improved, however, and it is expected that in the future a high percentage of vehicles on the road will be all-electric.

14   Hydrogen fuel cells are being developed as a new energy source for powering automobiles. Hydrogen and oxygen are mixed to create electricity, which powers a motor as in an electric car. Hydrogen

can be produced from renewable sources, but the process is expensive and uses a lot of energy.

Convenience and Comfort

15 New technological developments are also enhancing driver convenience and comfort. One focus is on new autonomous features. Advanced keyless entry systems can start the car remotely. The "parking assist" function can take over a car's controls from the driver and do parallel and reverse parking. And one new system can even park the car when the driver is outside the vehicle! Also, in many of today's automobiles, car seats can now not only be heated, but cooled by the delivery of cool air into the seat cushion.

16 High-tech dashboards contain the usual displays of vehicle systems and incorporate other functions, including audio, communications, entertainment, and maps. They can do things such as read text messages, answer calls, and play music. Some can even connect with apps on mobile phones. Through a "gesture control" system, in some cars the driver can control radio functions, answer phone calls, and

direct the navigation system with hand movements that are picked up by a camera.

17 Automobiles have changed dramatically since the first simple vehicles were produced. Though they still have the same basic purpose of transporting people from one place to another, there is a lot more to that process than there used to be. We can be sure that technology will continue to transform vehicles into ever more complex machines.

DID YOU UNDERSTAND?

1. What was the big development in the 1970s that began new types of innovations in automobiles?

2. In what three areas have modern automotive developments occurred?

3. What system controls engine functions?

4. What three main strategies for improving passenger safety are mentioned?

5. What causes most car accidents?

6. What is a blind spot?

7. What are some ways that a driver drowsiness detection system can detect when a driver is falling asleep?

8. What is another name for a self-driving car?

9. How should we interpret, "consumer demand for fuel-efficient vehicles tends to vary depending on the price of gasoline"?

10. What is one factor that limits the use of electric vehicles?

11. What is a hybrid vehicle?

12. What is the purpose of high-tech dashboards?

WHAT'S YOUR EXPERIENCE?

1. Have you driven a car that has some of the technology described here? How was the experience?

2. How does your concern for safety affect the way you drive?

WHAT'S YOUR OPINION?

1. What do you think is the best way to prevent car accidents?

2. You have probably seen drivers talking on the phone or messaging while driving. What do you think about that, and what do you think should be done about it?

3. How important to you is a car's fuel economy?

4. Would you like to have a car that can drive itself, or do you prefer to do the driving?

READING COMPREHENSION

1. The introduction of electronic technology has had a major impact on a car's _____.
   A. transmission system
   B. engine performance
   C. steering system
   D. braking system

2. What makes new airbags technologically "smart" is that _____.
   A. they open as soon as there is an impact
   B. they can force the airbag to open
   C. they operate based on information from sensors
   D. they communicate with the vehicle occupants

3. Which of the following features is not related to accident prevention?
   A. a lane departure system
   B. active lane-keeping assist
   C. a blind-spot detection system
   D. computerized engine control units

4. A blind-spot detection system _____.
   A. sees vehicles that aren't visible in the car's mirrors
   B. takes active control of a vehicle
   C. signals when a driver is moving out of a lane
   D. applies the vehicle's brakes to slow it down

5. Which paragraph describes safety systems that respond to weather conditions?
   A. Paragraph 3
   B. Paragraph 4
   C. Paragraph 5
   D. Paragraph 6

6. Based on the reading, which of the following does not yet exist?
   A. sensors that allow a car to drive itself without human control
   B. an electronic monitoring system that alerts a driver who has become drowsy
   C. technology that prevents all car accidents from happening
   D. tires that will support a car even when they are flat

7. From its usage in paragraph 11, it can be assumed that *turbocharging* is a mechanism for _____.
   A. controlling computers
   B. boosting an engine's power
   C. replacing the use of fuel
   D. consuming fuel

8. Keyless entry systems and parking assist are _____.
   A. new features related to driver convenience
   B. technological advances in fuel economy
   C. advances in vehicle-to-vehicle communication
   D. alternative power sources

9. Which of the following statements about electric vehicles is correct?
   A. They don't produce fuel emissions.
   B. They don't consume any energy.
   C. They use gasoline to charge their battery.
   D. Their battery life gives them unlimited range.

10. The major focus of the reading is to _____.
    A. demonstrate the latest developments in car safety
    B. describe the role of technology in the evolution of car manufacturing
    C. present the newest innovations in automotive design
    D. show how car manufacturing has responded to drivers' concerns

ACADEMIC VOCABULARY

1. The automobile industry has _____ significant changes through advances in technology.
   A. represented
   B. undergone
   C. enabled
   D. involved

2. There's a strong _____ on safety in contemporary automobile design.
   A. process
   B. goal
   C. function
   D. focus

3. The _____ of an automobile collision on passengers can be severe.
   A. impact
   B. input
   C. output
   D. function

4. Many new vehicles are _____ with a rear-facing back-up camera.
   A. implemented
   B. adapted
   C. equipped
   D. generated

5. In many of today's cars, there is a system that _____ the driver's behavior.
   A. achieves
   B. monitors
   C. assists
   D. investigates

6. It is essential for drivers to have _____ of road conditions.
   A. detection
   B. control
   C. an awareness
   D. an interpretation

7. Headlights that turn while the vehicle turns improve _____ during nighttime driving.
   A. visibility
   B. technology
   C. transmission
   D. economy

8. The goal of contemporary automobile design is for a vehicle to _____ maximum fuel efficiency.
   A. incorporate
   B. establish
   C. acquire
   D. achieve

9. Over the years, there have always been new and improved _____ to engine design.
   A. sources
   B. approaches
   C. structures
   D. policies

10. In the future, a high _____ of vehicles will be all-electric.
    A. range
    B. dimension
    C. alternative
    D. percentage

11. New technological developments have greatly _____ the driving experience.
    A. assessed
    B. ensured
    C. enhanced
    D. contributed

12. Automobiles have _____ changed since they were first introduced.
    A. dramatically
    B. approximately
    C. crucially
    D. securely

13. Air bags are designed to protect a vehicle's _____.
    A. participants
    B. components
    C. occupants
    D. elements

14. Lower fuel consumption can be achieved by using lightweight materials to _____ car parts.
    A. transform
    B. construct
    C. conduct
    D. select

UNIT 8 LISTENING

PART A

Practice: A B C   3. A B C
        1. A B C   4. A B C
        2. A B C   5. A B C

PART B

Practice: A B C   3. A B C
        1. A B C   4. A B C
        2. A B C   5. A B C

Look at pages 44–45 of the core text. Write the correct words to complete the description.

ambulance	checking	gloves	nursing	setting up	transport
ball	dietetic	gurney	orderly	surgeon	transporting
bed	discussing	measuring	oxygen	surgical	ventilator
certified	emergency	medication	perform	taking	weights
changing	entrance	monitor	sanitizing	therapist	wheelchair

The certified _____ **nursing** _____ ¹ assistants at this hospital are doing a variety of tasks. One CNA

is _____ ² a patient's blood pressure, another is _____ ³ an IV, another is

_____ ⁴ the linens on a patient's hospital _____ ⁵, and another has received some

_____ ⁶ from an RN that he will administer to a patient. A respiratory therapist is adjusting the

settings on a _____ ⁷ for a patient who is using _____ ⁸ inhalation equipment.

A _____ ⁹ aide is delivering a patient's meal. A _____ ¹⁰ SPD technician is

bringing a commode to a patient's room. An _____ ¹¹ wearing disposable _____ ¹²

is _____ ¹³ a bathroom. Another is _____ ¹⁴ a patient's output. A CNA is

_____ ¹⁵ a patient's status with family members. The patient is connected to a blood pressure

_____ ¹⁶. An _____ ¹⁷ has arrived at the _____ ¹⁸ room. An EMT is

_____ ¹⁹ a patient into the emergency room on a _____ ²⁰. An emergency room

technician is meeting them at the emergency room _____ ²¹. In the _____ ²² suite, a

surgical technician is _____ ²³ surgical instruments for a _____ ²⁴ who is operating on a

patient. A patient _____ ²⁵ attendant is transporting a patient in a _____ ²⁶ to physical

therapy, where a physical _____ ²⁷ and physical therapist assistant will _____ ²⁸

physical therapy using a therapy _____ ²⁹ and hand _____ ³⁰.

activities	evaluate	organizes	raised	safety	status
aide	homemaker	portable	ramp	sanitize	vital
belt	nurse	prepares	reports	shops	walker

This client in this home has 24-hour home health care. The home health _____ ³¹ who

comes during the day uses a gait _____ ³² to help him out of bed. She grooms and dresses him

and _____ ³³ his meals. She also helps him eat. In addition, she _____ ³⁴ to the

Home Health Service on his _____ ³⁵. A physical therapist comes in to _____ ³⁶

his PT progress and a visiting _____ ³⁷ comes in to check his _____ ³⁸ signs. Also,

a _____ ³⁹ comes to vacuum and clean the house and _____ ⁴⁰ the counters. The

client uses a two-wheel _____ ⁴¹ to get around his house. The aide who comes in the evening

_____ ⁴² for groceries and puts them away, bathes the client, _____ ⁴³ his medication

supply, does _____ ⁴⁴ with him, and puts him to bed. There's a _____ ⁴⁵ bar and

_____ ⁴⁶ toilet seat in the bathroom, _____ ⁴⁷ oxygen in the dining room, and a

handicap _____ ⁴⁸ outside the house.

CAREER RESEARCH

Using the O*NET Career Exploration Tools at mynextmove.org, search for information about one of the jobs in Unit 9. Write the information in the job profile below. Then prepare and give a presentation about the job.

Job Zone 2 (some job preparation)
certified nursing assistant (CNA), dietetic technician/aide, home health aide, homemaker, medical equipment preparer/certified SPD technician, orderly, patient transport attendant

Job Zone 3 (medium job preparation)
emergency medical technician (EMT), emergency room technician, licensed practical nurse (LPN), physical therapist assistant, registered nurse (RN), respiratory therapist, surgical technician, visiting nurse

Job Zone 5 (extensive job preparation)
anesthesiologist, doctor, physical therapist, surgeon

Job name: _____

What does a person do in this job?

_____

_____

_____

What tools and equipment does a person use in this job?

_____

What skills and abilities are important?

_____

_____

What technology might a person use in this job?

_____

What kind of person will be interested in this work?

_____

What level of education, job training, and experience is required?

_____

_____

What is the job outlook?   What is the average salary?

_____   _____

Read the home health care agency memo and answer the questions.

SUNSHINE HOME HEALTH

TO: New Home Health Aides

FROM: Carline Joseph, Director

Welcome to our agency. We are happy to have you on our health care team. Please be sure to follow these important guidelines.

1. All clients must be treated with courtesy, dignity, and respect. They have a right to not be discriminated against based on race, national origin, religion, age, sex, or handicap.

2. A client's living place and property must be respected at all times.

3. Clients have a right to privacy. Disclosure of a client's personal, financial, or medical information is strictly forbidden.

4. Caregivers may not accept gifts from clients, nor may they borrow funds from clients.

5. Caregivers shall not provide any form of medical care or assistance that is not in their job description or for which they are not trained or certified.

6. Notify the agency immediately of any change in the client's medical condition.

7. Know what to do in the event of an emergency.

8. Notify the agency of a planned absence as far in advance as possible so that alternative coverage can be arranged.

9. Have the client or a family member contact the agency regarding any request for a change in the visit schedule.

10. Notify the agency of any concerns about the client's welfare, including elder abuse/neglect and unsafe conditions in the home.

1. Which guideline relates to money matters?
   A. Guideline 2
   B. Guideline 4
   C. Guideline 6
   D. Guideline 9

2. What would be an example of *disclosure* as the term is used in Guideline 3?
   A. sharing information about the client with others
   B. talking with the client
   C. talking with the client's family about a change in schedule
   D. sharing information about the client's welfare with the agency

3. According to the memo, if an aide can't go to work, who will take care of the aide's client?
   A. a family member
   B. another client
   C. another caregiver
   D. a medical assistant

4. If this memo had a subject line, what would best express the director's main purpose for writing it?
   A. Your Client's Rights
   B. Welcome to Our Team
   C. When to Notify the Agency
   D. Guidelines for New Aides

DEMONSTRATING A PROCEDURE

Using YouTube, WikiHow, or another source, search online for a demonstration of how to treat a simple medical problem or do a first-aid procedure. Write out the instructions. Then prepare a media presentation. Make screenshots of the steps or video-record your demonstration. Present the procedure to the class.

Suggestions: how to treat a nosebleed; how to stop hiccups; how to apply a tourniquet; how to perform rescue breathing; how to perform the Heimlich maneuver

Science & Technology in Medicine Today & Tomorrow

1   Advances in science and technology are bringing about major changes in the field of medicine. From new methods for diagnosis and treatment to scientific breakthroughs in genetic medicine and remote robotic surgery, progress is being made at an ever-increasing pace.

Medical Diagnosis

2   Monitoring signals such as heart activity and glucose levels or studying sleep and activity levels currently requires a patient to be connected by wires to a machine that can record this data. For medical diagnosis in the future, scientists are working on the development of wearable skin patches with electronic sensors that can perform the same functions while allowing the patient to move freely and resume normal activity. Patches will transmit data wirelessly to a smartphone or computer and will transmit an alert or store information for later analysis. Another new type of patch will read biomarkers to determine levels of stress and anxiety.

3   Sensors that work from inside the body are also being developed. One example is a tiny ingestible sensor placed inside a pill that a patient swallows. The sensor turns on in the stomach, detecting when the patient has taken the medication, and monitors bodily systems. It sends this information to a skin patch that transmits it to the patient's smartphone.

4   Cancer continues to be one of the leading subjects of medical research, with early diagnosis being a main focus. Currently, doctors need to remove a tissue sample and conduct a biopsy to determine the presence of cancer. One new development is a small fiber optic probe that examines tissue with a laser light and a miniature microscope and collects images that can reveal the presence of cancer. Researchers hope to make the probe small enough so it can be inserted into the body to detect internal cancers. In the detection of skin cancer, a handheld scanner now helps doctors screen suspicious skin spots to see whether a biopsy is needed. In another approach, smartphone apps compare photos of suspicious spots to a data bank of cancerous moles, although their findings are not yet reliable. Smartphone apps are also being developed that

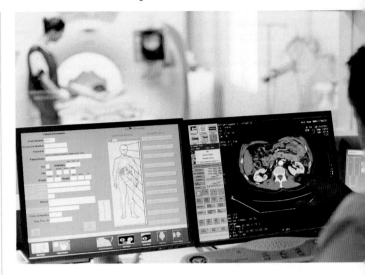

make use of the camera, flash, and microphone to help diagnose and monitor a variety of diseases or conditions.

5   Scientists have also devised a new method for detecting cancerous tissue using photoacoustic imaging. The new technique involves aiming a light beam on the area and then reading an image of sound waves that are released from cancerous cells. Surgeons are using it in breast cancer operations to see if they have removed all the cancerous tissue in the area.

6   Computer software that accesses data banks is aiding in the diagnosis of schizophrenia, a serious mental disorder. The software compares magnetic resonance imaging (MRI) scans of the patient's brain to a data bank of scans from patients with schizophrenia. Another software analyzes electrocardiograms in reference to a data bank to check for signs of cardiac arrhythmia, or irregular heartbeat.

Innovative Treatment

7   A new approach has been developed for delivering medication directly to an area needing treatment, as an alternative to pills or injections. A magnetic implant containing a drug is surgically inserted in the area to be treated. Passing a magnet over the device causes it to release a dose of the drug into the surrounding tissue.

8   Scientists are working on a more futuristic way of delivering treatment to specific points in the body.

They are developing tiny robots—"nanobots" less than one-millionth of a meter in length—that would travel inside veins, recognize cancer cells, and deliver drugs to a specific area. In another system, nanoparticles containing drugs are guided to their target by ultrasonic waves. Other researchers envision self-propelled nanobots with sensors and injectors that could destroy bacteria or repair cells.

9   Decades of research have focused on cancer treatment. One new approach is immunotherapy cancer vaccines that aim to use the body's immune system—its natural germ-fighting defense—to target and destroy cancer cells. New cancer-fighting drugs continue to be developed. Drug trials are now testing drug therapies that could work against similar cancers in any part of the body, not just a targeted area.

Genetic Medicine

10   The science of genetic engineering has progressed rapidly in recent years. An organism's genome can be manipulated by gene editing, which involves cutting natural DNA sequences and adding, removing, or altering DNA to achieve a particular effect. It has been used in plants and animals for many years for purposes such as promoting resistance to disease or producing desirable features. Gene-editing technologies have improved, and genetic engineering in humans is now under consideration. It could be used to correct genetic mutations or defects that cause certain diseases, or for purposes such as creating genetically-altered immune cells that can be used to attack cancer. A debate is currently underway over the ethics of changing DNA in human embryos to create "designer babies" that would have preferred characteristics.

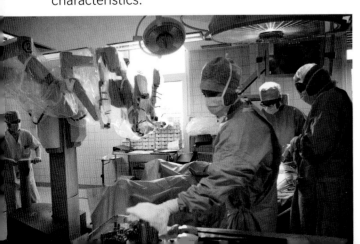

Prosthetic Limbs

11   Researchers are coming closer to achieving natural control and movement of artificial arms and legs. Brain-machine interface (BMI) technologies have made it possible for a patient to move a prosthetic computer-controlled limb by neural signals through use of an implant in the brain. Computer technology has enabled natural walking and stair-climbing movement in artificial legs. Scientists are making progress on research to create feeling in prosthetic hands through the use of sensors.

Telemedicine

12   Telemedicine is the delivery of medical care from a distance. It uses telecommunication and information technology to connect medical staff and patients who are in different locations for purposes such as remote monitoring of a patient's condition, interactive check-ups and consultations, and telenursing services. Remote surgery, or telesurgery, is possible through the use of a robotic surgical assistant. With this technology, the operating surgeon might even be located in another country!

13   In telepathology, laboratories can share images of tissue samples with specialists for diagnosis. Through teleradiology, specialists can get access to images such as X-rays and CT scans from a remote location.

Robots in Health Care

14   Various types of robots are appearing in many areas of the medical field. Some are actively involved in providing health care. Mobile medical robots move around a hospital floor and check on patients in their rooms. Their display screens allow medical specialists to consult with patients. Robotic surgical assistants are used for complex operations requiring precision and control. They are remotely operated at a workstation outside the operating room. Rehabilitation robots can be programmed to help a patient with physical therapy.

15   Other types of robots include: medical transportation robots that move around the hospital, delivering supplies, medications, and

meals to patients, and removing medical waste and soiled linens; mobile medical robots that clean and disinfect hospital rooms where dangerous microbes might be present, using an ultraviolet light that inactivates bacteria and kills pathogens such as Ebola and measles; and robots in research laboratories that are used to handle liquids and microplates and to perform a variety of precise, repetitive functions.

Other Developments

3-D Printing

16 Through the process of 3-D printing, scientists have created various artificial body parts, such as ears, skin cells, and parts of organs. They have also used 3-D printing to create physical models of a patient's artery and heart valve to help heart surgeons decide on effective surgical procedures.

Tissue Engineering

17 A different way of creating replacement tissue and organs is to grow them in a laboratory in a process that uses a patient's own stem cells. Through tissue engineering, scientists have created a variety of small internal body parts and successfully placed them in patients.

Artificial Heart Valves

18 As an alternative to open-heart surgery, an artificial heart valve has been designed that can be inserted through an artery and placed in the heart.

Microneedles

19 Scientists have designed a tiny patch containing microneedles that can effectively deliver a flu vaccine into the bloodstream through the skin. The microneedles are made of a material that dissolves in the skin. Researchers have found that the vaccine is more effective when delivered with microneedles than with an injection.

Surgical Glue

20 Surgical glue is sometimes used in operations to hold incisions together. Scientists have developed a new type of glue using proteins from mussels and other sea animals that holds tissues together even in wet conditions. In some cases, it may be preferable to using sutures or staples.

The Future

21 Many of the developments discussed previously are already being put into practice, and others will be appearing soon in one form or another. As science and technology continue to advance, and as new generations of scientists conceive of innovative ways to approach medical challenges, the future of medicine will continue to be exciting to watch. And we may be watching it for a long time: One area of current scientific research is in extending the human lifespan through antiaging drugs.

DID YOU UNDERSTAND?

1. What is the advantage of a wearable skin patch for monitoring health signals?

2. How do doctors currently test for cancer in tissue?

3. How does the smartphone app for detecting skin cancer work?

4. How are data banks used in diagnosing brain or heart conditions?

5. What are nanobots, and what can they be used for?

6. How does immunotherapy fight cancer?

7. How can gene editing be used to prevent disease?

8. What is a prosthetic limb?

9. How is remote surgery done?

10. How is light used to disinfect a room?

11. How does tissue engineering work?

12. What is the purpose of surgical glue?

WHAT'S YOUR OPINION?

1. What is your opinion about genetic engineering in humans? Do you think it is acceptable? For what purposes?

2. What are the pros and cons of extending human life?

READING COMPREHENSION

1. According to the reading, smartphones of the future will _____.
   A. be connected by wires to machines that record data
   B. receive information from a skin patch worn by a patient
   C. help with remote robotic surgery
   D. send signals to medication inside the body

2. Which of the following will be a new method of cancer detection in the future?
   A. Doctors will remove a tissue sample and perform a biopsy.
   B. A handheld scanner will screen biopsied tissue samples.
   C. A probe with a microscope will take images inside the body.
   D. Photos of cancerous cells will be analyzed using light and sound waves.

3. What do magnetic implants, nanobots, and nanoparticles have in common?
   A. They are all one-millionth of a meter in length.
   B. They are all surgically inserted.
   C. They are all guided by ultrasonic waves.
   D. They all deliver medication.

4. Which of the following uses of genetic engineering is most controversial?
   A. the ability to change DNA in human embryos
   B. the ability to correct genetic mutations
   C. the ability to create genetically altered immune cells
   D. the ability to produce desirable features in plants

5. In paragraph 11, what is the meaning of the term *prosthetic*?
   A. protective
   B. temporary
   C. artificial
   D. identical

6. _____ are programmed to administer physical therapy to patients.
   A. Robotic surgical assistants
   B. Mobile medical robots
   C. Medical transportation robots
   D. Rehabilitation robots

7. Which paragraph describes a process that would help doctors make surgical decisions?
   A. Paragraph 13
   B. Paragraph 16
   C. Paragraph 17
   D. Paragraph 19

8. Incisions can be held together during an operation through the use of _____.
   A. tissue engineering
   B. microneedles
   C. surgical glue
   D. artificial valves

9. Based on the context in paragraph 15, *pathogens* most likely _____ diseases.
   A. cause
   B. prevent
   C. kill
   D. reduce

10. The author's primary focus in this reading is to _____.
   A. describe current innovative treatments of diseases
   B. explore the role of technology in present and future medicine
   C. compare past, present, and future approaches to medical care
   D. describe innovations in medical diagnoses

ACADEMIC VOCABULARY

1. Machines are able to carefully _____ a patient's heart activity and glucose level.
   A. transmit
   B. monitor
   C. transfer
   D. promote

2. One of the main focuses of medical research is on the early _____ of cancer.
   A. consultation
   B. operation
   C. inspection
   D. detection

3. The goal of new treatments is to deliver medication aimed at _____ points in the body.
   A. specific
   B. accurate
   C. internal
   D. complex

4. Medical researchers continue to develop innovative strategies for _____ medication to patients.
   A. projecting
   B. administering
   C. adjusting
   D. assisting

5. New approaches are being explored to develop effective _____ to pills and injections.
   A. techniques
   B. methods
   C. alternatives
   D. processes

6. Gene editing involves altering DNA to _____ a particular result.
   A. perform
   B. achieve
   C. design
   D. transform

7. Medical professionals are researching ways to _____ resistance to certain diseases.
   A. require
   B. involve
   C. protect
   D. promote

8. Research is underway on how to _____ feeling in prosthetic hands.
   A. create
   B. transfer
   C. insert
   D. involve

9. It is possible to get _____ to X-ray images and CT scans from remote locations.
   A. input
   B. analysis
   C. access
   D. focus

10. Complex medical operations require _____ and control.
    A. precision
    B. conditions
    C. functions
    D. instruction

11. The sharing of patient medical information is _____ doctors in the diagnoses of many diseases.
    A. assessing
    B. aiding
    C. targeting
    D. assuring

12. Robots are able to deliver supplies and _____ medical waste.
    A. reveal
    B. receive
    C. resolve
    D. remove

13. Artificial heart valves can be _____ through an artery into the heart.
    A. located
    B. converted
    C. inserted
    D. retained

14. New generations of scientists will undoubtedly _____ of innovative ways to deal with complex medical problems.
    A. conceive
    B. identify
    C. achieve
    D. initiate

UNIT 9 LISTENING

PART A

Practice: A B C   3. A B C
1. A B C   4. A B C
2. A B C   5. A B C

PART B

Practice: A B C   3. A B C
1. A B C   4. A B C
2. A B C   5. A B C

Look at pages 136–137 of the core text. Write the correct words to complete the description.

assistant	clinical	diagnoses	needle	scheduling	transcriber
assisting	coder	escorting	receptionist	suturing	transcribing
blood	coding	giving	record	taking	transcriptionist
checking in	collecting	measuring	retrieving	technician	

It's a typical busy day at this medical office. The medical _____receptionist_____ ¹ is _____ ²
a patient. An administrative medical assistant is _____ ³ a patient's next appointment. Another
is _____ ⁴ a medical file. The medical _____ ⁵, wearing a _____ ⁶
headphone, is _____ ⁷ the doctor's notes, and the medical _____ ⁸ is
_____ ⁹ procedures and _____ ¹⁰. There are several _____ ¹¹ medical
assistants doing many different tasks. One is _____ ¹² a patient's height and weight and another
is _____ ¹³ a patient to an exam room. One is _____ ¹⁴ a lab specimen in a specimen
cup and another is doing a fingerprick for a _____ ¹⁵ test. One is updating a patient's medical
_____ ¹⁶ and another is _____ ¹⁷ vital signs. One is _____ ¹⁸ an injection
and another is _____ ¹⁹ a wound with a surgical suture _____ ²⁰ and thread. In addition,
an EKG _____ ²¹ is doing an EKG, and a physician _____ ²² is _____ ²³
a doctor with a medical procedure.

adjusting	dilating	grinding	making	optometrist	preparing
analyzed	display	hygienist	MRI	pharmacist	radiologist
assisting	drawing	imaging	optical	pharmacy	radiology
cleaning	filling	injecting	optician	phlebotomy	reading
dental	giving	lab	optometry	phlebotomists	taking

In the _____ ²⁴ office of this medical building, a dental _____ ²⁵ is
_____ ²⁶ a patient's teeth. One of the dental assistants is _____ ²⁷ dental X-rays and
another is _____ ²⁸ the dentist with a procedure. In the dental _____ ²⁹,
dental lab technicians are _____ ³⁰ dentures. In the radiology _____ ³¹ center, a
_____ ³² technician is taking a patient's X-ray and a _____ ³³ is _____ ³⁴
an X-ray. A nuclear medical technician is _____ ³⁵ radiopharmaceutical material into a patient and
an MRI technician is _____ ³⁶ a patient for an _____ ³⁷. In the _____ ³⁸
lab, _____ ³⁹ are _____ ⁴⁰ patients' blood, which is then _____ ⁴¹ in
the diagnostic lab by medical lab technicians. In the _____ ⁴² exam room of the vision center, an
optometric assistant is _____ ⁴³ a patient's eyes before the _____ ⁴⁴ examines him.
In the optometry lab, an _____ ⁴⁵ lab technician is _____ ⁴⁶ and polishing lenses. And
in the eyeglass _____ ⁴⁷ area, an _____ ⁴⁸ is _____ ⁴⁹ eyeglass frames.
In the _____ ⁵⁰, a _____ ⁵¹ is _____ ⁵² a prescription and a pharmacy
assistant is _____ ⁵³ medication instructions.

Using the O*NET Career Exploration Tools at mynextmove.org, search for information about one of the jobs in Unit 10. Write the information in the job profile below. Then prepare and give a presentation about the job.

Job Zone 2 (some job preparation)

dental lab technician, medical receptionist, optical lab technician, pharmacy assistant

Job Zone 3 (medium job preparation)

administrative medical assistant, dental assistant, dental hygienist, EKG technician, medical coder, medical lab technician, medical transcriptionist, MRI technician, nuclear medicine technician, optician, optometric assistant, pharmacy technician, phlebotomist, radiology technician, X-ray technician

Job Zone 4 (high job preparation)

clinical medical assistant

Job Zone 5 (extensive job preparation)

dentist, doctor/physician, optometrist, pharmacist, physician assistant, radiologist

Job name: _____

What does a person do in this job?

_____

_____

_____

What tools and equipment does a person use in this job?

_____

What skills and abilities are important?

_____

_____

What technology might a person use in this job?

_____

What kind of person will be interested in this work?

_____

What level of education, job training, and experience is required?

_____

_____

What is the job outlook?   What is the average salary?

_____   _____

A Community Health Coordinator

1   My name is Gita Banerjee. I'm the community health coordinator at the Central Public Health Clinic, the largest public health provider in our city. In this role,  I create and manage our clinic's community-based health and wellness programs.

2   We offer free education programs to residents to help them improve their health and well-being. These include classes in nutrition, stress management, and fitness, and support groups for cancer survivors, caregivers, and families that have lost a family member to drug abuse or violence.

3   Another important part of my job is to coordinate with the school system, social service agencies, and other community organizations so that we have better integration of our services to promote the health of families and children. We have monthly leadership meetings at City Hall.

4   Our biggest event of the year is our community health fair—a popular free event held on the last weekend in August every year. At the two-day health fair, we offer blood pressure checks, vision and hearing tests, glucose and cholesterol blood tests, diabetes screening, and flu vaccinations if available. We also have information booths with lots of educational material about all aspects of health and wellness. There's always free food, children's activities, and live entertainment.

5   My pathway to this job has been interesting. After graduating high school, I studied for two years at my local community college while working as a home health aide. I continued that work for two more years so I could save up enough to afford tuition and enroll in a four-year college, where I studied biology and environmental science. During my senior year, I became interested in public health as I did research on the effects of environmental problems on urban neighborhoods—problems such as lead poisoning and asthma. After graduating, I worked for a few years for a local environmental action coalition, and then I went to graduate school and earned a Master of Public Health (M.P.H.) degree. This clinic was my practicum site during graduate school, and the health coordinator position here happened to open up just as I completed my degree. It was definitely a case of being in the right place at the right time.

1. Which paragraph describes this person's first experience with the clinic?
   A. Paragraph 1
   B. Paragraph 2
   C. Paragraph 3
   D. Paragraph 5

2. Select the paragraphs that best describe the services this clinic offers directly to residents.
   A. Paragraphs 1 and 2
   B. Paragraphs 2 and 3
   C. Paragraphs 2 and 4
   D. Paragraphs 3 and 5

3. What information about the community health fair ISN'T provided in Paragraph 4?
   A. the location
   B. the activities
   C. the cost
   D. the days it occurs

4. How many different education programs did this person attend after high school to prepare for her career?
   A. one
   B. two
   C. three
   D. four

CLASSROOM VISITOR

Invite the coordinator of a community health clinic to visit your class. Ask about the medical services the clinic provides, the health and wellness programs it offers, the types of jobs that exist there, and the training required for these occupations. (Or, attend a community health clinic class or event or search the clinic's website to learn about its services and programs.)

Health Informatics

¹ A relatively new field in health care has been getting a lot of attention, not only for its role in improving the provision of medical services, but for its potential as a growing area of employment. It is called *health informatics*, and it is made possible by recent advances in computers, information technology (IT), and telecommunications. Health informatics involves storing patients' health-care information electronically and making it accessible to health-care providers for the purpose of improving collaboration, efficiency, cost-effectiveness, and results for patients.

Health Information

² Patients often have several medical providers, including their primary care doctor, specialists for certain health conditions, nurses, and therapists, all producing medical data on the patient. Information may also be generated by radiologists, laboratories, and pharmacies, and by providers in hospitals and in community and public health clinics. The key to making it possible to share this data in a data-exchange system is for the information to be stored in electronic format on computers. A transition from paper medical records to electronic medical records (EMRs) has been happening for several years as part of a policy requiring public and private medical providers to record information in digital form so that it can be accessed by computers. The information on individual EMRs is recorded in another format called an electronic health record (EHR) that contains a broader view of the patient's medical history. This record can be shared among medical providers who need access to all records pertaining to a patient's health situation and treatment.

Interoperability

³ Electronic health records are one of two basic elements of health informatics. The other is an interconnected and interoperable system through which providers and others seeking the records can communicate with each other and successfully access them. Currently, individual health-care providers or agencies hold their health data on

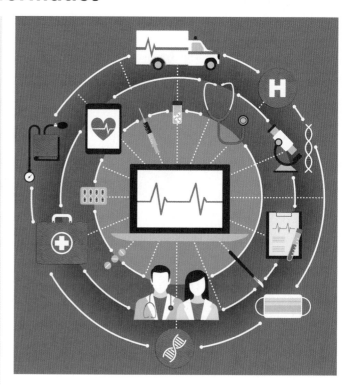

their own computer systems, and there is no overall system through which others can access it. A huge effort is now underway to set up standards for all health-care providers that will achieve the needed interoperability of their data systems and allow the quick, accurate, secure, and private exchange of patient health records and information.

Working in Health Informatics

⁴ Health informatics specialists work on creating and improving procedures and systems that manage data and transmit it to agencies that need it, with the goal of better informing providers of health services and improving health care delivery and outcomes. These specialists work for hospitals, large health-care organizations, nursing care facilities, dental practices, community clinics, public health offices, and insurance companies. They integrate and manage health data, monitor and improve computer networks and databases, analyze communication systems, and help develop and implement security and privacy policies.

⁵ Most jobs in health informatics require skills in information technology, data management, computer systems, and in software related to these

efficient way of analyzing and handling the massive amounts of health-care data being collected. The coded information is used in documenting health insurance claims, building databases, and maintaining patients' medical histories.

7   Jobs for health informatics specialists usually involve technical specializations that require a higher level of educational preparation. At the highest levels, informatics managers and directors are responsible for managing information systems and coordinating health information data across an organization. Here are some examples of jobs for health informatics specialists:

8   *Clinical Analysts* evaluate data generated by a health-care facility and help maintain its clinical information systems. They may also be involved in creating health information database systems. The job requires proficiency in information technology and an understanding of federal regulatory standards.

9   *Nursing Informatics Specialists* have expertise in both the medical field and informatics. They are registered nurses who have training in IT and related software systems. They evaluate the operation and services of health-care facilities and determine how information systems can improve efficiency. The job can also involve training staff in the use of the systems.

areas. Health informatics specialists in general need to be familiar with the basic elements of medical care and health services, the typical responsibilities of departments and staff, and common medical procedures and terminology, but most do not normally need in-depth medical knowledge. It is helpful for them to understand organizational structure, administrative functions, common lines of communication, and an organization's internal and external informational needs. Health informatics specialists also need to stay up-to-date on policies and regulatory standards related to electronic recordkeeping and data management.

6   At the entry level are health information technicians who work directly with patients' medical information and enter the data into electronic medical record systems. They play an important role in preparing health data in EMR and EHR formats according to regulatory standards. Medical transcriptionists listen to voice recordings made by doctors and other health-care workers and write them as reports that can be entered in digital data banks. Medical coders analyze health-care information in reports, records, and documentation and classify it according to a coding system. The information includes diagnosis of health conditions such as illnesses, symptoms, and injuries; procedures, treatments, surgeries, and other services; medications and prescriptions; and many other aspects of health and health care. Coding provides a standardized method of documenting health-care information and is an

MEDICAL TERMINOLOGY
Medical coders need to know the special vocabulary medical providers use to refer to parts of the body. Are you familiar with any of these terms?

Abdominal	Abdomen
Cranial	Skull
Digital	Fingers and toes
Femoral	Thigh
Lumbar	Lower back
Manual	Hand
Nasal	Nose
Oral	Mouth
Pedal	Foot
Thoracic	Chest

10   *Health Informatics Specialists* have responsibilities similar to those of Nursing Informatics Specialists, but their focus is more on the use of technology in health care settings. They work with clinical and clerical staff to implement computerized health information systems, producing educational materials and providing training and assistance.

11   *Health Informatics Consultants* are health IT specialists who work independently or for a health consulting firm. They assist health-care facilities or companies with EMR/EHR adoption, review and improve health information and computer systems, analyze needs in data storage and management, and train staff in the use of special software tools.

12   A *Director of Clinical Informatics* oversees clinical information systems and electronic records delivery systems and makes sure that they are up-to-date and work efficiently. The director adjusts and improves the systems to meet the needs of internal and external users in an effective way.

The Future of Health Informatics

13   As a large segment of the population ages, health care will become an increasingly large part of the overall economy. The number of health-care facilities and providers will increase, as will the amount of data that is generated from patients and services. The need to be able to manage this data

efficiently is vitally important not only for the health-care industry but for achieving the best health outcomes possible for every individual patient. Health informatics plays a key role in meeting this need. As one of the fastest-growing job sectors, health informatics is providing many opportunities for those who have or would like to acquire skills in both health care and information technology.

DID YOU UNDERSTAND?

1. What is health informatics?

2. Why is it important for health-care data to be stored in electronic format?

3. What does *interoperability* mean?

4. Where do health informatics specialists work?

5. What kinds of skills are usually required for jobs in health informatics?

6. What does a medical transcriptionist do?

7. Why is it important to code health-care information?

8. What is coded health-care information used for?

9. Which of the jobs listed as examples requires extensive knowledge in both informatics and the medical field?

10. What is the main focus of a health informatics specialist?

1. A data-exchange system is only possible _____.
   A. if patients have several medical providers
   B. if patient information is stored in electronic format
   C. if patients are able to use a computer
   D. if patients are treated in community and public health clinics

2. The advantage of interoperability is that _____.
   A. individual health-care providers are able to store their own data
   B. patients can have computerized electronic health records
   C. different health-care providers can communicate with each other about patient data
   D. patients can exchange health information with each other

3. According to the reading, informatics is not only an advance in medical recordkeeping, but it is also creating many potential new _____.
   A. medical services
   B. health-care providers
   C. organizations
   D. jobs

4. Which of the following is NOT required of health informatics specialists?
   A. familiarity with the basics of medical care
   B. knowledge of organizational structure and administrative functions
   C. in-depth medical knowledge
   D. an understanding of current medical policies and standards

5. What do the jobs mentioned in paragraph 6 have in common?
   A. They are for workers who are starting out in the health informatics field.
   B. They require familiarity with the insurance industry.
   C. They involve assisting in patient care.
   D. They offer training in providing health services.

6. Which of the following professionals are involved in classifying patients' medical information?
   A. medical transcriptionists
   B. medical coders
   C. clinical analysts
   D. informatics managers

7. According to the reading, which of the following statements is true?
   A. Nursing informatics consultants must understand federal regulations.
   B. Health informatics specialists are usually employed by consulting firms.
   C. Clinical analysts must be registered nurses with IT training.
   D. The director of clinical informatics is in charge of information and records systems.

8. In paragraph 10, what would be the best synonym for the word *implement*?
   A. study
   B. evaluate
   C. put into use
   D. understand

9. The primary focus of the reading is to _____.
   A. describe the duties and responsibilities of health informatics specialists
   B. describe the importance and benefits of keeping electronic health records
   C. explain how a patient's medical information is coded
   D. predict future changes in medical record keeping

10. According to the reading, we can predict that in the future _____.
    A. there will be less need for health-care providers
    B. there will be fewer jobs for informatics specialists
    C. there won't be as many health-care facilities as there are today
    D. there will be a greater amount of patient medical data

ACADEMIC VOCABULARY

1. It is essential that patients' health-care information be _____ to health-care providers.
   A. contributed
   B. assisted
   C. accessible
   D. efficient

2. A _____ from paper to electronic medical records has been taking place for the past several years.
   A. procedure
   B. transition
   C. process
   D. translation

3. An interconnected system of medical files makes it easier for providers who are _____ patients' records.
   A. seeking
   B. achieving
   C. involving
   D. allowing

4. Our company is always looking for ways to improve _____ for managing data.
   A. objectives
   B. assignments
   C. requirements
   D. procedures

5. We are working hard to _____ the new security and privacy policies that have been established.
   A. innovate
   B. implement
   C. interact
   D. instruct

6. My job _____ skills in information technology and data management.
   A. promotes
   B. acquires
   C. requires
   D. receives

7. We need to _____ all of our systems to see if they need to be improved.
   A. clarify
   B. evaluate
   C. demonstrate
   D. create

8. Our specialists will be able to provide training and any _____ you might need.
   A. assistance
   B. approach
   C. aspects
   D. responsibilities

9. For this job, you will need to have _____ in both the medical field and information technology.
   A. methods
   B. systems
   C. opportunities
   D. expertise

10. We work with hospitals, community clinics, and nursing care _____.
    A. facilities
    B. securities
    C. capacities
    D. economies

11. A large amount of health-care _____ needs to be collected and coded.
    A. storage
    B. data
    C. technology
    D. outcome

12. A patient's medical information is used to _____ health insurance claims.
    A. relate
    B. provide
    C. document
    D. detect

13. We are responsible for _____ a large amount of health-care information.
    A. interacting
    B. cooperating
    C. determining
    D. coordinating

14. A great deal of patient information is _____ by doctors, laboratories, and pharmacies.
    A. assisted
    B. involved
    C. generated
    D. participated

UNIT 10 LISTENING

PART A

Practice: A B C   3. A B C
     1. A B C   4. A B C
     2. A B C   5. A B C

PART B

Practice: A B C   3. A B C
     1. A B C   4. A B C
     2. A B C   5. A B C

Look at pages 150–151 of the core text. Write the correct words to complete the description.

apprehending	control	fingerprinting	gear	operators	testing	victim
booking	detective	firefighters	handcuff	paramedic	ticketing	witnesses
chasing	directing	forensics	holding	parking	traffic	
collecting	entering	frisking	interview	rescuing		

Public service workers are hard at work! 911 ___**operators**___ 1 are responding to emergency calls. Police officers are helping to keep the city safe. One is _____ 2 a suspect down the street. Another is holding a gun while _____ 3 a suspect. Another is _____ 4 a suspect for a weapon. Another is using handcuffs to _____ 5 a suspect. A public safety officer is directing _____ 6. An animal _____ 7 officer is attempting to catch a dog. A _____ 8 enforcement officer is _____ 9 an illegally parked car. A forensic identification specialist is _____ 10 evidence at a crime scene. An EMT and a _____ 11 are helping a _____ 12 and a _____ 13 is interviewing _____ 14. At the police station, a police officer in the _____ 15 area is _____ 16 a suspect who will then wait in the _____ 17 cell before being questioned by detectives in the _____ 18 room. In the _____ 19 lab, specialists are _____ 20 evidence. At the fire station, _____ 21 are dressing in turnout _____ 22, ready to respond to a fire. At a fire scene, firefighters are _____ 23 a water spray on a fire, _____ 24 a burning building, and _____ 25 victims.

apprehending	confiscating	detectors	locker	patrolling	screeners	watching
asset	contraband	escorting	luggage	probation	searches	watchman
badge	corrections	guards	parole	probationer	searching	
checking	defending	images	parolee			

A bailiff is _____ 26 a defendant into a courtroom, where the public defender will be _____ 27 her. A _____ 28 officer is bringing food to an inmate in his jail cell. Other corrections officers are _____ 29 a prison cell for _____ 30. A _____ 31 agent is reviewing conditions of parole with a _____ 32. A _____ 33 officer is checking an ankle monitor on a _____ 34. At the airport, TSA _____ 35 are _____ 36 photo IDs, searching carry-on _____ 37, checking X-ray _____ 38 of carry-on bags, and sometimes _____ 39 illegal carry-on items. They're also viewing AIT screening images, using handheld metal _____ 40, and performing pat-down _____ 41 on passengers. There are security _____ 42 at a guard house at the entrance of a company. One is _____ 43 security monitors and the other is checking an employee's ID _____ 44. At a school, a safety officer is checking a student's _____ 45 for illegal items. In a department store, an _____ 46 protection specialist is _____ 47 a shoplifter. A _____ 48 and a security patrol officer are _____ 49 buildings. All of these professionals are working to keep the community safe.

CAREER RESEARCH

Using the O*NET Career Exploration Tools at mynextmove.org, search for information about one of the jobs in Unit 11. Write the information in the job profile below. Then prepare and give a presentation about the job.

Job Zone 2 (some job preparation)

911 operator, animal control officer, asset protection specialist, bailiff, corrections officer, emergency services dispatcher, parking enforcement officer, security guard, TSA agent, TSA officer, TSA screener, watchman

Job Zone 3 (medium job preparation)

detective, emergency medical technician (EMT), engine chauffeur, firefighter, K9 officer, law enforcement officer, paramedic, police officer, public safety officer, school safety officer, security patrol officer

Job Zone 4 (high job preparation)

fingerprint analyst, forensic identification specialist, parole agent, probation officer

Job Zone 5 (extensive job preparation)

judge, public defender

Job name: _____

What does a person do in this job?

_____

_____

_____

What tools and equipment does a person use in this job?

_____

What skills and abilities are important?

_____

_____

What technology might a person use in this job?

_____

What kind of person will be interested in this work?

_____

What level of education, job training, and experience is required?

_____

_____

What is the job outlook?   What is the average salary?

_____   _____

Read the memo about security guard patrol procedures and answer the questions.

TO: All Security Personnel
FROM: Amir Basri, Security Director
SUBJ: New Patrol Procedures

Our long-planned switchover to the new patrol data management system will occur tomorrow. Here is a reminder of the key procedures covered in last month's training sessions.

1. Patrolling routes have changed. Be sure to follow the new routes and check in at all checkpoints. Also, note that the new system will continually change routes and include backtracking in order for routes to be unpredictable.

2. Record tour times and enter notes on tour activities and observations using the new mobile app.

3. Record **your own** patrol data and checkpoint activity. Buddy punching has always been prohibited and grounds for dismissal. With the new app, it is now detectible.

4. The app provides reminders of your patrol duties. Be alert for ad hoc requests during your tour from the security supervisor on duty.

5. Report incidents immediately using the mobile app. If appropriate, take photos of the situation.

6. In the event of an emergency, push the panic button on the app. This will instantly alert emergency contacts, record your GPS location, and take photos. (The app tracks and stores your GPS location at all times.)

7. The phone you have been issued for the new patrolling management system may only be used for official work responsibilities. Personal use is prohibited.

8. Do not allow interaction with the mobile device to distract from focusing on your surroundings.

1. Which feature of patrolling probably didn't exist before the switchover to the new system?
   A. making notes and observations
   B. tracking guards' locations at all times
   C. reporting emergencies
   D. checking in at checkpoints

2. In Procedure 3, what does the term *buddy punching* probably refer to?
   A. not getting along with a co-worker
   B. taking breaks at the wrong time
   C. reporting an incident for another guard
   D. recording another guard's patrol data

3. In Procedure 4, what does the term *ad hoc requests* refer to?
   A. special instructions
   B. reminders of regular duties
   C. reports about incidents
   D. new patrolling data

4. What is the purpose of Procedure 8?
   A. to prohibit personal use of the phone
   B. to not allow interaction with other guards by phone
   C. to make sure guards pay attention during their tours
   D. to make sure guards use the focus feature on the phone's camera correctly

DEMONSTRATING A PROCEDURE

Using YouTube, WikiHow, or another source, search online for a demonstration of how to do a procedure related to public safety. Write out the instructions. Then prepare a media presentation. Make screenshots of the steps or video-record your demonstration. Present the procedure to the class.

Suggestions: how to report a crime; how to report a home emergency; how to report a car accident; how to go through airport security; how to testify in court

The Science and Technology of Identification

1   Driver's licenses, photo IDs, passports, passwords—these are the most common forms of identification that we use to verify who we are. But scientists are creating new ways of establishing a person's identity. Modern identification systems are now being used for a variety of everyday purposes, such as authorizing access to buildings, logging in and out at workplaces, and processing travelers at immigration checkpoints at airports and borders. They are also being used in banking, retail businesses, and government social service agencies to quickly and conveniently identify individuals with a high degree of accuracy.

2   The most widespread use of identification technology is by law enforcement agencies and by government security and intelligence organizations. Police departments now rely heavily on new technologies in doing criminal investigations and in forensics—analyzing physical evidence from crime scenes to identify criminals and sometimes victims.

Biometrics

3   The new identification systems are based on biometrics, the unique physical characteristics every individual possesses. These characteristics— or biometric indicators—include fingerprints, facial features, eyes, voice, DNA, and even behavior.

FINGERPRINTS

4   The most commonly used type of biometric identification is fingerprinting. Everyone's fingerprints are unique and can be used to establish a person's identity with great certainty. When criminal suspects are *booked*—entered into police records—they are routinely fingerprinted. A technician using the department's fingerprint identification system can check a suspect's fingerprints against a data bank of prints. Matching prints can identify a person who has a criminal record. Police departments sometimes also provide fingerprinting services for employers so that they can do background checks before hiring child-care providers, teachers, health-care workers, truck drivers, and others.

5   Most police departments still use the *rolled ink method*, which places prints on a card. However, *live scan fingerprinting*, which uses an optical scanner, is becoming more common. Optical scanning is a process similar to photocopying or scanning a document. A bright light shines on the finger and a charge coupled device (CCD) camera, or light sensor system, takes a digital picture that records the tiny lines or ridges that make up the fingerprint. A computer analyzes the fingerprint pattern by looking at a set of up to sixteen features and measuring distances and angles from point to point, and an algorithm creates a unique numeric code from this information. In a fingerprint identification system, these codes are stored in a data bank and can be used to compare different sets of prints.

6   Capacitance scanners use a different technology to record fingerprints. They capture an image of the fingertip using electric current rather than light. The scanners contain semiconductor chips, other electronic components, and tiny sensors that read the ridges and low areas of the fingerprint. These scanners create and save a mathematical representation of the fingerprint. This system is used in mobile phones that use touch identification.

7   Palm prints are also used in identification, primarily in criminal investigations. They are recorded by scanning in the same way that fingerprints are scanned.

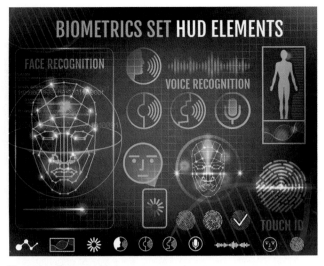

FACIAL FEATURES

8   With advances in computer technology, facial recognition systems have been developed that can identify individuals based on the shape and layout of their facial features. The primary use is in law enforcement, to compare an individual—in person or recorded on surveillance cameras—to a database of known faces in searching for criminal suspects. The systems are also used to verify a person's identity at border checkpoints and for granting access to secure buildings. Some airports have begun using facial recognition to allow passengers to move easily through check-in, immigration, and boarding. The technology is also used on some mobile phones as a way for the user to unlock a device.

9   Working from an image of a person's face, facial recognition software analyzes features such as the eyes, nose, and cheekbones. It identifies their shape and relative position, and takes measurements such as the distance between a person's eyes. This data is used to create a template, or *faceprint*, that can be stored in a database and compared to other faceprints. An improved identification technology is three-dimensional (3-D) facial recognition, in which special sensors capture more information about the shape of a face. In a 3-D image, measurements of the depth and curvature of facial features add to the quality of the data collected. 3-D facial recognition is not affected by lighting, can recognize faces from side angle views, and generally provides more accurate identification than traditional facial recognition systems.

EYES

10   There are three different features of the eye that are used for identification purposes: the iris, the sclera, and the retina. In each of these, there are unique patterns in the eyes of different people that identification systems can use to distinguish one individual from another.

- The iris is the colored portion of the eye surrounding the central pupil. An infrared camera is used to capture an image of the pattern of the iris. An analysis of the pattern is created that can be stored and compared to a data bank of iris patterns. Systems based on irises are becoming more widely used because they are almost 100% accurate.

- The sclera is the white part of the eye. Regular white light is used to capture an image that shows the patterns of the tiny blood vessels in the eye. The pattern is analyzed and stored. This system is also extremely accurate.

- The retina is the innermost layer of tissue at the back of the eyeball. Retinal scanning was the first type of identification system based on the eye. It uses infrared light to capture an image of retinal patterns. It is mainly used in access systems for high-security areas.

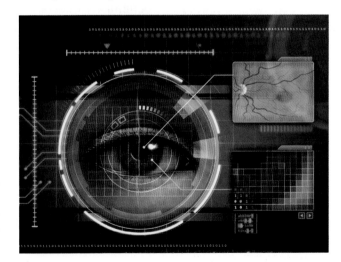

VOICE

11   Voice biometrics analyzes the characteristics of a person's voice, including the sound of the voice and the manner of speaking. Acoustic features of speech, which are determined by the size and shape of the mouth and throat, differ between individuals. In addition, each person speaks in a unique way that computer technology can analyze. An initial sample is used to create a voice print or template,

and other speaking samples can be compared to it. Voice verification, or speaker authentication, is now becoming widely used in the banking industry to identify customers on the phone.

BEHAVIOR

12   Behavioral biometrics deals with the way people move and act. It analyzes many different actions, such as walking, speaking, gesturing, and standing, and derives a mathematical model that can identify a unique individual. Identification systems based on behavioral biometrics are being used in law enforcement, border management, and counter-terrorism. Patterns in typing and moving a mouse have applications in financial institutions and businesses for authenticating the identity of online customers and detecting fraud. A new area of biometrics used by security agencies is called the biometrics of intent. This technology analyzes signals such as a person's heart rate, breathing, eye movements, and body temperature to try to determine if the person intends to commit a hostile act.

DNA

13   Scientific advances in biochemistry have allowed testing of DNA—the unique genetic material in every living organism—to become a practical way of determining the identity of specific individuals. It is widely used in criminal and forensic investigations to identify both the criminal and the victim. DNA and fingerprints are among the few types of biometric indicators that can be left behind by criminals at a crime scene. It is also the only biometric that can establish a connection to genetic relatives. Through a chemical process, DNA is extracted from small samples of tissue or blood. For forensic purposes, scientists use advanced techniques to analyze Short Tandem Repeat (STR) sequences in the nuclear or mitochondrial DNA. An STR is a unit of two to thirteen elements repeated multiple times on a strand of DNA. STR analysis measures the number of repeating units. In looking at multiple sets of STRs in a single sample, a personal DNA profile or "DNA fingerprint" can be created, which can distinguish one individual from another and can link two DNA samples from the same individual.

Legal and Privacy Issues

14   Collection of personal biometric information brings up concerns about privacy. Even if the original intended purpose of the data is to gain access to a building or unlock a device or identify a friend's face in a photo, who knows what other purposes it could be used for? Once a person's information is in a data bank, that person has no control over who sees it or uses it, or how it is shared with other organizations. There are serious concerns when the government and law enforcement agencies are involved. They might use biometrics to identify criminals; however, they could also use it to identify people taking part in a peaceful protest. There is also always a danger that data banks of personal information might be hacked into and the data might be stolen and possibly used to access someone's bank account or make purchases. Data privacy advocates raise legal questions about collecting a person's biometric data, and about who owns it. These issues will become more prominent as the collection of biometric data increases.

Working in Identification Technology

15   Job opportunities in the field of biometrics are increasing as the use of biometric identification systems grows. Most employment opportunities are in law enforcement, security, and intelligence agencies. Examples of entry-level jobs are a fingerprint technician and a fingerprint examiner. These individuals work with a fingerprint

identification system and operate a variety of other biometric systems. A biometric examiner works in a government agency performing face and iris biometric examinations and processing the images. At a higher level, a forensic analyst analyzes, compares, and evaluates fingerprints using various techniques. Biometric intelligence analysts usually work for a defense contractor, collecting and analyzing biometric data and performing other functions to support biometric intelligence missions. Biometric engineers create and maintain biometric systems for a variety of purposes, including monitoring physical and online access control points and secure ID systems as well as defense-related functions. These positions require a university degree in computer science and a certificate or experience in biometrics.

DID YOU UNDERSTAND?

1. What is biometrics?

2. What are some examples of biometric indicators?

3. Why are fingerprints an accurate way of identifying and differentiating people?

4. In modern systems, how are fingerprints compared?

5. Which type of fingerprint scanner is used for unlocking mobile phones?

6. How is a faceprint created?

7. What three features of the eye are being used for identifying people?

8. What is a common use for voice verification?

9. What are some of the physical actions or movements analyzed in behavioral biometrics?

10. What is DNA, and how is it used to identify a person?

11. What are some of the privacy concerns about collecting biometric information?

12. What are some examples of jobs in the field of biometrics?

WHAT'S YOUR OPINION?

1. How do you feel about your bank, a retail business, the government, or your mobile phone using your biometric information to identify you?

2. Do you think the government should record the fingerprints and other biometric data of all residents? Of foreign visitors? Give reasons for your answer.

READING COMPREHENSION

1. The main use of biometric indicators is to _____ people.
   A. analyze
   B. authorize
   C. evaluate
   D. identify

2. *Live scan*, the *rolled ink method*, and *capacitance scanning* are ways of _____.
   A. scanning documents
   B. analyzing electronic images
   C. recording fingerprints
   D. creating numeric codes

3. Which of the following statements about facial recognition is implied in the text?
   A. It is an accurate method of identifying individuals.
   B. It is the most widely used identification system.
   C. It is the system most popular with travelers.
   D. It respects people's right to privacy.

4. According to the reading, which of the following statements is true?
   A. Features of each portion of the eye can be captured through the use of infrared light.
   B. Identification based on eye features is the most accurate type of biometric identification.
   C. Different identification systems are based on the unique patterns of each portion of the eye.
   D. Identification systems based on eye features are mainly used in high-security areas.

5. Based on the context in paragraph 5, an *algorithm* is most likely _____.
   A. an image created by a computer
   B. a formula or set of rules for solving a problem
   C. someone with expertise in computer systems
   D. a scanning system

6. Acoustic features are especially effective for _____.
   A. describing physical characteristics
   B. authenticating the identity of online customers
   C. creating phone banks
   D. identifying customers on the telephone

7. If someone wishes to establish a genetic connection to another individual, which biometric marker would be most reliable?
   A. a voiceprint
   B. DNA
   C. fingerprints
   D. a faceprint

8. Which paragraph warns of the risks of collecting biometric data?
   A. Paragraph 4
   B. Paragraph 13
   C. Paragraph 14
   D. Paragraph 15

9. Based on the context in paragraph 8, a *surveillance camera* most likely _____.
   A. continuously observes a scene to gather information
   B. is worn by a law enforcement officer
   C. takes identification photos for travelers
   D. is used in making surveys

10. It can be assumed from the reading that the majority of individuals developing identification technology _____.
    A. are employed by law enforcement agencies
    B. perform functions involving intelligence missions
    C. create and maintain biometric systems
    D. have expertise in computer science

ACADEMIC VOCABULARY

1. Fingerprints can be used to _____ a person's identity.
   A. create
   B. establish
   C. involve
   D. display

2. Criminal investigators _____ a great deal on technology.
   A. proceed
   B. require
   C. rely
   D. investigate

3. Physical evidence from crime scenes helps the police to _____ criminals.
   A. identify
   B. notify
   C. indicate
   D. deduce

4. Computers are able to _____ people's facial features.
   A. distribute
   B. resolve
   C. interact
   D. analyze

5. Identification is required for a visitor to be granted _____ to this building.
   A. license
   B. access
   C. identity
   D. security

6. Eye patterns can be used to distinguish individuals because they are _____.
   A. physical
   B. colored
   C. unique
   D. secure

7. The iris is the colored _____ of the eye.
   A. portion
   B. position
   C. image
   D. sequence

8. There have been many advances in developing ways to _____ fraud.
   A. derive
   B. deliver
   C. detect
   D. display

9. DNA can be _____ from an individual using a special medical process.
   A. undertaken
   B. indicated
   C. differentiated
   D. extracted

10. The position _____ a university degree in computer science.
    A. requires
    B. reveals
    C. relates
    D. refers

11. Modern identification systems are used to _____ travelers at immigration checkpoints.
    A. implement
    B. define
    C. process
    D. enable

12. A variety of identification systems are used in law _____.
    A. detection
    B. authority
    C. coordination
    D. enforcement

13. Palm prints are often used in criminal _____.
    A. encounters
    B. investigations
    C. innovations
    D. inspections

14. Sophisticated new technology can determine if an individual intends to _____ a hostile act.
    A. commit
    B. transmit
    C. involve
    D. capture

UNIT 11 LISTENING

PART A
Practice: A B C
1. A B C
2. A B C
3. A B C
4. A B C
5. A B C

PART B
Practice: A B C
1. A B C
2. A B C
3. A B C
4. A B C
5. A B C

Look at pages 164–165 of the core text. Write the correct words to complete the description.

accessing	bag	counting	explaining	information	reconciling	vault
application	check	drive-through	greeting	officer	standing	windows
auto loan	checking	establish	handling	printer	teller	withdrawal

It's a busy day at the bank today. A customer service associate is _____greeting_____ 1 a customer at the _____ 2 desk. A new account associate is helping a customer _____ 3 a new account. A financial services rep is _____ 4 investment account options. An _____ 5 officer is helping a customer with an auto loan. A mortgage loan officer is helping with a mortgage _____ 6. A small business loan _____ 7 is helping a customer with a small business loan. Many customers are _____ 8 in the waiting line waiting for a _____ 9. All the tellers are busy helping customers at their teller _____ 10. One is depositing a customer's _____ 11. Another is helping a customer with a _____ 12. Another is preparing a bank check using a check _____ 13. One of the tellers is _____ 14 and banding money. Another is _____ 15 a customer's ID. Another is _____ 16 a commercial deposit for a customer who has brought money to the bank in a bank deposit _____ 17. Another is _____ 18 a cash drawer. A _____ 19 teller is handling a drive-through window transaction. In the _____ 20 area, a safe-deposit clerk is _____ 21 a customer's safe-deposit box.

activating	associates	collecting	handling	preparing	returns	tax
agency	calling	damage	investigates	processing	reviewing	verifying
appraiser	center	examiner	obtaining	property	selling	video

At the insurance _____ 22, two of the insurance agents are _____ 23 customer information and another agent is _____ 24 someone's policy. At the insurance company call _____ 25, insurance sales agents are on their phones, _____ 26 insurance to customers. Customer service _____ 27 are also assisting people on the phone. A claims processing specialist is _____ 28 a claim submitted by a customer and an insurance _____ 29 is reviewing a claim submitted by another customer. At the auto appraisal facility, an auto damage _____ 30 is appraising _____ 31 to someone's car. At an insurance inspection, an insurance adjuster is using a _____ 32 camera as he examines _____ 33 damage. An insurance investigator is in his car. He's taking photos as he _____ 34 an insurance claim. At the credit card company, a sales associate is _____ 35 a customer's credit card, a member services representative is _____ 36 a customer problem, a fraud detection associate is _____ 37 transactions, and a collection associate is _____ 38 about a late payment. At the collection agency, a collection specialist is _____ 39 an unpaid bill. At the _____ 40 preparation service, tax preparers are _____ 41 customers' tax _____ 42.

Using the O*NET Career Exploration Tools at mynextmove.org, search for information about one of the jobs in Unit 12. Write the information in the job profile below. Then prepare and give a presentation about the job.

Job Zone 2 (some job preparation)
bank security guard, collection associate, collection specialist, customer service associate, drive-through teller, member services representative, new account associate, sales associate, teller

Job Zone 3 (medium job preparation)
auto damage appraiser, auto loan officer, call center supervisor, financial services rep, insurance adjuster, insurance appraiser, insurance examiner, insurance investigator, loan officer, mortgage loan officer, safe-deposit clerk, small business loan officer, tax preparer

Job Zone 4 (high job preparation)
bank manager, claims processing specialist, fraud detection associate, insurance agency manager, insurance agent, insurance sales agent

Job name: _____

What does a person do in this job?

_____

_____

_____

What tools and equipment does a person use in this job?

_____

What skills and abilities are important?

_____

_____

What technology might a person use in this job?

_____

What kind of person will be interested in this work?

_____

What level of education, job training, and experience is required?

_____

_____

What is the job outlook?

_____

What is the average salary?

_____

A Bank New Account Associate

1   I'm Martin Estrada. I work as a new account associate at Community Financial, a relatively new bank that was founded to provide banking services to individuals and families that have not usually been served by the larger banking institutions.

2   In some parts of our city, more than 50 percent of residents are unbanked or under-banked. They either have no account at any bank, or they have an account but still rely on storefront businesses for some financial transactions. This can be expensive. Check-cashing stores may charge two to four percent or more to cash a person's paycheck. Payday lenders usually charge a high fee for a cash advance against an upcoming paycheck. The costs can be even higher on pre-paid debit cards that charge a monthly fee whether the card is used or not and charge fees for ATM cash withdrawals, reloading money onto a card, and even balance inquiries.

3   However, banks can also be expensive places to put your money, especially if you can't afford to maintain a large minimum balance in an account to avoid monthly fees or per-check fees. The overcharge fee for writing a check that exceeds an account balance can also be costly.

4   Community Financial is a federally-insured

bank with a mission to provide safe and affordable banking services to all members of our community regardless of their income. We want to build a relationship with them, contribute to their financial security and success, and have them as loyal customers in the years ahead.

5   We offer a free checking account with no monthly fee, no minimum balance requirement, no per-check charges, and free withdrawals at our ATMs. Its only drawback is that the interest rate it pays on deposits is very low for accounts with balances under $10,000. We also offer a prepaid card linked to the account. It has a modest $2.00 monthly fee, and ATM withdrawals are free.

6   When I help new customers open accounts, I'm also able to offer information about our auto and home mortgage loans. And for clients who plan to open small businesses in the community, we have a special community lending program with low-interest loans. It's a great program that's revitalizing some neighborhoods as empty storefronts give way to new businesses.

---

1. What role does Paragraph 2 play in this article?
   A. It describes the bank's services.
   B. It recommends using storefront businesses.
   C. It explains how financial transactions can be expensive.
   D. It describes expensive bank fees

2. What is the meaning of *modest* as used in paragraph 5?
   A. automatic
   B. monthly
   C. shy
   D. low

3. Which term in the article DOESN'T refer to borrowing money?
   A. check-cashing
   B. auto loan
   C. mortgage
   D. cash advance

4. Select the paragraphs that best describe the reason the bank was established.
   A. Paragraphs 1 and 2
   B. Paragraphs 1 and 4
   C. Paragraphs 3 and 4
   D. Paragraphs 3 and 5

CLASSROOM VISITOR

Invite an employee of a local bank to visit your class. Talk about the kinds of financial institutions students use and problems that exist with check-cashing stores, payday lenders, and the cost of using banks. Ask about the types of accounts and financial services that the bank offers. Ask about the types of jobs at the bank and the training required.

(Or, do an Internet search to find information about the best banks in your area, and compare the features of their different checking and savings accounts.)

The Mathematics of Personal Finance

1   Money is a fundamental part of modern life. We earn money, we spend money, and we save money. We also have to manage our money. Personal finance is about using and managing our money. Managing our money wisely can help us achieve financial security throughout life.

2   To make good decisions about handling our finances, we need to understand details about banking options and how purchases and transactions are made. Some of these details involve banking policies and financial industry practices, and others have to do with fees, charges, and interest rates.

Bank Accounts

3   Banks generally offer two main types of accounts: savings and checking. There are usually no fees involved in opening a savings account, but it is common for banks to charge a monthly fee of $10 or more for a checking account. However, if a depositor maintains a monthly minimum balance of $1,200 or perhaps $1,500 in the account, the fee is waived—not charged. If the balance goes below that amount, the bank will apply the charge. Also, if the account holder tries to make a payment and there isn't enough money in the account to cover it, the bank may charge a penalty fee. In addition, most banks charge customers a fee if they use an ATM at a different bank. Consumers need to inform themselves about the fees and requirements associated with bank accounts at different banks before deciding on where to open an account.

Interest

4   A main business of most banks is to lend money (including money they get from their depositors) to people and to businesses that want to borrow money. When a bank makes a loan such as an auto loan, home mortgage loan, or small business loan, the bank earns money by charging the borrower interest. Interest is usually calculated as a percentage of the amount of money that is borrowed, and is sometimes expressed as an annual percentage rate (APR), the amount of interest averaged over the full length of the loan period.

5   Savings accounts usually earn interest, since the bank is using that money to make loans. Some checking accounts earn interest and some do not. A bank usually pays 1% interest or less to depositors and charges borrowers 4% or more.

Credit Card Accounts

6   Store cashiers sometimes ask, "Debit or credit?" The price is the same either way. How much difference does it make for the customer? A purchase made with an ATM card or debit card draws money directly from the depositor's account—in effect, it is the same as a cash purchase. Buying things using a credit card is actually borrowing money to pay for the purchases. In a credit purchase, the bank pays the seller and later collects the purchase amount from the card holder. The purchase is listed on the account statement, which the account holder needs to pay by the due date.

7   Making purchases with a credit card is very convenient. But if consumers are not careful about managing their account, they can have problems. If they pay the full amount due on their statement, and pay by the due date, there are no extra charges. However, if they do not pay the entire balance, they will have to pay a finance charge—interest on the unpaid amount. On the next bill, the customer must pay the balance from the previous month plus the finance charge, in addition to the amount for new purchases. If unpaid bills continue for many months, the debt will accumulate. If consumers also have credit cards from other banks or from

PAYING A CREDIT CARD BILL – OPTIONS AND CONSEQUENCES

LINFIELD BANK	Account #: 12345-67890	Minimum payment due: $25.00
	Period: 07/19/20 – 08/18/20	Interest rate: 16% APR
	Balance total: $649.00	Payment due date: 09/15/20

(1) Paying full balance on time		(2) Paying minimum payment by due date		(3) Not paying minimum payment for 60 days	
Amount paid	$649.00	Amount paid	$ 25.00	Amount paid	$ 0.00
Balance to add to next payment	$0	Balance to add to next payment	$624.00	Balance to add to next payment	$649.00
		Interest on $624	$ 8.30	Interest on $649 (30 days)	$ 8.66
		Balance to add to next payment	$632.30	Late fee #1	$ 35.00
				Interest on $692.66 (60 days)	$ 17.32
				Late fee #2	$ 35.00
				Balance to add to next payment	$744.98

There are no extra charges if the total amount due is paid on time (1). The option to make a minimum payment (2) avoids a late fee, but leaves a balance to carry forward to the next statement, along with a finance charge. If the bill is unpaid for 60 days (3), there will be two late fees and two finance charges added, the second one at a higher rate of interest.

stores, which can issue their own credit cards, the combined amount the consumers owe could be substantial and more than they might be able to pay off easily.

8   Interest rates for finance charges on credit cards can vary from about 12% to 24% APR. But if the customer is more than 60 days late in making even the small required minimum payment, the bank can raise the interest rate to almost 30%. In addition, the bank adds a late fee of $20 to $30 or more on any late payments.

9   Fees and policies can work in both directions. For example, some banks charge an annual fee for a credit card. But some cash-back credit cards pay account holders 1%, 2%, or 3% of the price of their purchases. Consumers need to be aware of the fees and benefits at different banks before they decide where to open a credit card account.

Borrowing Money

10   In getting a loan, such as for buying a car, borrowers usually make a down payment—paying a small part of the price in cash—and borrow the rest of the purchase price from the auto dealer or from a bank. They make payments on the loan every month for a specified period of time, or term.

11   The details of an auto loan can be seen in this example:

Total cost of auto:	$ 10,000	Monthly payment:	$ 183.00
Down payment:	$ 1,000	Total cost of loan:	$ 10,980.00
Amount of loan:	$ 9,000	Total finance charge:	$ 1,980.00
Interest rate:	8.0%		
Term:	0 months		

Here, the borrower is borrowing $9,000 at 8% interest, and has to pay $183.00 every month for five years. At the end of the term, the borrower will have paid back $10,980, which includes $1,980 in interest.

12   Payday loans are another way some people borrow money, but this type of loan is very costly. People who are "living paycheck-to-paycheck" often don't have extra cash on hand for their immediate needs. Payday lenders lend borrowers a small amount of money—averaging around $400—for a period of two or three weeks, and charge fees of about $15 to $30 per $100 borrowed. Fees are often the equivalent of an interest rate of 400 to 800%! Many people cannot pay the loan back and have to take out another loan to pay the first one, and in the end, they spend hundreds of dollars on loan fees.

Home Mortgages

13   With a home loan—or mortgage loan—the loan amount is very large, often more than $100,000, and the lender wants to be sure that the borrower will be able to repay the loan. Borrowers must have a stable job and a regular income that is high enough for them to be able to make monthly loan payments for the home they will buy, usually over a term of 30 years. Lenders usually say that borrowers should not spend more than 28% of their income on mortgage payments. Lenders also need to know if borrowers have other fixed expenses such as auto loan or student loan payments, or credit card balances that need to be paid. The amount of real estate taxes and the cost of home insurance are additional expenses involved in owning a home. Mortgage insurance is also required when the down payment is less than 20% of the purchase price of the home.

14   Another consideration in the loan approval process is the borrower's *credit rating* or *credit score*, which indicates whether the person is reliable financially. People who always pay their bills on time and pay back money they borrow will have a good credit score. Credit scores are also important when people apply for a credit card account, an auto loan, insurance, and even when they apply for a job.

15   The most important element of a mortgage loan is the interest rate. There are two types of mortgages—fixed-rate mortgages and adjustable-rate mortgages (ARM). A fixed-rate mortgage is preferable because the interest rate will not increase during the life of the loan. In contrast, the interest rate of an ARM might increase, along with the borrower's monthly payment amount. A borrower who has a bad credit score and cannot make a down payment of 10% of the purchase price will probably have to pay a high interest rate or will be given an ARM. In the end, a calculation of the maximum monthly payment that a borrower can afford will determine the size of the loan and the price limit on the house the person can buy.

16   Examining the loan figures shows how much interest a borrower would pay over a full 30-year term:

Loan amount:	$200,000.00
Interest rate:	5%
Monthly payment:	$ 1,073.64
Total paid after 30 years:	$ 386,510.40
Amount of interest paid:	$ 186,510.40

Saving

17   When interest is paid on money in a savings account, it makes the money in that account grow. Interest rates are different from bank to bank and they also vary over time. In recent years, bank savings accounts have been earning less than 1% interest annually. Putting money into a CD, or certificate of deposit, is another way to save. CDs typically have a fixed term, such as one, two, or three years, and pay more interest than a standard savings account (usually around 2%), but there are often restrictions in terms of when money can be withdrawn. The earnings in savings and CD accounts increase through *compounding*, a means of calculating interest not just on the principal amount of money in the account, but on previously earned interest—in other words, earning interest on interest.

COMPOUND INTEREST CALCULATOR	
Savings amount	$20,000
Length of time	10 years
Interest rate	2.00%
Compounded	Annually
Total savings amount at end of period	$24,379.89

Investment Accounts

18   In a typical investment account, investors buy company stocks, bonds, and real estate. Most accounts do not earn interest, though some investments may pay small dividends to their investors. The value of the investments usually grows over time. Investments can also decrease in value, so there is risk involved in addition to the opportunity to make money. Investment funds also charge management fees, which can decrease fund balances over time.

19   Many workplaces offer retirement savings plans for their employees to invest in, such as a 401(k) plan. Employees put an amount of their salary into their account every month, and sometimes the company participates by adding money to the amount the employee invests. If they can, employees should at least put into these accounts the amount that their company will match. Another advantage of these accounts is that they are tax-deferred. The employee doesn't pay income taxes on the salary that goes into the plan. Instead, taxes are paid later when the money is withdrawn from the account.

20   It may be a long way off, but it is a good idea to start saving for retirement as soon as you can and to continue saving throughout your career.

DID YOU UNDERSTAND?

1. What are the two main types of bank accounts?

2. Who pays interest?

3. Why is it a good idea to do research before opening a checking account?

4. What are some examples of fees banks can charge on checking accounts?

5. How is making a purchase with a debit card different from buying something with a credit card?

6. What is a finance charge?

7. What is the term of a loan?

8. What are the dangers of payday loans?

9. What are some things a lender will want to know about a borrower before deciding to approve a mortgage loan?

10. Why is a fixed-rate mortgage better than an adjustable-rate mortgage?

11. What is compounding?

12. How does an investment account make money?

WHAT'S YOUR EXPERIENCE?

1. Do you have a checking account? What factors did you consider when you decided on a bank?

2. How do you usually pay for purchases—with cash, with a debit card, or with a credit card? Why do you pay that way?

3. If you have a credit card, do you always pay off your bill completely, or do you sometimes pay a finance charge?

4. How much money do you try to save every month?

CAN YOU FIGURE IT OUT?

Answer the questions. Show your calculations in the space provided.

1. Dan's credit card gives him back 3% cash back on purchases of gas. If he buys gas at $3.00 per gallon, how much per gallon will the gas cost him, counting his cash back?

2. Marissa owes $7,200 on several credit cards, and she is paying a high interest rate on finance charges every month. She heard about consolidating her debt with a balance transfer credit card that has an introductory interest rate of 0% for 18 months. There is a transfer fee of 3%. (a) How much will she pay in transfer fees to move her debt to the new card, and (b) how much will she have to pay each month to pay off the whole $7,200 before the new card starts charging her interest?

3. Erica is planning to buy a condominium, and the loan officer is checking her income and other expenses. Erica makes $4,400 a month and is paying off her student loan at $220 a month. With the "28% of income" requirement for a mortgage loan, what is the maximum monthly payment she would be approved for?

4. Carlos and Laura are applying for a loan to buy a home at a price of $275,000. Their down payment will be $50,000. Will they have to pay for mortgage insurance? Why, or why not?

5. The total of monthly payments over 30 years on a loan of $250,000 with a fixed interest rate is calculated at $469,482.60. Taxes, insurance, and other fees are not included in the payments, only the loan amount and interest. How much total interest will be paid?

6. Jason is thinking of investing in an investment fund that has an annual management fee of 3%. If his account balance continues to average about $10,000, about how much will he pay for management fees over five years?

READING COMPREHENSION

1. According to the reading, financial security can best be achieved by understanding how to _____ money.
   A. earn
   B. manage
   C. save
   D. spend

2. Interest is charged when a bank customer _____.
   A. borrows money from the bank
   B. uses an ATM at a different bank
   C. doesn't maintain a minimum checking account balance
   D. writes a check that exceeds the customer's account balance

3. Which of the following paragraphs warns about the risks involved in using credit cards?
   A. Paragraph 6
   B. Paragraphs 6 and 7
   C. Paragraphs 6, 7, and 8
   D. Paragraphs 7 and 8

4. Based on the "Options and Consequences" statement from Linfield Bank, which of the following would be a *consequence*?
   A. paying a credit card balance on time
   B. making a minimum payment with an interest charge
   C. being charged interest and late fees
   D. not paying a minimum balance for more than 60 days

5. What does it mean that a family is *living paycheck-to-paycheck*?
   A. They are spending most of their earnings every month.
   B. They have problems cashing their paychecks.
   C. They are not managing their money well.
   D. They have been borrowing too much money.

6. According to the reading, borrowers are considered *financially reliable* if they _____.
   A. have fixed expenses
   B. have mortgage insurance
   C. maintain a high credit card balance
   D. pay back money they owe

7. Which paragraphs describe different types of information lenders need to know about borrowers?
   A. Paragraphs 13 and 14
   B. Paragraphs 13 and 15
   C. Paragraphs 14 and 15
   D. Paragraphs 15 and 16

8. One reason an individual might avoid putting money into a CD is that _____.
   A. the earnings do not increase through compounding
   B. interest rates are lower than regular savings accounts
   C. interest rates differ from bank to bank
   D. there are often restrictions on when the money can be withdrawn

9. In paragraph 19, the meaning of *deferred* is _____.
   A. reduced
   B. preferred
   C. postponed
   D. invested

10. The main point of the reading is that by understanding banking and credit card practices, consumers will _____.
    A. better understand how to set up accounts
    B. learn to make sound financial decisions
    C. learn the importance of paying their bills on time
    D. begin early to save for retirement

ACADEMIC VOCABULARY

1. Your goal should be to _____ financial security.
   A. assist
   B. achieve
   C. advise
   D. afford

2. Will there be any fees _____ in setting up this account?
   A. acquired
   B. contained
   C. involved
   D. informed

3. You must _____ a minimum balance in your account.
   A. receive
   B. cover
   C. obtain
   D. maintain

4. It is convenient to make _____ with a credit card.
   A. finances
   B. purchases
   C. policies
   D. benefits

5. Unfortunately, debt will _____ if your bills continue to be unpaid.
   A. accumulate
   B. participate
   C. distribute
   D. calculate

6. Interest rates can _____ from 15 percent to 25 percent.
   A. borrow
   B. transfer
   C. vary
   D. revise

7. Consumers need to be _____ of fees they might be charged.
   A. aware
   B. acknowledged
   C. confirmed
   D. considered

8. If you wish to borrow money, you must have a _____ job and regular income.
   A. minimal
   B. capable
   C. stable
   D. sufficient

9. With this loan, you will be _____ to purchase mortgage insurance.
   A. issued
   B. specified
   C. insisted
   D. required

10. With some accounts there are _____ that limit the number of withdrawals that can be made.
    A. adjustments
    B. restrictions
    C. revisions
    D. deductions

11. Fixed-rate mortgages are _____ to adjustable-rate mortgages.
    A. reliable
    B. eligible
    C. preferable
    D. affordable

12. All of our employees _____ in the company's retirement plan.
    A. participate
    B. incorporate
    C. associate
    D. regulate

13. Interest on a loan is calculated as a _____ of the amount that is borrowed.
    A. payment
    B. rating
    C. purchase
    D. percentage

14. A borrower's credit rating _____ whether the person is financially reliable.
    A. indicates
    B. approves
    C. refers
    D. requires

UNIT 12 LISTENING

PART A

Practice: A B C   3. A B C
       1. A B C   4. A B C
       2. A B C   5. A B C

PART B

Practice: A B C   3. A B C
       1. A B C   4. A B C
       2. A B C   5. A B C

Look at pages 178–179 of the core text. Write the correct words to complete the description.

accounting	client	distributing	payroll	reviewing	signing
applicant	composing	handling	receivable	secretaries	spreadsheets
applications	conference	interviewing	reception	setting up	switchboard
assigning	delivery	payable	receptionist	sign in	

It's Monday morning and the office is open. An administrative assistant has come to the

_____reception_____ [1] area to greet a _____ [2]. A _____ [3] is asking a visitor to

_____ [4] at the reception station. Another receptionist is _____ [5] an incoming call on

the _____ [6] phone. A mail clerk is _____ [7] for a _____ [8] of a package.

Two office assistants are _____ [9] videoconference equipment in the _____ [10] room.

The office manager is _____ [11] tasks to office assistants who have come to his office. Human

resource assistants are _____ [12] job _____ [13] and resumes. One of the assistants

is _____ [14] a job _____ [15]. In the _____ [16] department, the accounts

_____ [17] clerk is verifying invoices and the accounts _____ [18] clerk is paying them.

The _____ [19] clerk is processing employee forms and a mail clerk is _____ [20] mail.

The _____ [21] in this office are doing different tasks. One is _____ [22] correspondence,

another is proofreading, and another is creating _____ [23].

answering	copy	fixing	marketing	repair	sorting	updating
calling	faxing	inventory	materials	sales	supplies	website
clients	file	lounge	postage	scale	taking	weighing
copiers	filing	mailroom	preparing	shorthand		

There are several executives in this company. Each has an administrative assistant. One of the assistants

is _____ [24] the telephone and another is _____ [25] documents on the fax machine.

The general manager is dictating a letter to an executive assistant, who is taking _____ [26]. In

the _____ [27] department, one of the marketing associates is _____ [28] promotional

_____ [29] and another is _____ [30] the company's _____ [31] and

social media sites. In the _____ [32] department, sales associates are _____ [33]

potential _____ [34]. Mail clerks in the _____ [35] are _____ [36] incoming

mail and _____ [37] and metering outgoing mail using a postal _____ [38] and

_____ [39] meter. An office assistant is making copies in the _____ [40] room. There's a

problem with one of the _____ [41], and a _____ [42] technician is _____ [43]

it. File clerks are _____ [44] documents in the _____ [45] room. Office assistants

are putting away _____ [46] and checking _____ [47] in the supply room. And some

employees are _____ [48] a break in the employee _____ [49].

Using the O*NET Career Exploration Tools at mynextmove.org, search for information about one of the jobs in Unit 13. Write the information in the job profile below. Then prepare and give a presentation about the job.

Job Zone 2 (some job preparation)
delivery person, file clerk, mail clerk, office assistant, office clerk, payroll clerk, receptionist

Job Zone 3 (medium job preparation)
accounts payable clerk, accounts receivable clerk, administrative assistant, executive assistant, executive secretary, office manager, repair technician, secretary

Job Zone 4 (high job preparation)
general manager, human resource assistant, human resource director, marketing associate, marketing manager, sales associate, sales manager

Job Zone 5 (extensive job preparation)
executive

Job name: _____

What does a person do in this job?

_____

_____

_____

What tools and equipment does a person use in this job?

_____

What skills and abilities are important?

_____

_____

What technology might a person use in this job?

_____

What kind of person will be interested in this work?

_____

What level of education, job training, and experience is required?

_____

_____

What is the job outlook?   What is the average salary?

_____   _____

Read the memo about office procedures and answer the questions.

1 **TO:** All Personnel
2 **FROM:** Roland Makamba, Office Manager
3 **SUBJECT:** New Mailroom Procedures

4 Please be advised that our new mailroom equipment is now operational.

5 The upgraded folding and inserting equipment allows for up to five letter- or legal-sized sheets to be folded
6 and inserted into a standard number 10 envelope. One of the inserted items can be a business reply envelope.
7 Do not staple items.

8 The new tabbing machine will apply adhesive tabs to brochures and other open-ended media, including double
9 postcards and direct mail pieces. (No more peeling and sticking one-by-one!)

10 The new postage metering equipment will streamline mail processing, but please remember these long-standing
11 procedures for preparing outgoing mail:

12 Keep all different-sized mail pieces separate. Use rubber bands to bundle similar-sized items together.

13 Label each piece or bundle of mail with your department number so that it can be charged correctly to your
14 department's account. No mail will be processed without an account code.

15 All outgoing business mail is metered. Employees' personal mail must not be mixed in with business mail.
16 Employees' mail must be stamped, envelopes sealed, and placed in the separate bin for outgoing personal mail.

17 Large mailings should be in the mailroom by 1:30 P.M. for same-day processing due to the amount of time
18 required to complete them. For large mailings that need to be sealed, stack all envelopes with flaps facing up,
19 nested, and rubber-banded together.

20 All international mail and items that must be sent as certified or insured mail should be placed in the bin labeled
21 Special Handling. Due to the expense, all overnight mail must be approved by your department manager. Use
22 the company's approved local courier service for time-sensitive documents that require same-day local delivery.

23 Also, please note two important policy changes related to incoming mail:

24 If a package addressed to you looks suspicious or potentially dangerous, we will inform the security department
25 and it will be removed to an off-site facility for X-ray scanning.

26 With the expansion of online shopping and the problem of theft of delivered packages from employees'
27 apartments or houses, we appreciate the desire to have packages sent for delivery to your daytime work
28 location rather than to your home. However, we do not have the space to store these items. Therefore,
29 effective immediately, employees are not allowed to have personal mail or packages sent to our office location.

30 Thank you for your cooperation.

---

1. Who is the intended audience for this memo?
  A. all mailroom staff
  B. all mailroom staff and the security department
  C. everyone in the company
  D. all staff who visit the mailroom

2. Before the new tabbing machine, the tabbing task was done _____.
  A. by a slower tabbing machine
  B. by hand
  C. by the old folding and inserting equipment
  D. automatically

3. As used in Line 17, the term *large mailings* refers to _____.
  A. the amount of mail
  B. a high number of pages in each piece of mail
  C. the size of the envelopes
  D. mail that requires same-day processing

4. Based on the memo, what problem has this company been experiencing?
  A. employees sending suspicious packages
  B. employees sending too much personal mail
  C. employees sending too much mail that requires Special Handling
  D. employees receiving personal packages at work

DEMONSTRATING A PROCEDURE

Using YouTube, WikiHow, or another source, search online for a demonstration of how to do a procedure or operate equipment in an office setting. Write out the instructions. Then prepare a media presentation. Make screenshots of the steps or video-record your demonstration. Present the procedure to the class.

Suggestions: how to use a copier; how to scan a document; how to sit properly at a computer; how to write a business letter

Designing the Office of the Future

1   As the economy evolves, work changes—not only in the kinds of jobs we work at, but also *how* we work and *where* we work. New approaches to work are changing workplaces and influencing workplace design. Office work and office space are seeing the first major changes in a generation.

The Office Workplace

2   Office work has been a common type of employment for the last hundred years. Early large business offices had open work floors with many workers seated at rows of desks. This configuration maximized the use of floor space and accommodated a large number of workers who labored under the eyes of supervisors. Furniture designers in the 1960s, responding to concerns about distraction and lack of privacy, introduced workstations consisting of low, movable walls that could be used to create convenient workspaces. By the 1980s, these modules had evolved into individual cubicles with higher walls. Since cubicles provided an economical way for a company to accommodate a large number of workers on a work floor, they became the most common office plan.

3   By the early 2000s, developments in computer and Internet technology made it possible for employees to work at home or in other locations away from the office. Many companies began to allow staff to work remotely, or "telecommute," connecting to the office over the Internet. For employees who continued to work in an office, the portability of laptops and other equipment made it possible for them to work from anywhere inside the office. They did not have to be confined to cubicles, and as a result, office floor plans became more flexible. These developments led to the next big change in office design.

The Open Office

4   In recent years, there has been a trend toward a new office workplace design called the *open office*. It features an open floor plan with few walls, and tables where employees sit side-by-side at computers. It is especially popular with small business startups.

5   Several factors have contributed to this new design. In an economic environment where businesses must closely manage their budgets to survive, keeping office space to a minimum cuts expenses. Remote working has reduced the number of staff working in the office, and the new design has reduced the amount of space and furniture needed for each employee. At the same time, a new generation of workers and managers finds the old "cubicle farm" workspace design unappealing, isolating, and not conducive to communication and collaboration.

6   The new open floor plans allow personal interaction and promote information sharing and

teamwork. Staff working at different jobs in different departments often work together in an open workspace rather than in separate departmental offices. Supervisors and managers sometimes work in the same spaces as the staff rather than in private offices, giving a less hierarchical feel to an office.

7 Offices with open floor plans commonly have long shared tables where computers are set up and high counters where staff can work in a standing position. For companies with larger budgets, another approach is to install individual workstations with lower walls that divide but do not isolate, as cubicles do. New office furniture is easy to move around, and tables and modular units can be reconfigured as needs change. Another feature of open-space plans is that, with the lack of interior walls, natural light can reach across the work floor.

8 Assignment of personal workstations is sometimes flexible in these new arrangements, as staff that work remotely on some days may not need to have their own permanent space in the office. Instead, they can "float" or share a workstation. Staff can set up their computers at any location inside the office or outside and access the information and other resources they need for doing their jobs.

9 To provide a place to take a break from the intensity of prolonged computer work and to facilitate contact among the staff, modern offices often include a lounge area, which can also serve as a place to hold meetings and to greet guests.

The Modern Office in Urban Architecture

10 In some cities with a declining manufacturing sector, unused factory and warehouse spaces have been converted into new-era workplaces. The large open spaces in these buildings lend themselves well to being redesigned into modern open-space workplaces. These facilities are marketed to attract new types of small businesses, which are often technology-based. Examples include software and web development companies, 3-D printing workshops, and advertising design studios.

Co-working

11 By the early years of the 21st century, working remotely had become common. Another trend

was for people to work as independent consultants, contracted by companies but not working at company offices as employees. While remote work gave workers flexibility and freedom, some felt isolated. They missed the stimulation and socialization that working around other people provides.

12 Entrepreneurs, seeing a need, created locations called co-working spaces where people, often working at very different jobs, work side-by-side in a shared space. Empty warehouses and factory spaces were redesigned, creating open areas with few walls where people from many different fields could work around each other, often at shared workstations. Tenants range from small businesses that rent space for their operations, to people working for their companies remotely, to "freelancers" working on their own. Business startups and other entrepreneurs feel that close contact with people working in a wide variety of fields facilitates an exchange of information and ideas and fosters creativity. Some co-working centers attract clients by offering amenities such as a gym or exercise area, a kitchen, and a salad bar.

13 Co-working facilities are also practical workplaces for employees who work primarily over the Internet, collaborating via online work platforms with colleagues who are often in distant locations. Given the nature of their jobs, they can work from any location that has Internet access. In some cases, the company may not even have a traditional office to work at. People doing this sort of work often prefer going to communal worksites such as co-working

centers, libraries, or coffee shops, rather than working from home in isolation.

Reaction to the New Approaches

14 Companies that have experimented with open office design are generally satisfied with the concept, but many of their employees dislike it. Although proximity to other workers may promote interaction and collaboration, the noise and other distractions at group work tables can detract from an employee's ability to focus on work tasks. Workers also say there is no sense of personal space in the open arrangements. In a desire for quiet and privacy, some employees wear headphones all the time, even though they are not listening to anything, just to block the outside noise. Many workers also find that not having a fixed workstation can cause disorientation and a feeling of impermanence.

15 Some new designs are now taking into account the type of work tasks employees are engaged in. Accommodations for those whose work requires concentration include quiet zones, areas for focused work, and places for telephoning and for small group meetings. Another modification is to cluster workers who do similar work into groups.

16 Many companies are rethinking remote working arrangements and have been requiring

telecommuting staff to work at company offices. Although this means higher office space costs, the companies see advantages in "co-locating" their employees and having them work side-by-side in the same facility. They think that having employees all present in the same location promotes face-to-face collaboration as well as a sense of connection among the staff. Tech companies especially think that staff interaction can lead to more innovation and that encounters with others can stimulate ideas and creativity. Many employees who have enjoyed being able to work at home are not happy about this change. In response to this, some big companies are serving free food and offering onsite child care and laundry services to help build more positive feelings among employees about their workplaces.

DID YOU UNDERSTAND?

1. What was the most common type of configuration for work floors in offices before the open office?

2. What is telecommuting?

3. What are the main characteristics of the open office design?

4. What factors contributed to the development of the open office design?

5. What are some of the advantages of the open office design?

6. Why are unused factories and warehouses easy to adapt to open-space workplaces?

7. What is a co-working space?

8. Why do new businesses think co-working is a good idea?

9. What are some of the criticisms of open office designs?

10. Why have some companies stopped allowing remote working?

WHAT'S YOUR EXPERIENCE?

1. Have you worked in or seen an office with an open office design? If you did, what did you think about it?

2. Can you concentrate on your work when there are distractions around you?

3. Have you ever worked remotely? If you did, how did you like it? If not, do you think you would like working from home instead of in an office? What are your reasons?

READING COMPREHENSION

1. Workstations of the 1960s were designed in order to _____.
   A. maximize the use of floor space
   B. give workers some privacy
   C. allow workers to be easily supervised
   D. accommodate a large number of workers

2. According to the reading, the "open office" design was made possible as a result of _____.
   A. work cubicles
   B. telecommuting
   C. the flexible use of laptops
   D. the emergence of small business startups

3. The financial benefits of an open office are explained in _____.
   A. Paragraph 4
   B. Paragraph 5
   C. Paragraph 6
   D. Paragraph 7

4. In paragraph 7, which of the following would be the best synonym for *reconfigured*?
   A. removed
   B. replaced
   C. received
   D. rearranged

5. According to the reading, which of the following statements is correct?
   A. Large open spaces in redesigned buildings are particularly suitable for new-era workplaces.
   B. More companies are now located in older remodeled buildings than in traditional office spaces.
   C. Many of the manufacturing companies that had closed factories are reopening them in new buildings.
   D. Warehouses are using new technologies to redesign their facilities and make them more attractive.

6. Which paragraph reveals the underlying reason for the establishment of co-working facilities?
   A. Paragraph 11
   B. Paragraph 12
   C. Paragraph 13
   D. Paragraph 14

7. Which of the following is most important for a co-working location to have?
   A. shared workstations
   B. amenities for exercise and food preparation
   C. Internet access
   D. warehouse space

8. As described in paragraph 14, what is the reason some workers might experience a feeling of *impermanence* in an open office?
   A. There are a lot of distractions around them.
   B. They feel the lack of personal space.
   C. They have to wear headphones to block out the noise.
   D. They don't have a workstation of their own.

9. According to the reading, some companies are serving free food in order to _____.
   A. promote face-to-face collaboration
   B. stimulate the generation of ideas
   C. make the worksite more appealing
   D. develop connections between workers

10. The author would probably agree that the greatest influence on the evolution of the modern workplace has been _____.
    A. worker preferences
    B. technology
    C. innovations in office design
    D. changing work tasks

ACADEMIC VOCABULARY

1. It is essential that we come up with a different _____ to solving this problem.
   - A. access
   - B. approach
   - C. schedule
   - D. priority

2. The goal of the company's office design is to _____ the use of floor space.
   - A. equip
   - B. occupy
   - C. maximize
   - D. construct

3. We need to _____ a large number of workers at our new headquarters.
   - A. accommodate
   - B. accompany
   - C. interact
   - D. collaborate

4. In your opinion, what factors have _____ the most to your company's success?
   - A. responded
   - B. facilitated
   - C. influenced
   - D. contributed

5. Our company's goal is to _____ communication and the sharing of information.
   - A. encounter
   - B. promote
   - C. contact
   - D. display

6. Many unused warehouses in our city have been _____ to modern workplaces.
   - A. converted
   - B. evolved
   - C. created
   - D. generated

7. People who work remotely from home without much socialization sometimes tend to feel _____.
   - A. implicated
   - B. implemented
   - C. isolated
   - D. estimated

8. It is difficult to _____ on work tasks when there are too many distractions.
   - A. commit
   - B. emphasize
   - C. devote
   - D. focus

9. Some organizations are now _____ staff members to work at the company offices.
   - A. insisting
   - B. requiring
   - C. enforcing
   - D. offering

10. Many technology companies believe that staff _____ will result in more innovation.
    - A. isolation
    - B. administration
    - C. demonstration
    - D. interaction

11. Our company's new office design _____ an open floor plan with few walls.
    - A. acquires
    - B. selects
    - C. features
    - D. encounters

12. What has the _____ of employees been to your company's revised organizational plan?
    - A. concept
    - B. motivation
    - C. reaction
    - D. satisfaction

13. We do not want our workers to be _____ to small work cubicles.
    - A. confined
    - B. engaged
    - C. provided
    - D. prohibited

14. Sometimes employees need to take a break from the _____ of prolonged computer work.
    - A. input
    - B. intensity
    - C. participation
    - D. collaboration

UNIT 12 LISTENING

PART A

Practice: A B C   3. A B C
1. A B C   4. A B C
2. A B C   5. A B C

PART B

Practice: A B C   3. A B C
1. A B C   4. A B C
2. A B C   5. A B C

Look at pages 192–193 of the core text. Write the correct words to complete the description.

caregiver	drill	handyman	lock	repairing	technician
cleaner	exterminator	insecticide	locksmith	sitter	tutor
cleaning	feeding	install	mounting	snack	vacuuming
delivery	giving	installers	nanny	supplies	walker

These personal service workers are working hard today. A pet _____sitter_____ [1] has filled a pet

bowl with pet food and is _____ [2] a pet. A _____ [3] has come with his toolbox to

_____ [4] shelving in someone's apartment. A home appliance repair _____ [5] is

_____ [6] a washing machine. Housekeepers have come with their cleaning _____ [7]

and are _____ [8] a kitchen and washing a floor. A carpet _____ [9] is

_____ [10] a customer's carpet. A _____ [11] is taking care of children and

_____ [12] them a _____ [13]. A _____ [14] is providing care for an

elderly person. An _____ [15] has set up a bait station and is using a pump sprayer to spray

_____ [16] under a kitchen sink. A _____ [17] is using a _____ [18] to install

a deadbolt _____ [19] on an apartment door. A dog _____ [20] is about to walk

the neighbors' dogs. Home entertainment equipment _____ [21] are installing speakers and

_____ [22] a TV on a wall. A _____ [23] is tutoring a young boy in math and

a _____ [24] person is delivering a package.

accepting	assisting	clinic	driver	make	research	supervising
aerobics	checking out	coordinator	fitness	paralegal	shelving	tow
aide	child-care	courier	handler	playground	sorting	veterinarian
assistant	clerk	director	leading			

A senior citizen activities _____ [25] is leading an activity at the senior center. A teacher's

_____ [26] is _____ [27] a teacher at the school. A _____ [28] at city hall

is _____ [29] a tax payment. At the recreation center, a recreation worker is _____ [30]

equipment. A recreation program leader is _____ [31] a recreation program at the

_____ [32]. A library _____ [33] is sorting and _____ [34] books at the

library. A mail _____ [35] at the post office is _____ [36] mail. At the health club,

a _____ [37] trainer is instructing a client on exercise equipment and an _____ [38]

instructor is _____ [39] an exercise class. A _____ [40] worker is reading to a group at

the child-care center. A _____ [41] is doing legal _____ [42] at the law office, where

a _____ [43] is delivering documents. At the veterinary _____ [44], a _____ [45]

is preparing to give a shot to a dog. And at the funeral home, the funeral _____ [46] is helping

a family choose a casket and _____ [47] funeral arrangements. Across the street, a tow truck

_____ [48] has arrived with his tow truck to _____ [49] a vehicle.

CAREER RESEARCH

Using the O*NET Career Exploration Tools at mynextmove.org, search for information about one of the jobs in Unit 14. Write the information in the job profile below. Then prepare and give a presentation about the job.

Job Zone 1 (little or no job preparation)
dog walker, lawn care worker, pet sitter

Job Zone 2 (some job preparation)
caregiver, carpet cleaner, child-care worker, clerk, courier/messenger, delivery person, exterminator, funeral attendant, handyman, housekeeper, library assistant, locksmith, mail carrier, mail handler, tow truck driver

Job Zone 3 (medium job preparation)
aerobics instructor, fitness trainer, funeral director, home appliance repair technician, home entertainment equipment installer, legal secretary, nanny, paralegal/legal assistant, senior citizen activities coordinator, teacher's aide, veterinary technician

Job Zone 4 (high job preparation)
recreation program leader, recreation worker, teacher, tutor

Job Zone 5 (extensive job preparation)
lawyer, librarian, veterinarian

Job name: _____

What does a person do in this job?

_____

_____

What tools and equipment does a person use in this job?

_____

What skills and abilities are important?

_____

_____

What technology might a person use in this job?

_____

What kind of person will be interested in this work?

_____

What level of education, job training, and experience is required?

_____

_____

What is the job outlook?   What is the average salary?

_____   _____

A Neighborhood Volunteer Program Coordinator

1   I'm Amy Lin—the founder and coordinator of Friendly Neighbors, a network of volunteers that helps senior citizens in our neighborhood. Our mission is to help elderly residents in our community who wish to stay in their apartments and age in place safely rather than move to a senior residence or nursing home.

2   There are many benefits to staying at home as long as possible, but there are also challenges. Many seniors live alone, and many don't have family members nearby to provide help and companionship. As they get frailer, it becomes more difficult for them to take care of things at home and do shopping and other errands. Loneliness is also a big problem.

3   Friendly Neighbors offers companionship, friendship, and basic services to help seniors stay in their homes. All of our services are free. Most of our volunteers participate by visiting a senior for a couple of hours once or twice a week. They might play cards, watch a movie together, listen to music, or just chat. Some volunteers may bring a pet along on the visit (if approved).

4   Although supermarkets in our area have delivery services, getting out of the home helps our seniors stay socially connected to people. So, our volunteers will escort them on trips to shop for groceries or prescription refills. They also accompany them to medical appointments or a coffee shop or restaurant to meet a friend, or just enjoy a walk in the park.

5   We also provide basic services such as cleaning, laundry, minor home repairs, and dog-walking. Although many smartphone apps can be used to obtain such services, the costs can add up. There's also a safety issue. Many apps provide reviews from customers, but they don't do background checks on the people whose services are available. Instead, we have volunteers who provide these services at no cost. (All volunteers are screened to assure the safety of our seniors.)

6   We're a local organization, but we're part of a national trend as more and more programs are formed to connect neighbors with elderly residents. The senior population is growing, and volunteer programs such as ours will have a greater role to play in helping seniors age in place and maintain their independence.

---

1. What is the meaning of *age in place* as used in reference to elderly residents in paragraph 1?
A. to live at home
B. to live in a senior residence
C. to live in a nursing home
D. to volunteer to help senior citizens

2. Which quote from the article provides the best statement of the purpose of the organization?
A. "All of our services are free."
B. "We're a local organization."
C. "We're a network of volunteers that helps senior citizens in our neighborhood."
D. "All volunteers are screened to assure the safety of our seniors."

3. In paragraph 5, which words relate most to the term *screened* in that same paragraph?
A. reviews from customers
B. basic services
C. background checks
D. another important aspect

4. Which paragraphs provide the best information about the volunteer services offered by this program?
A. Paragraphs 1 and 2
B. Paragraphs 1, 2, and 6
C. Paragraphs 2 and 3
D. Paragraphs 3, 4, and 5

CLASSROOM VISITOR

Invite the coordinator of a neighborhood volunteer program to visit your class. Ask about the types of services offered and the opportunities for volunteering that are available. Or, invite someone from your city or town's department of elder affairs or senior services to visit and talk about the types of assistance, services, and programs that are available to help seniors in your community.

(Or, do an Internet search for information about a volunteer organization similar to the one described in the article.)

There's an App for That: How Technology Is Transforming the Service Economy

1   People often need help with tasks in their daily lives that they can't do themselves or don't have time to do, and they seek businesses or specialists who provide the services they need. In "the old days," to find someone to repair a washing machine, move furniture, clean carpets, or walk a dog, people would usually ask family, friends, neighbors, or co-workers for references, look at business listings in the telephone directory or yellow pages, or in more recent times check websites that list local service providers by category. However, nowadays, mobile phones have become a tool that consumers can use not only to *find* service providers, but also to *contract* them, *schedule* them, *pay* them, and even *evaluate* them. This all happens through the use of mobile apps.

Apps

2   An app—short for application—is a computer software program that lets the person using it perform certain functions. Computer applications, or desktop apps, include many of the common everyday applications we use to send e-mail, write documents, browse the Internet, plan schedules, or play music. Some apps are already installed on computers and devices when they are sold. Other apps can be downloaded from websites and installed. An app designed for mobile phones and other mobile devices is called a mobile app.

3   Mobile apps can serve as an alternative to using a browser on a computer to go to a website on the Internet to access information or services. Websites were originally designed to be viewed on personal computers. Their pages are formatted in a layout that fits a computer screen, and they have menus and commands that are accessed by using a mouse or trackpad. To be able to easily and conveniently see and manipulate content on the small screen of a mobile phone, a different presentation is needed. The layouts of mobile apps are constructed to fit the size of the small screen of a mobile device, and functions and commands are designed to be operated through a touch screen. Many companies, such as banks, retail stores, media organizations, and airlines, have mobile apps in addition to their websites, to offer an easy and convenient way for customers to connect with them and access their services.

4   Millions of mobile apps have been created by software developers, and more are becoming available every day on websites and at online app stores. Games, social media, messaging, and business apps are some of the main categories of apps in use. Some apps are free, and others require users to pay. Most apps are "native apps"—they are developed for a particular operating system, such as Apple iOS, Android, or Windows, and cannot be used on other systems. There are also web apps on websites that all mobile users can access through a browser. They are cheaper to develop, but their performance is limited compared to native apps. A hybrid app is a third type that can operate on multiple systems.

5   Many apps use other capabilities of a phone, such as geolocation, which uses GPS (the

GPS

The Global Positioning System (GPS) was originally developed as a secret project by the United States military for use as a navigation system to pinpoint exact locations on land or sea or in the air. Today's system, which is operated by the United States Air Force, is provided free by the U.S. government as a global public service. It uses a "constellation" of at least 24 satellites circling the Earth. A receiver chip in a smartphone or other mobile device receives signals sent out by multiple satellites to establish the device's location. Future improvements to the system will make it even more precise.

Global Positioning System) to identify the exact location of the phone. Geolocation is used not only in map and transportation apps, but in apps that do things such as identifying nearby businesses, measuring the distance a jogger has run, and directing a shopper to specific areas inside a department store. Apps may also access personal information about people who use them, such as their age and gender. In addition, some apps are designed to access users' contacts, photos, messaging history, and other data contained in their phones. Privacy can be a concern, as users may not realize how an app company will use their personal information.

Mobile Apps for Accessing Services

6   Entrepreneurs have started companies—sometimes called "on-demand" businesses—that help people find and connect with providers who offer services, such as carpet cleaning, home appliance repair, tutoring, and pet sitting. These companies have apps that make this process easy for customers. Service providers—for example, carpet cleaners—sign up with the company. People looking for someone to clean their carpets use the app to describe the work they need to have done, and the company provides this information to carpet cleaners who have registered with them. Carpet cleaners who want to do the work contact the customer and offer to do the service, and the customer selects and communicates with one of them. Customers use the app to schedule the work with the carpet cleaner. They might even pay for the job through the app when the work is done, and they can sometimes rate the service on a scale, such as one to five stars. These ratings help other customers identify capable service providers.

A typical rating scale

7   With the transition in recent years from a production economy to a service economy, new service businesses have continued to appear, and new apps that can help people connect with these services are being created. In addition, apps are also being developed that help service providers manage their businesses. Through these apps, managers can connect with their employees as well as customers, monitor jobs, collect information they need to get the work done, prepare invoices, and keep business records.

8   Many new apps make use of multiple features of mobile phones and other technology. A new app from a national home improvement store uses a phone's camera to measure furnishings or spaces in the home. After buying groceries on a well-known food store app, customers can watch on their phones as in-home video shows a delivery person entering the customer's house and putting food into the refrigerator. Apps for fitness training connect with wearable sensors that monitor physical exercise, collect information, and send signals through vibration and earphones that transmit feedback to the person exercising. Wearable technology is an example of the growing *Internet of things*, in which objects, such as medical devices and household appliances, can transmit data and communicate with computers and mobile devices. Other advances include apps that can process business transactions and make payments,

and devices with apps that respond to voice input and can answer questions and perform tasks.

Developing Apps

9   Thousands of new apps are being created every day. They are usually created by professional software developers, but it is possible for anyone with an idea for an app to create one. Most people creating apps want to make money from them. Developers usually have a business plan in mind from the beginning, as there are costs involved.

10   The starting point is the idea for the app: What will this app do? Planning begins as the designer thinks about the purpose of the app, its functions and components, how elements will be connected, and the steps that a user will go through to use it. The designer makes a diagram of sequences of screens that illustrates how the user would move from screen to screen by selecting commands. The diagram has branches showing different options. For example, a user selects a command on Screen A and goes to Screen B, or selects a different command on Screen A and goes to Screen C. The designer makes a complete list of all of these operations and outcomes.

11   At this stage, the person creating an app may need to engage outside help from a development studio or hire a designer to write the software and give advice on the app's functionality—how to make it work most effectively. App developers have to decide whether to make a native app for only one operating system, a hybrid app for multiple operating systems, or a web app. This determines the kind of mobile phone hardware or other devices the app will need to work with. A major element of the design is the *user interface*—how the user interacts with the app and provides input to operate it. This involves both the hardware and software, or programming. The developer's goal is to create a clear, logical, and well-organized design that makes the app easy to operate through simple commands and signals from the user.

12   To publish an app, creators must register with the companies that manage the major operating systems so they can get their new app into the companies' app stores and make it available to the public. Creators of new apps often market their app through advertising, for example, on social media. Effective advertising can make more people aware of new apps. If apps are innovative enough, they can get more attention by being reviewed on websites for computer products and compared to other apps in their category, such as "the top five messaging apps" or "the best apps for finding home service providers."

13   Creating an app can seem complicated, and technical knowledge and ability play a part in the process. But it is possible to create an app without being a computer expert. Educators have

developed simplified courses to teach students how to create apps without knowing computer programming, and resources are available that can guide amateur developers through the process. There are even DIY (do it yourself) app builders—apps for making apps.

14   Apps have changed the way that we interact with technology and participate in the service economy. As mobile technology continues to develop in the coming years, we are sure to see a continuing flow of new apps and uses for these small devices we hold in our hands.

DID YOU UNDERSTAND?

1. What is an app?

2. Why is the layout of a mobile app different from the layout of a website?

3. Why do many companies have mobile apps in addition to websites?

4. What are some of the main categories of apps?

5. What does geolocation do on a mobile phone?

6. Why should app users be concerned about privacy?

7. What are on-demand businesses?

8. How does an app rating system for service providers work?

9. Give one example of an app that uses multiple features of a mobile phone.

10. What does the *Internet of things* refer to?

11. Why is the user *interface* a major element in the design of an app?

12. What is an app developer's goal?

WHAT'S YOUR EXPERIENCE?

1. How do you find services you need? Have you ever used apps to find these services? If so, describe them and how you have used them.

2. What are your favorite apps? What do they do? How do you use them?

BRAINSTORMING

Think of an idea for a new app. What will it do? How will it work? What will it look like? Why will people want or need it?

READING COMPREHENSION

1. We use _____ to send e-mails and write documents on a home computer.
   A. desktop applications
   B. mobile apps
   C. websites
   D. browsers

2. A mobile app is operated by using _____.
   A. a website
   B. a touch screen
   C. a mouse or trackpad
   D. a browser

3. Which paragraph warns of possible risks associated with the use of apps?
   A. Paragraph 3
   B. Paragraph 4
   C. Paragraph 5
   D. Paragraph 6

4. Why would companies that connect people to service providers be called *on-demand* businesses?
   A. Customers demand good quality work.
   B. There is a big demand for competent home service providers.
   C. Service providers must follow customers' instructions exactly.
   D. The companies connect consumers to services at the time they need them.

5. Which of the following is an example of an app that utilizes wearable technology?
   A. an app for preparing invoices and keeping business records
   B. an app that enables managers to monitor their employees' work
   C. an app that allows customers to watch food being delivered to their homes
   D. an app that receives data through sensors that monitor a person exercising

6. What motivates people to create apps is described in _____.
   A. Paragraph 2
   B. Paragraph 4
   C. Paragraph 9
   D. Paragraph 13

7. In paragraph 11, the term *functionality* refers to an app's _____.
   A. design
   B. operation
   C. user interface
   D. all of the above

8. According to the reading, an app has a better chance of being reviewed by a tech website if it is _____.
   A. innovative
   B. in an app store
   C. available to the public
   D. well-advertised

9. The main purpose of the reading is to describe _____.
   A. how businesses create successful apps
   B. why the number of service providers has increased since the development of mobile apps
   C. how the development of apps has changed access to the service industry
   D. how computer technology has improved business services

10. The purpose of the graphic is to depict _____.
    A. the steps for getting to the home screen
    B. the outcomes of choosing different commands
    C. the stages of app development
    D. how an idea can evolve into an app

1. A mobile app is specifically _____ for use on a mobile phone.
   A. incorporated
   B. scheduled
   C. designed
   D. equipped

2. Mobile apps must be _____ to fit the small size of a mobile device.
   A. formatted
   B. functioned
   C. implemented
   D. exhibited

3. Movement from one screen to the next is accomplished by _____ commands.
   A. promoting
   B. selecting
   C. offering
   D. deciding

4. A good app design enables users to easily _____ content.
   A. involve
   B. manipulate
   C. register
   D. construct

5. The purpose of a rating scale is to help customers _____ competent service providers.
   A. achieve
   B. display
   C. ensure
   D. identify

6. Geolocation is an important _____ of mobile phones.
   A. process
   B. responsibility
   C. capability
   D. entity

7. A large number of new apps are being _____ every day.
   A. created
   B. conducted
   C. determined
   D. interacted

8. There has been a _____ in recent years from a production economy to a service economy.
   A. translation
   B. transmission
   C. transition
   D. transportation

9. Many costs are _____ in the development of a new product.
   A. influenced
   B. occupied
   C. arranged
   D. involved

10. Service providers _____ with on-demand businesses as a way of attracting customers.
    A. identify
    B. register
    C. regulate
    D. incorporate

11. Some apps are able to _____ business transactions and make payments.
    A. impose
    B. encounter
    C. process
    D. pursue

12. The developer's _____ is to simplify the operation of the app.
    A. goal
    B. status
    C. foundation
    D. format

13. User interface is an important _____ in the design of a product.
    A. image
    B. circumstance
    C. event
    D. element

14. In recent years, there have been many changes in the ways people _____ with technology.
    A. invest
    B. interact
    C. interpret
    D. involve

UNIT 14 LISTENING

PART A

Practice: A B C
   1. A B C
   2. A B C
   3. A B C
   4. A B C
   5. A B C

PART B

Practice: A B C
   1. A B C
   2. A B C
   3. A B C
   4. A B C
   5. A B C

Look at pages 206–207 of the core text. Write the correct words to complete the description.

baker	cobbler	designing	helping	photographer	specialists
bakery	cooked	floral	limo	photography	studio
caterer	day-care	food truck	newsstand	proprietor	supervising
chauffeur	designer	greets	owner	service	temp

The small business owners and their employees in this community are working in their stores and shops today.
At a _____temp_____ [1] agency, temporary staffing _____ [2] are helping their clients find temporary
jobs. A coffee shop owner is standing at the cash register in his coffee shop where he _____ [3] and
checks out customers. A _____ [4] designer is making a flower arrangement at his flower shop.
A jewelry designer is _____ [5] jewelry at her jewelry store. A _____ [6] is repairing
shoes at his shoe repair shop. A _____ [7] is baking a pie at her _____ [8]. A newsstand
_____ [9] who sells newspapers and magazines at his _____ [10] is talking to a customer.
A _____ [11] is doing a photo shoot at her _____ [12] studio. A licensed _____ [13]
operator and two child-care workers are _____ [14] children today. A food truck owner is selling tacos
that she has _____ [15] in her _____ [16]. A bookstore owner is _____ [17] a
customer at her bookstore. A _____ [18] service owner is watching a _____ [19] clean one of
the limos. A pet food shop _____ [20] has prepared pet food she is selling at her shop.
A _____ [21] is busy preparing food at her catering _____ [22]. An interior
_____ [23] is meeting with a client at her interior design _____ [24].

changing	copy	grooming	owner	selling	shop	training
clothing	distributor	making	packaging	service	sporting	vendor
copies	esthetician	operates	repairer	serving	studio	

A personal trainer is offering fitness _____ [25] at his personal trainer's _____ [26]. One
tailor is measuring a client and the other is making _____ [27] at the tailor shop. An _____ [28]
is doing a skin treatment at her skin care salon. A smoothie shop owner and her employee are making smoothies
at the smoothie _____ [29]. A _____ [30] center manager and his employee are making
_____ [31] at the copy center. A _____ [32] goods store manager is helping a customer at
his sporting goods store. A _____ [33] store manager is packaging items for shipping at his mailbox
store. An auto glass _____ [34] has arrived in her mobile auto glass _____ [35] truck to repair
a windshield. A route _____ [36] is delivering supplies to a convenience store. A convenience store
owner who _____ [37] his business 17 hours a day is talking with a customer. A hardware store manager
is _____ [38] hardware items at her hardware store. A sandwich shop owner is _____ [39]
sandwiches at his sandwich shop. An ice-cream shop owner is _____ [40] ice cream at her ice-cream
shop. A pet groomer is _____ [41] a dog. A food cart _____ [42] is selling food at her food cart.
And an auto lube shop _____ [43] is speaking to a customer while a technician is _____ [44]
the oil in the customer's car.

CAREER RESEARCH

Using the O*NET Career Exploration Tools at mynextmove.org, search for information about one of the jobs in Unit 15. Write the information in the job profile below. Then prepare and give a presentation about the job.

Job Zone 1 (little or no job preparation)
barista, limo driver/chauffeur, pet groomer

Job Zone 2 (some job preparation)
auto glass repairer, baker, child-care worker, cobbler, floral designer, food cart vendor, food truck owner, jobber/route distributor, newsstand proprietor, picture framer

Job Zone 3 (medium job preparation)
auto lube shop technician, barber, esthetician, jewelry designer, personal trainer, photographer, photography assistant, tailor

Job Zone 4 (high job preparation)
auto lube shop owner, bookstore owner, caterer, coffee shop owner, convenience store owner, copy center manager, hardware store manager, ice-cream shop owner, interior designer, licensed day-care operator, limo service owner, mailbox/packaging store manager, pet food shop owner, pet shop owner, sandwich shop owner, smoothie shop owner, sporting goods store manager, temp agency owner, temporary staffing specialist

Job name: _____

What does a person do in this job?

_____

_____

What tools and equipment does a person use in this job?

_____

What skills and abilities are important?

_____

_____

What technology might a person use in this job?

_____

What kind of person will be interested in this work?

_____

What level of education, job training, and experience is required?

_____

_____

What is the job outlook?   What is the average salary?

_____   _____

Read the memo and answer the questions.

1 **TO:** All Neighborhood Merchants Association Members
2 **FROM:** Wanda Jackson, Board President
3 **SUBJECT:** Small Business Crime Prevention

4 As most of you are aware, there has been a rise in burglaries and robberies of small businesses in our area over the past several weeks. Please keep in mind these crime prevention suggestions from the Los Angeles Police Department.

5 **Preventing Burglaries:**
6 All outside entrance doors and inside
7 security doors should have deadbolt
8 locks.

9 Windows should have locks and burglar-
10 resistant glass. Install metal grates on
11 all windows except display windows.
12 Remove expensive items from window
13 displays at night.

14 Use good lighting inside and outside—at
15 doors, windows, other entry points, and
16 in the parking lot.

17 Keep the cash register empty and open
18 after closing. It should be visible from
19 outside so police can monitor it.

20 Your safe should be fireproof and
21 anchored so it cannot be removed. It
22 should be open when it is empty. Keep
23 it locked when it contains valuables.
24 When an employee who knows the
25 combination leaves your employment,
26 change it.

27 If you have an alarm system, check
28 it daily.

29 **Preventing Shoplifting:**
30 Keep the business orderly and neat.
31 Keep merchandise away from store exits to prevent
32 grab-and-run incidents.

33 Use mirrors to be able to view corners or other blind spots
34 that shoplifters may use to hide their activities.

35 Keep expensive merchandise in locked cases. When a
36 customer wishes to examine items, do not remove too
37 many items at once.

38 Keep dressing rooms locked and limit the number of items
39 customers can bring into them at one time.

40 A store employee or security person should be stationed
41 at or near the exit.

42 **Preventing Robberies:**
43 Give a friendly greeting to each person who enters.
44 (Personal contact sometimes deters a criminal.)

45 Keep windows clear and the inside of the business well-lit so
46 that inside activity can be viewed from the outside.

47 Place the cash register near the front of the business so a
48 robbery in progress might be seen by someone and reported.

49 Do not keep large amounts of cash in the register. Have
50 employees place excess cash and large bills into a drop safe
51 that cannot be opened by them.

52 For complete information, see the Small Business Crime Prevention page on the LAPD website.

1. What is the primary source of the crime prevention information in the memo?
   A. small business owners
   B. Wanda Jackson
   C. the Neighborhood Merchants Association
   D. the Los Angeles Police Department

2. What type of crime is given the least attention in the memo?
   A. thefts by employees
   B. break-ins by burglars
   C. thefts by shoplifters
   D. robberies

3. In Line 37, what does *at once* mean?
   A. immediately
   B. one at a time
   C. at the same time
   D. for one customer

4. Which statement is true based on the information in the memo?
   A. Most association members didn't know about the increase in crime.
   B. Being able to see inside a store from the outside can prevent crimes.
   C. Most of the businesses have alarm systems.
   D. The memo appears on the LAPD website.

DEMONSTRATING A PROCEDURE

Using YouTube, WikiHow, or another source, search online for information about how to start a small business. Write out the information about the steps in the process. Then prepare a media presentation or video-record your demonstration. Present the information to the class.

Suggestions: how to start a _____ (bakery, coffee shop, flower shop, sandwich shop, etc.); how to start a food truck business; how to start a small business at home

The Economics of Starting a Small Business

1   When we think of work, we usually think about jobs. Most people work as employees of a company or an organization, but some people take a different approach and decide to go into business for themselves. They may like the idea of being their own boss, or they may feel motivated to build their own business around an idea or a passion or special skills they have, or they may just think that they will be able to make money. These entrepreneurs see a challenge in bringing a dream to reality through their own hard work.

Small Businesses

2   New businesses start out small. Some may grow into big businesses, but most remain small. Despite their size, *small* businesses make up a *big* part of the economy. Some small businesses, such as bakeries, flower shops, and frame shops, make products. Some businesses, such as jewelry stores, book stores, and beauty supply stores, sell merchandise. Others, such as tailor shops, barber shops, photography studios, and child-care centers, provide services.

need their own physical place of business. This is also true for certain small businesses that exist only online.

4   A lot is involved in owning and running a business—from hiring and managing staff to maintaining a place of business, dealing with property managers, buying equipment, ordering supplies, handling the finances, advertising and promotion, and complying with government requirements. According to figures from the U.S. Bureau of Labor Statistics, 20% of new businesses with employees fail within the first year, and 50% fail within the first five years. Factors that contribute to these failures may include low market demand, limited cash supplies, poor management skills, strong competition, inappropriate pricing, poor quality of products or services, unsuitable location, and an unfavorable economic environment. Entrepreneurs are willing to take a risk, but it helps if they prepare themselves as well as they can before they start out. Fortunately, many government and community agencies offer information and training on opening a small business.

Starting a Small Business

3   Most small businesses are located in a shop or an office and may have from 5 to 50 or 100 employees. Many businesses are franchises, branches of a big company such as a fast-food restaurant chain. And some small-business service providers, such as plumbers, home repair workers, and babysitters, work as individuals or with a few helpers and do not

5   The first step in starting a business is to make sure there is a need for what the business intends to sell or the service it plans to provide. It is also important

to consider what other similar businesses already exist that serve the target customers. If the business needs to have a shop or store, deciding on a location for the business may be an important factor in its chances for success. If the situation looks hopeful, writing a business plan is the next step. This can be done informally. However, if a loan from an investor or bank is required, a more formal business plan document must be drawn up. This business plan needs to include a detailed description of the company and its products or services, a market analysis, the strategy for marketing and sales, and a financial analysis.

6   Financial aspects are important considerations. First and foremost is funding—anticipating how much money will be needed to start up the business and to keep it running, since it can take up to two or three years for new businesses to begin to earn money. A business partner or other investor may be needed to contribute to the funding. If a loan is necessary, bank requirements will have to be met. The financial plan must include the establishment of an accounting system for the business and a separate bank account.

7   Legal and governmental issues are also involved. The proposed business must have one of four business structures: sole proprietorship, partnership, limited liability company (LLC), or corporation. Each type of business structure has different legal and tax implications. Government licenses, permits, and taxation requirements are also part of registering a new business. In addition,

the business needs to take a name that is not already used by someone else.

Calculating Startup Costs

8   Financial matters are an important part of planning a business. The reality is that businesses are about money. It takes money to run a business, and a business needs to make money in order to survive. But first of all, it takes money to *start* a business, and calculating startup costs is an important initial step in planning.

9   The types of startup costs depend on the business. Some businesses must have an office or other type of facility, while a service or an online business may not need any type of physical location. Most businesses require equipment and supplies, along with costs for communication services. A retail business will need to acquire inventory, a supply of things to sell. There are fees for licenses and permits, and lawyers often need to be consulted. Advertising and printed marketing materials are other common expenses.

10   Many of the costs are one-time expenses, such as for equipment or permits, but other costs will be ongoing, for example, rent and employee salaries. The cost of starting up a business is the total of all the one-time expenses plus expenses for the first month. Figuring startup costs includes just the expenses, and does not consider any money the business may make.

STARTUP COSTS WORKSHEET – Pooch Palace Dog Day Care

One-time Expenses

Rent

First month's rent	1,800.00
Deposit	3,600.00
First month's utilities	300.00

Construction

Fencing, gates	2,000.00
Sanitation facilities	2,000.00
Play yard	1,300.00

Equipment

Recreational equipment	650.00
Sanitation equipment	1,300.00
Other	800.00

Miscellaneous

Permits, fees	525.00
Legal services	400.00
Computer equipment	500.00
	$15,175.00

Monthly Expenses

Rent

Rent	1,800.00
Property insurance	350.00
Utilities	300.00
Water	300.00

Staff

Salaries	2,200.00
Payroll taxes, etc.	800.00

Professional

Accounting	130.00
Legal	220.00

Supplies

Pet food	750.00
Grooming supplies	300.00

Miscellaneous

Advertising	300.00
Liability insurance	750.00
Maintenance	200.00
	$8,400.00

The total startup costs for opening this business would be $23,575: $15,175 for one-time expenses and $8,400 for monthly expenses. The estimated annual cost of operation would be $100,800 ($8,400 per month times 12 months.)

Total Startup Costs: $15,175.00 + $8,400 = $23,575.00

Estimated Annual Cost of Operation: $8,400 x 12 = $100,800

11   The worksheet above is based on guidelines from the U.S. Small Business Administration detailing startup costs for establishing a business. The name of this proposed business is "Pooch Palace"—a day-care center for dogs.

Financial Analysis

12   It takes money to start up and operate a business, and money needs to come in to make the business profitable. The first step in planning a business is to determine how much demand there would be for the product or service. This is done through market research, trying to determine the need for what the business is selling or the service it is offering, and looking at competitors in the field. Research also has to be done to set a selling price for the product or service, estimating how much people would be willing to pay for it. The big question is whether the business will be able to earn enough money to be profitable.

13   If the research shows enough demand, a business plan must be developed that includes a financial projection of costs, ongoing expenses, and income. A financial analysis should also include estimating a *break-even point*—the number of units that must be sold to cover costs, so that revenue (money coming in) exceeds expenses (money going out).

14 For example, for a business that is selling a product, figuring a break-even point requires determining the following:

(1) the selling price of the product

(2) the cost of producing and selling the product, including materials and labor

(3) the business overhead (operating costs) and other fixed monthly costs

By subtracting (2) from (1), the profit margin per unit can be calculated. Dividing this number by (3) will determine how many units must be sold to cover operating expenses. This is the break-even point.

15 Below is a table that can be used to calculate startup costs for a small startup company named Maskaria that intends to produce antipollution face masks.

Break-even planning:
Maskaria – Smart antipollution face masks

Selling price		$39.95
Cost per unit		$10.49
Materials	$5.93	
Labor	$4.56	
Profit margin per unit		$29.46
Overhead (monthly)		$4,415.00
Salaries	$1,500.00	
Rent	$1,800.00	
Utilities	$320.00	
Misc. business expenses	$425.00	
Advertising, marketing	$370.00	

Break-even point:
$4,415.00 ÷ $29.46 = 149.86 = 150 units

The numbers show that the Maskaria company would have to sell 150 face masks per month to *break even*—to cover its overhead for the month. For every mask it sells beyond 150, the company would earn a clear profit of $29.46. With this information, a profit projection can be done to determine if the earnings would be sufficient to justify establishing the company. There are additional ways to increase profit, such as raising the selling price or lowering production costs or other expenses, although these steps could have an effect on sales numbers.

Profit Margins

16 A company's profit margins provide a way of looking at its profitability. One type of profit margin is gross profit margin, which is figured by subtracting the cost of goods sold from the total sales revenue, and dividing that amount by the total revenue to get a percentage. It is sometimes called a gross margin ratio.

Gross Profit Margin =
   (Sales Revenue – Cost of Goods Sold) ÷ Revenue

If the Maskaria company sold 200 masks per month, the gross profit margin ratio for this product for the month would be 74%. Here are the calculations:

($39.95 x 200) $7,990.00 (Sales Revenue)
($10.49 x 200) $2,098.00 (Cost of Goods Sold)
_____

   $5,892.00 ÷ $7,990.00 = 0.74 (74%)
   (Sales Revenue)   (Gross Margin Ratio)

17 Another type of profit margin is net profit margin. In addition to product costs, the net profit margin takes into consideration overhead and all other company expenses, such as taxes and loan interest payments. For this reason, net profit margin is a better indication of a company's profitability.

Net profit margin = (Revenue – Total Expenses) ÷ Revenue

If Maskaria sold 200 masks in a month, and in addition to overhead paid $500 in interest and $600 in taxes in the month, the net profit margin ratio for the month would be 4.7%. Here are the calculations:

$7,990.00 (Sales Revenue)
$7,613.00 ($2,098 Cost of Goods Sold + $4,415 Overhead
             + $500 Interest + $600 Taxes)
_____

$377.00 ÷ $7,990.00 = .047 (4.7%)
   (Sales Revenue)   (Net Profit Margin)

With a net profit margin of 4.7%, and assuming its sales projection is accurate, the startup business would be making money. It would be a good beginning, but the owners would have to find ways to make the business more profitable.

18   Business is basically about money and numbers. Starting and operating a business involves a lot of money, a lot of numbers, and a lot of math. To be successful, entrepreneurs and business owners need to stay on top of the numbers and be aware of "the bottom line"—the company's net profitability.

DID YOU UNDERSTAND?

1. What are some of the reasons people start a new business?

2. What kinds of businesses might not have their own store or other physical place of business?

3. What percentage of new businesses with employees fail within the first year?

4. What is the first thing to consider about an idea for a new business?

5. What is included in a business plan?

6. What two general types of expenses are counted when figuring business startup costs?

7. In planning a new business, what is the break-even point?

8. What are two ways of increasing unit profit margin?

9. How is gross profit margin calculated?

10. How is net profit margin calculated?

CAN YOU FIGURE IT OUT?

1. If the monthly expenses listed on the Pooch Palace worksheet are correct, how much gross (total) revenue would the business have to take in in one month to make a 20% profit for that month? (One way to think about this is: $8,400 is 80% of what number? 0.80x = $8,400.) How much would the profit be?

2. In the preliminary business plan for his food truck, Jason estimated employee salary expenses of $4,000 a month based on a wage of $12.00 an hour. However, the city just raised the minimum wage to $15.00 an hour. What percent salary increase is this? What will the new estimate of monthly salary expenses need to be?

3. What percent of the product cost for a Maskaria face mask is for materials and what percent is for labor?

4. The owners of Maskaria found another supplier for one of the components of the face mask that would lower the unit materials cost by $0.72. By what percent will this increase the profit margin per unit?

READING COMPREHENSION

1. According to the reading, _____ can depend on factors such as competition, cash supplies, and location.
   A. market demand
   B. government requirements
   C. the economic environment
   D. the success of a new business

2. Which of the following sections of the reading best describes the various types of expenses involved in starting a business?
   A. Starting a Small Business
   B. Calculating Startup Costs
   C. Financial Analysis
   D. Profit Margins

3. Sole proprietorship and partnership are two types of _____.
   A. financial arrangements
   B. business structures
   C. business plans
   D. financial plans

4. Unlike businesses that provide services, retail businesses require _____.
   A. inventory
   B. equipment
   C. a facility
   D. supplies

5. Which of the following statements about startup costs is incorrect?
   A. Startup costs are based on company earnings.
   B. Permits and equipment are a one-time expense.
   C. Rent and employee salaries are ongoing expenses.
   D. Startup costs differ depending on the type of business.

6. Based on the Pooch Palace startup costs worksheet, which of the following is true?
   A. Fees for a lawyer will not be necessary after the business has begun operating.
   B. Miscellaneous monthly costs are greater than miscellaneous one-time costs.
   C. Costs for construction of the facility are ongoing.
   D. The rental deposit is the equivalent of two month's rent.

7. Market research is done to determine _____.
   A. a company's profitability
   B. the break-even point
   C. demand for the product or service
   D. operating costs

8. Why is net profit margin a better indicator of profitability than gross profit margin?
   A. Gross profit margin is just a ratio, not a calculation.
   B. Gross profit margin does not include sales revenue.
   C. Net profit margin considers all of a company's expenses.
   D. Net profit margin is expressed as a percentage.

9. A company's *bottom line* refers to the company's _____.
   A. total sales revenue
   B. income after deduction of production costs
   C. sales projections
   D. earnings after costs and operating expenses have been deducted

10. The goal of the reading is to _____.
    A. encourage entrepreneurs to start a new business
    B. explain the financial factors involved in starting a new business
    C. describe potential problems in starting a new business
    D. explain why many small businesses are not profitable

ACADEMIC VOCABULARY

1. Businesses must comply with various government _____.
   A. responsibilities
   B. requirements
   C. establishments
   D. foundations

2. Many factors have _____ to the success of the company.
   A. participated
   B. generated
   C. contributed
   D. attributed

3. Many _____ agencies offer information on starting a new business.
   A. community
   B. communication
   C. institutional
   D. technical

4. There are several _____ involved in determining the best location for a business.
   A. formulas
   B. functions
   C. features
   D. factors

5. It is essential to _____ how much money will be needed to start a business.
   A. detect
   B. require
   C. anticipate
   D. intend

6. You must _____ an accounting system and separate bank account for a business.
   A. establish
   B. allocate
   C. legislate
   D. facilitate

7. Every type of business structure has different legal and tax _____.
   A. correspondences
   B. implications
   C. indications
   D. processes

8. Before a retail business can operate, it must _____ inventory.
   A. construct
   B. utilize
   C. inquire
   D. acquire

9. Anyone wishing to start a new business must _____ with a lawyer.
   A. consult
   B. consent
   C. consider
   D. conclude

10. They will need to estimate the cost of sanitation _____.
    A. components
    B. equipment
    C. networks
    D. sources

11. For a business to succeed, revenue must _____ expenses.
    A. ensure
    B. achieve
    C. exceed
    D. maximize

12. A company's net profit _____ is a good indication of its profitability.
    A. margin
    B. equation
    C. amount
    D. distribution

13. _____ costs are expenses that continue month after month.
    A. Startup
    B. Miscellaneous
    C. Outgoing
    D. Ongoing

14. A business plan must include a financial _____ of costs, expenses, and income.
    A. operation
    B. promotion
    C. projection
    D. organization

UNIT 15 LISTENING

PART A

Practice: A B C

1. A B C
2. A B C
3. A B C
4. A B C
5. A B C

PART B

Practice: A B C

1. A B C
2. A B C
3. A B C
4. A B C
5. A B C

Look at pages 222–223 of the core text. Write the correct words to complete the description.

agency	checking	dropping off	line service	screener	ticket
boarding	counter	flight deck	overhead	serviceperson	weighed
boarding pass	demonstrating	food service	recording	shuttle	wheelchair
check-in	directing	handler	rental	skycap	

People are traveling! Customers are making travel arrangements at a travel ___**agency**___ 1. A taxi driver

is _____ 2 a passenger at the airport. A _____ 3 is bringing in luggage on a baggage

cart. A _____ 4 agent is providing wheelchair assistance. There are several _____ 5

agents at the check-in counter. One is _____ 6 a passenger's ID, another is printing a passenger's

_____ 7, and another has just _____ 8 and tagged a passenger's luggage. A TSA

_____ 9 is checking boarding passes and IDs in the security _____ 10 area. A gate agent

is checking tickets at the _____ 11 gate. An airplane is being serviced before boarding.

A cabin _____ 12 is checking the cabin, a _____ 13 worker is stowing food carts,

a _____ 14 technician is servicing the plane, and a baggage _____ 15 is loading baggage.

In another airplane, a pilot and first officer are in the _____ 16, communicating with a ground

crew member who is _____ 17 aircraft. One of the flight attendants is _____ 18 safety

procedures, and another is checking _____ 19 compartments. When passengers arrive at their

destination, many of them will rent cars. At the auto _____ 20 agency, auto rental agents are helping

customers at the reservation _____ 21. The _____ 22 driver is sitting in the shuttle bus

and service agents are _____ 23 mileage and gas level on cars that have been returned.

attendant	concierge	entrance	housekeeping	maintenance	planner	setting up
bellhop	coordinator	function	inspecting	observing	reviewing	valet
checking in	doorman	housekeeper	leading	operating	servers	wall

At the Grand Hotel, guests are checking in. A _____ 24 is giving an arriving guest a valet ticket.

A _____ 25 has welcomed an arriving guest at the hotel _____ 26. At the front desk,

one front desk clerk is _____ 27 a guest and the other is _____ 28 a departing guest's

folio. In the lobby, the _____ 29 is making reservations for a hotel guest and a _____ 30 is

bringing luggage to a guest's room. On one of the guest floors, a room service _____ 31 is delivering

food and a hotel _____ 32 worker is doing a repair. On a different floor, the _____ 33

manager is _____ 34 rooms and a _____ 35 is making one up. The hotel has a large

_____ 36 room that can be divided by a retractable _____ 37. There's going to be an event

in one half of the room. An event _____ 38 is designing the floor plan and an event _____ 39

is giving instructions to the housepeople who are _____ 40 for the event. There's a banquet in

the other half of the room. Banquet _____ 41 are serving meals while the banquet manager is

_____ 42 the wait staff. There's a tourist site nearby. Tour bus drivers are _____ 43 tour

buses and tour escorts are _____ 44 tours.

CAREER RESEARCH

Using the O*NET Career Exploration Tools at mynextmove.org, search for information about one of the jobs in Unit 16. Write the information in the job profile below. Then prepare and give a presentation about the job.

Job Zone 1 (little or no job preparation)
auto rental agent, banquet server, busperson, food service worker, houseperson, room service attendant, taxi driver/cab driver, wheelchair agent

Job Zone 2 (some job preparation)
baggage handler, banquet manager, bellhop, cabin serviceperson, curbside check-in agent, doorman, front desk clerk, gate agent, housekeeper, housekeeping manager, service agent, shuttle driver, skycap, ticket agent, tour bus driver, TSA screener, valet

Job Zone 3 (medium job preparation)
concierge, flight attendant, ground crew member, group tour guide, hotel maintenance worker, line service technician, tour escort, travel agent

Job Zone 4 (high job preparation)
event coordinator, event planner, first officer, pilot

Job name: _____

What does a person do in this job?

_____

_____

What tools and equipment does a person use in this job?

_____

What skills and abilities are important?

_____

_____

What technology might a person use in this job?

_____

What kind of person will be interested in this work?

_____

What level of education, job training, and experience is required?

_____

_____

What is the job outlook?   What is the average salary?

_____   _____

Read the memo to motorcoach operators and answer the questions.

1 **TO:** All Motorcoach Operators
2 **FROM:** Cheryl Wilson, General Manager
3 **SUBJ:** Passenger Safety Instructions

4 Effective immediately, please follow these updated procedures for presenting safety information
5 to passengers.

6 After passengers have boarded and prior to moving the motorcoach, make an announcement to
7 ask passengers to review the information card in the seat back pocket in front of them. Then play
8 the automated presentation over the audio or video system.

9 This should be repeated at all major stops or terminals after new passengers have boarded.

10 In the event that the automated presentation isn't operational, you must read aloud the following
11 passenger safety instructions:

12   Welcome and thanks for traveling with us. We are happy to have you aboard. Your safety and
13   comfort are very important to us. Before we get started, we want you to be familiar with the safety
14   features on this vehicle and how to use them properly.

15   First, please stay seated while the vehicle is in motion.
16   Newer buses have seat belts. If your bus has seat belts, please be sure to use them.
17   Never block the center aisle.
18   Follow all safety instructions made by the driver.
19   If necessary, notify authorities of an emergency by using a cellular telephone to call 911.

20   There is a fire extinguisher on this vehicle. It will be located behind the driver's seat, or beneath the
21   front row passenger's seat, or in the front-most overhead compartment.

22   Remember: the primary exit from this vehicle is the same door at the front through which you
23   entered. In an extreme emergency situation, the windows can also serve as exits. Follow the
24   instruction markings on the windows or the window frames. Also note that there is an emergency
25   exit hatch in the roof above the center aisle. Please take a moment to locate the emergency exits
26   nearest to you.

27   If you have any questions about the safety procedures, ask the driver. Thank you again for riding
28   with us today.

29   This message has been provided in cooperation with the Federal Motor Carrier Safety
30   Administration, U.S. Department of Transportation.

Federal Motor Carrier Safety Administration, U.S. Department of Transportation

1. Which line of the memo indicates that these procedures have changed?
   A. Line 1
   B. Line 4
   C. Line 11
   D. Line 14

2. Which is not a safety feature of the vehicle?
   A. seat belts
   B. fire extinguisher
   C. overhead compartments
   D. emergency exit hatch

3. What is the meaning of *primary* as used in Line 22?
   A. main
   B. only
   C. nearest
   D. most extreme

4. Who is the likely writer of the passenger safety instructions?
   A. the company's general manager
   B. one or more of the company's best operators
   C. the bus manufacturer
   D. one or more government employees

DEMONSTRATING A PROCEDURE

Using YouTube or another search engine, search online for passenger safety instructions for a form of transportation. Write out the instructions. Then prepare a media presentation. Make screenshots of the steps or video-record your demonstration. Present the procedure to the class.

Suggestions: passenger safety instructions for an airline, an interstate bus company, a commuter ferry, a cruise ship

A Hospitality Industry Executive and Philanthropist

1   Henri Landwirth was born on March 7, 1927, in Antwerp, Belgium. He was a survivor of the Holocaust, separated from his family and imprisoned in the Nazi death camps during World War II. He and his twin sister survived, but their parents were killed.

2   Henri arrived in the United States after the war and soon after served in the Army. After his military service, he studied hotel management and began a lifelong career in the industry, starting out as a bellhop. He moved to Florida in 1954 and managed a hotel near Cape Canaveral, where he became friendly with guests that included the original Mercury 7 astronauts and the news reporters who covered the space program.

3   He became very successful in Florida's hospitality industry as the state became an increasingly popular family destination, especially the Orlando area in central Florida with its many theme parks and attractions. The area is the desired destination for half of all children with life-threatening illnesses and their families who are involved with wish-granting organizations. In 1986, Henri started Give Kids the World, and three years later he opened Give Kids the World Village, a non-profit resort that offers weeklong free vacations to these families. The Village becomes their home during their visit. It includes accommodations and an amusement park full of fun activities and entertainment.

4   Give Kids the World is able to make these dream vacations happen on very short notice in order to assure that terminally-ill children have their wishes fulfilled. In fact, that is the reason the Village was created. In the 1980s, a six-year-old girl with a critical illness was scheduled to stay at Henri's hotel in Orlando, but she died before she was able to make the trip. Henri was determined that this wouldn't happen again. He created a wonderful place to make sure children's dreams would come true. Since its opening, Give Kids the World Village has hosted more than 160,000 families from every state in the U.S. and 76 countries.

5   Henri Landwirth passed away at the age of 91 on April 16, 2018. His inspiring legacy includes the wonderful institution he created and the happiness it will continue to bring into the lives of children and families in the years ahead.

1. Select the paragraph that provides information about the person's education.
   A. Paragraph 1
   B. Paragraph 2
   C. Paragraph 3
   D. Paragraph 4

2. Based on the article, what is the most likely definition of a *philanthropist*?
   A. an industry executive
   B. a successful businessperson
   C. a person who helps others
   D. a person who served in the military

3. Which words in Paragraph 3 are closest in meaning to *dream vacation* in Paragraph 4?
   A. accommodations
   B. non-profit resort
   C. family destination
   D. desired destination

4. What word in the article best describes the writer's opinion about this person's life?
   A. inspiring
   B. friendly
   C. successful
   D. determined

CLASSROOM VISITOR

Invite a local philanthropist to visit your class—someone who donates money or time or takes action to help people or institutions in your community, or someone who works for a charity or philanthropy such as the wish-granting organizations described in the article. Ask about the person or organization's mission and work.

(Or, do an Internet search for information about a wish-granting organization or other philanthropy.)

The Future of Travel

1   With the expansion of the middle class and increased availability and affordability of air travel and hotels in the second half of the 20th century, the travel and hospitality industries have become a major part of the world economy. In the 21st century, new developments in information technology, transportation technology, and electronics are leading to significant changes in the travel experience.

Travel Services

2   Before the growth of the Internet, the most common way for people to make travel arrangements, particularly for airline flights, was to go to a travel agency. Travel agents worked with clients to identify their requirements and preferences, present them with options, and book their travel. They also helped in booking hotels and tours. However, in recent years, travel agencies have lost business since most people now make travel bookings by themselves on the Internet. In addition, travel for business purposes has declined somewhat as telecommuting and teleconferencing have become more common. Travel agencies are now working mostly with clients who prefer to have their travel arrangements taken care of by someone else, people interested in booking tour packages, and large companies booking travel arrangements for their employees.

3   Online travel companies that allow customers to book flights, hotels, rental cars, and other services are very popular. Travelers can book several of these services for their trips at the same time. For flights, customers enter destinations and dates, which brings up a list of flight options. They can compare flight times and prices and make their selection. Payment is made by credit card, and booking is done electronically, with notifications sent by e-mail and messaging. Travelers can also book flights on the websites of individual airlines and on smartphone mobile apps. Prior to their flight departure, customers can print boarding passes from an airline website or receive them on their smartphones to be scanned at the gate when they board the plane.

4   It is also possible for travelers to book a hotel or rental car in a similar way at various types of online travel booking companies. A search for hotel room vacancies by location, dates, and number of occupants generates a list of options that includes prices, picture galleries showing the interior of the hotel and typical guestrooms, descriptions of the hotel and its services, and a map showing its location. Customers can check room availability for their desired dates and make reservations and payments. They can also consult reviews that previous hotel guests have posted on websites about their experiences—with ratings of one to five stars, poor to excellent, often along with detailed comments.

5   Travelers who need lodging but prefer not to stay in a hotel now have an alternative to hotels through online rental service companies. Property owners who want to rent out their houses or apartments list them with the rental service company. Travelers wishing to use the service register with the company, and then they can search the company's website for rentals at their travel destinations. Rentals arranged on this basis are more informal and personal than hotels and provide more of a home-like experience. There are companies all over the world now engaged in this business, and they are taking a growing share of the lodging market.

Air Travel

6   The technology of air travel is changing. Aircraft manufacturers are building more fuel-efficient

airplanes that have new wing designs and use advanced, lightweight materials such as carbon fiber. The planes have attractively designed interiors and larger windows. Seating space is getting tighter, however, as designers attempt to maximize the use of space and the number of seats, while still trying to pay attention to passenger comfort. In-flight entertainment options are increasing, and onboard Wi-Fi is more common. Jet engines are achieving greater fuel economy, and new designs are making them quieter. Electric aircraft that can be used for short flights, including solar-powered planes, are in development, and a futuristic supersonic passenger aircraft has been proposed.

7   Airports in many parts of the world are using new technologies. One development is the use of biometrics, such as facial recognition, at passenger check-in, baggage drops, immigration checkpoints, and boarding, to move travelers through quickly and efficiently. As a way of reducing the incidence of lost bags, an innovation in handling and tracking baggage uses electronic baggage tags and a smartphone app in a cloud-based system that stores travelers' travel documents. Beacon technology at locations inside airports can transmit signals to travelers' smartphone apps to provide flight and gate updates and load a boarding pass that appears on the passenger's phone. Robots are being used in some airports to answer travelers' questions and provide information such as flight departure schedules and weather at their destinations.

Trains

8   High-speed rail travel has proven to be an effective mode of transportation in many countries. Most of these train lines use electric-powered locomotives, but trains using a different technology called magnetic levitation, or maglev, are now being developed. The trains do not travel on wheels, but are raised up by a magnetic force in the track or guideway that pushes against magnets at the bottom of the cars. The train is propelled forward by a flow of electric current in the rails that pulls and pushes the magnets on the cars. Without the friction of wheels on rails, these trains are able to achieve much higher speeds than conventional trains, and they use much less energy.

9   The latest idea in transport technology, called the Hyperloop, involves passenger carriers or pods traveling inside a long tube to their destination. The tube is sealed, and the air pressure inside is reduced in order to lower air resistance on the moving pods. The latest version of this idea uses magnetic levitation to raise the pods and a linear induction motor using electromagnetic fields to propel them. Theoretically, speeds faster than jet aircraft can be reached. Many independent teams are working on creating prototypes, but it is uncertain whether the Hyperloop could become a practical means of long-distance transportation.

Ground Transportation

10   Once travelers reach their destinations, they often need a vehicle to get around. Although there are still many auto rental companies, ridesharing

businesses have become a popular option. In these businesses, private drivers register with the rideshare company and use their own vehicles to give rides to customers. Passengers register with the company and provide their credit card information. They use the service's mobile app to find and contact a driver, who picks them up and takes them to their destinations. The fee is set beforehand and is charged to the passenger's credit card. Some travelers prefer ridesharing services over renting a car, especially when they are in a city they are not familiar with. In some cases, ridesharing services are less expensive than renting a car. Ridesharing services are also very popular with local residents. However, these services are having a negative impact on traditional taxi companies.

11   The development of autonomous vehicles (self-driving cars, or driverless cars) will be bringing even bigger changes to the ground transportation business. Automakers are designing vehicles that can be controlled effectively and safely by computers with little or no input from human drivers. Self-driving cars will eventually change the nature of short- and long-distance road travel, and will no doubt be put into service as taxis. There are also great expectations that autonomous vehicles will reduce the number of traffic accidents and fatalities.

Hotels

12   With strong competition for customers, especially those who are willing to pay more for their hotel

experience, hotels are feeling the need to keep up with the latest trends and innovations. This is especially true in the area of technology. Guests at some hotels can use apps on their mobile phones to manage their booking, check in, enter their rooms, control the room temperature and lighting, and access hotel services and information. Some hotel companies now have systems that enable guests to check in online. They may receive a barcode that they can scan at a kiosk when they arrive at the hotel lobby to get their room key, or the phone itself can serve as the key. Some hotel rooms have touchscreens that guests can use to communicate directly with hotel services, and in the future, there will be voice-activated information and control systems. Guests want connectivity for their electronic devices, so hotels are investing in hotel-wide, high-capacity WiFi networks. They are also upgrading in-room services by providing streaming entertainment to guestroom televisions.

13   In the future, guests will receive wearable devices that the hotel can use to identify them. Beacons in hotel lobbies and other areas will be able to communicate with guests' smartphones, including sending messages about promotions in hotel restaurants and other facilities, and helping guests find their way to locations in the hotel. Geolocation technology will allow hotels to track where guests are and what facilities they use. However, there will be concerns about privacy and the hotel's use of guests' personal information.

14   Hotel companies will make use of virtual reality (VR) in marketing and other ways. Using special

headsets or devices that hold smartphones, potential guests will be able to take VR walking tours through hotels and their facilities. When planning excursions, hotel guests will use VR to view local neighborhoods and attractions.

15   Finally, in the future, technological advances in virtual reality might actually reduce the need to travel! Through virtual tourism, people will be able to enjoy life-like presentations of exotic destinations, historic locations, or cultural attractions by strapping on a VR viewer, sitting back, and taking in the sights from the comfort of their own homes.

DID YOU UNDERSTAND?

1. Why have travel agencies lost business in recent years?

2. What information about hotels can customers find on booking websites?

3. How do online vacation rental services work?

4. What effect have online vacation rental services had on the hotel industry?

5. What changes are making new airplanes more fuel-efficient?

6. How is biometric technology being used in airports?

7. What do beacons do?

8. How can maglev trains run without wheels?

9. What services have taken business away from taxi companies?

10. What are some new uses for guests' mobile phones in hotel rooms?

11. What can hotels use geolocation technology for?

12. What are two ways hotel companies will use virtual reality?

WHAT'S YOUR EXPERIENCE?

1. Have you ever used the services of travel agencies? If you have, what was your experience?

2. What do you find to be the most difficult part of making travel arrangements?

3. Have you ever used a vacation rental service for lodging when you traveled? If you have, what was your experience?

4. Do you use rideshare services? If you do, how well has it worked for you?

5. Do you consider customer reviews on websites when you are going to purchase goods or services? Have you ever written an online review or comment about a hotel stay or for some other purpose? What was it about?

WHAT'S YOUR OPINION?

1. Do you enjoy air travel? What do you like and dislike about it?

2. Would you feel safe riding in a super high-speed train?

3. Most taxi companies think ridesharing services are not fair to them because ridesharing companies do not have to follow the same rules, regulations, and licensing requirements that governments make taxi companies follow. What do you think about this?

4. Would you pay extra for luxury hotel accommodations and services? Why, or why not?

5. What's your opinion about hotels following the movement of guests inside the hotel?

READING COMPREHENSION

1. As a result of travelers preferring to book their own travel online, _____.
   A. travel for business purposes has declined
   B. travelers are booking more tour packages
   C. travel agencies are less popular than they used to be
   D. large companies are booking travel for their employees

2. Which of the following is stated in the reading?
   A. Customers save money when they book online.
   B. Most travelers prefer to print their boarding passes from airline websites.
   C. Home and apartment rentals have become more popular than hotel stays.
   D. Travelers are able to simultaneously book flights, hotels, and rental cars online.

3. Which of the following is an example of changing aircraft technology?
   A. a modification of airplane seating arrangements
   B. the use of carbon fiber materials
   C. an increase in the size of airplane windows
   D. an increase in the number of in-flight entertainment options

4. Biometrics is used at airports to _____.
   A. transmit messages to mobile devices
   B. provide information to travelers
   C. analyze travelers' physical characteristics
   D. monitor the location of baggage

5. Which of the following statements about maglev trains is NOT stated in the reading?
   A. Maglev trains are more energy-efficient than conventional trains.
   B. Maglev trains are able to travel faster than regular trains.
   C. Maglev trains are powered by electricity.
   D. Maglev trains are more expensive to produce and operate than traditional rail vehicles.

6. In paragraph 9, which of the following would be a synonym for *prototype*?
   A. model
   B. diagram
   C. presentation
   D. engine

7. According to the reading, what type of transport is popular with both travelers and local residents?
   A. rental cars
   B. autonomous vehicles
   C. taxis
   D. rideshare vehicles

8. Which paragraph warns of a possible risk that technology may pose to personal privacy?
   A. Paragraph 12
   B. Paragraph 13
   C. Paragraph 14
   D. Paragraph 15

9. Which of the following is predicted in the reading?
   A. Hyperloop trains will become a practical means of transportation in the future.
   B. There will be fewer hotels in the future due to the increased use of online rental services.
   C. With advances in virtual reality, people in the future may travel less.
   D. Driverless cars may lead to an increase in traffic accidents.

10. Of all the technological advances mentioned in the reading, which of the following is not yet in use?
    A. robots
    B. solar powered planes
    C. virtual reality
    D. beacon technology

ACADEMIC VOCABULARY

1. With an increase in the use of teleconferencing, travel for business purposes has _____.
   A. reversed
   B. excluded
   C. declined
   D. suspended

2. The customer would like to know if seat _____ can be done after a flight has been booked.
   A. regulation
   B. selection
   C. structure
   D. registration

3. Many people _____ reviews of hotels from previous guests.
   A. consult
   B. construct
   C. convert
   D. conceive

4. New aircraft designs allow airplanes to _____ greater fuel economy.
   A. contribute
   B. release
   C. resolve
   D. achieve

5. The airline's goal is to reduce the _____ of lost luggage.
   A. implementation
   B. incidence
   C. circumstance
   D. generation

6. High-speed rail travel is an effective _____ of transportation.
   A. framework
   B. structure
   C. media
   D. mode

7. Through the use of magnetic levitation, it is _____ possible for trains to travel faster than jet airplanes.
   A. theoretically
   B. approximately
   C. accurately
   D. consistently

8. Ridesharing has become a popular transportation _____ for many people.
   A. encounter
   B. position
   C. option
   D. outcome

9. Robots are being used in some airports to provide information on weather and flight _____.
   A. schedules
   B. networks
   C. systems
   D. monitors

10. It is predicted that self-driving cars will _____ change the nature of future road travel.
    A. particularly
    B. differently
    C. eventually
    D. exactly

11. An increasing number of hotels are _____ in high-capacity WiFi networks for the convenience of their guests.
    A. establishing
    B. investing
    C. contributing
    D. undertaking

12. In the future, hotel guests will have wearable _____ that a hotel can use to identify them.
    A. structures
    B. implements
    C. displays
    D. devices

13. Rideshare passengers use the service's mobile app to _____ a driver.
    A. require
    B. contact
    C. indicate
    D. transmit

14. Teams of engineers are working on _____ prototypes of future modes of transportation.
    A. creating
    B. undergoing
    C. perceiving
    D. deciding

UNIT 16 LISTENING

PART A

Practice: A B C

1. A B C
2. A B C
3. A B C
4. A B C
5. A B C

PART B

Practice: A B C

1. A B C
2. A B C
3. A B C
4. A B C
5. A B C

Look at pages 236–237 of the core text. Write the correct words to complete the description.

art	columnist	designer	editing	photojournalist	producer	technician
assignment	creating	desktop	illustrator	presentation	reporter	writing
binding	creative	digital	manuscript	printing	stories	

Creative professionals are hard at work. At the publishing company, a _____desktop_____ 1 publisher is laying out a page of an author's _____ 2. An _____ 3 is doing an illustration, and a graphic _____ 4 is designing a publication. At the printing company, a prepress _____ 5 is using a CTP plate maker. A digital press operator is operating _____ 6 equipment, and a finisher is _____ 7 documents. At the advertising and marketing company, the _____ 8 director is meeting with her assistant. In the _____ 9 department, a graphic designer is _____ 10 graphics and a copywriter is _____ 11 ad copy. In the conference room, the creative director is giving a _____ 12 to clients.

A _____ 13 is doing an interview at the scene of a fire and a _____ 14 is taking news photographs. At the newspaper office, the _____ 15 editor is talking to a reporter at the assignment desk, other reporters are writing news _____ 16, an assistant copy editor is _____ 17 copy, and a _____ 18 is writing a column. In the web development department, an online content _____ 19 is creating website content and a digital editor is working with a _____ 20 staff writer.

booth	directing	hooking up	news	report	technician
broadcaster	engineering	meteorologist	operator	session	vocal
camera	field	monitoring	production	studio	weather
desk	giving	musicians	recording	switching	

At the TV _____ 21, a camera _____ 22 is operating a studio camera. Newscasters are reading the _____ 23 at the anchor _____ 24. The _____ 25 is ready to report the _____ 26. On the _____ 27 floor, the floor manager is _____ 28 timing cues. In the production control room, the program director is _____ 29 the program, the broadcast technician is _____ 30 video feeds, and the sound engineer is _____ 31 sound levels. From a remote location, a _____ 32 reporter is doing an on-location _____ 33, a field _____ 34 operator is operating a field camera, and an ENG operator is _____ 35 the remote news feed. At the radio station, a radio _____ 36 is doing a radio broadcast from the broadcast _____ 37 and the radio broadcast _____ 38 is engineering the broadcast. At the music studio, _____ 39 are playing their instruments, a sound technician is _____ 40 sound equipment, a singer is singing in the _____ 41 booth, and in the control room, the _____ 42 engineer is engineering the recording _____ 43.

(continued)

CAREER VOCABULARY

Look at pages 238–239 of the core text. Write the correct words to complete the description.

auditioning	casting	director	Foley	mixer	script
boom	changes	dresser	gaffer	operating	software
cables	clapper	editor	grip	operator	soundstage
cart	creating	evaluating	mix	prop	updating

Many people are involved in movie production. A screenwriter is writing a _____ **44** and a story analyst is _____ **45** it. At this _____ **46** agency, an actor is _____ **47** for a part with an assistant casting director. A movie is being shot on a _____ **48**. An actor and actress are taking direction from the _____ **49**. The _____ **50** is adjusting lighting. The on-set _____ **51** is dressing the set. The _____ **52** is adjusting the camera crane. The camera _____ **53** and her assistant are _____ **54** the camera. The _____ **55** is holding the production slate. The _____ **56** operator is operating the boom microphone. The sound assistant is managing the sound _____ **57**. The assistant _____ **58** master is handling props at the prop _____ **59**. The writer assistant is noting _____ **60** in the script. In the producer's office, the assistant producer is _____ **61** the production schedule. In the post production department, the film _____ **62** and his assistant are using film editing _____ **63** to edit the film and a recording _____ **64** is using rerecording software to _____ **65** audio. In the _____ **66** room, a Foley artist is _____ **67** sound effects.

architectural	carpenter	equipment	lighting	photographer	routine	selecting
artist	ceramic	fashion	marking	photographs	scenery	tape
artist's	choreographer	gels	painter	pottery	sculptor	
building	drafting	glassblower	pattern	rehearsing	sculpture	

Backstage at the theater, a set _____ **68** is building a stage set and a set _____ **69** is painting _____ **70**. On and above the stage, a _____ **71** technician is setting up stage lighting with lighting _____ **72**, an assistant stage manager is _____ **73** the stage with stage marking _____ **74**, and a sound technician is setting up sound _____ **75**. An actor and actress are _____ **76** their lines with the director and an assistant _____ **77** is helping the dancers with their dance _____ **78**.

At the _____ **79** firm, an architectural model maker is _____ **80** an architectural model and a draftsperson is _____ **81** building plans. A _____ **82** is sculpting at the _____ **83** studio. An abstract _____ **84** is painting at the _____ **85** studio. At the glass studio, a _____ **86** is blowing glass, and at the _____ **87** studio, a ceramicist is making _____ **88**. At the _____ **89** design house, a _____ **90** maker is laying out a garment pattern, a fashion _____ **91** is taking fashion _____ **92**, and a buyer is _____ **93** clothing designs for a store.

Using the O*NET Career Exploration Tools at mynextmove.org, search for information about one of the jobs in Unit 17. Write the information in the job profile below. Then prepare and give a presentation about the job.

Job Zone 1 (little or no job preparation)
fashion model

Job Zone 2 (some job preparation)
actor, actress, clapper, finisher, glassblower, intern, on-set dresser, prop master, set carpenter, set dresser, set painter, singer

Job Zone 3 (medium job preparation)
abstract artist, board operator, boom operator, broadcast technician, buyer, camera operator, ceramicist, dancer, desktop publisher, digital press operator, ENG operator, fashion designer, fashion photographer, field camera operator, film editor, Foley artist, gaffer, grip, illustrator, lighting technician, pattern maker, photography assistant, portrait painter, prepress technician, press operator, radio broadcast technician, recording engineer, recording mixer, scenic artist, sculptor, set production assistant, sound assistant, sound engineer, sound technician, web designer, web developer

Job Zone 4 (high job preparation)
architect, architectural model maker, art director, assignment editor, author/writer, CAD operator, casting director, choreographer, columnist, conductor, copywriter, creative director, digital editor, digital staff writer, director, draftsperson, field reporter, floor manager, graphic designer, meteorologist/weather reporter, musician, newscast producer, newscaster, online content producer, photojournalist, producer, program director, prop manager, publication assistant, radio announcer, radio broadcaster, reporter, screenwriter, staffer, stage manager, story analyst/script reader, technical writer, writer assistant

Job Zone 5 (extensive job preparation)
assistant set designer, researcher/archivist, set designer

Job name: _____

What does a person do in this job?

_____

What tools and equipment does a person use in this job?

_____

What skills and abilities are important?

_____

What technology might a person use in this job?

_____

What kind of person will be interested in this work?

_____

What level of education, job training, and experience is required?

_____

What is the job outlook?   What is the average salary?

_____   _____

ON-THE-JOB INSTRUCTIONS

Read the memo to the movie crew and answer the questions.

1 **TO:** All Production Crew
2 **FROM:** Tommy Brewster, 1st Assistant Director
3 **COPY:** Construction, Transportation, Special Effects, and Stunt Coordinators
4 **SUBJECT:** Safety on the Set

GALAXY PICTURES

5 As we begin production today on *Freddy and Fern's Fantastic Zoo*, please review the major safety
6 guidelines covered in last week's Production Safety Orientation and Emergency Action Plan meetings.

7 **Emergency Instructions:**
8 Know the location of emergency equipment, first-aid kits, exits, and evacuation plans in case of an
9 emergency. On-lot and off-lot emergency procedures and nearest hospital locations will be posted on
10 the Stage Safety Poster or Location Safety Poster at the worksite. Alert First-Aid staff immediately if
11 there is an injury.

12 **PPE:**
13 All crew must wear Personal Protective Equipment and fall protection equipment as required, including
14 goggles, masks, gloves, helmets, earplugs, and harnesses.

15 **General Hazards:**
16 Make sure cables in trafficked areas are covered to avoid trip hazards.
17 Keep all work areas and walkways clear of equipment, materials, and trash.
18 Before lifting and moving objects, check them for any hazardous conditions (nails, rough or slippery
19 surfaces, etc.), check the intended path, and get assistance when needed.

20 **Safety Pass certification:**
21 All operators of cranes, dollies, scissor lifts, forklifts, aerial lift platforms, and other specialized equipment
22 must have proper Safety Pass certification for their job classification. (Safety Pass training is obligatory
23 and must be completed before starting work. Safety Pass cards will be checked.)

24 **Equipment Safety:**
25 Do not wear loose sleeves, exposed shirt tails, ties, or other loose clothing when working with or near
26 machinery. Tie back long hair.
27 Do not remove or bypass machine safety guards that protect hands from contact with any moving parts.
28 Do not use any tools or equipment without proper training and certification.

29 **Fall Prevention:**
30 Fall protection equipment must be used when you are working more than 30 inches above the floor
31 (California general work regulation) or 6 feet above the floor (construction regulation) if guardrails or
32 other protection measures are not available.
33 Do not alter scaffolds. All guardrails, mid rails, and toe boards must be in place.
34 Observe ladder safety: Use two hands when climbing, do not stand on the top two rungs, and do not
35 place ladders in or near doorways unless they are protected.

36 **Electricity:**
37 Maintain required overhead clearances to avoid contact with power lines. This applies to ladders,
38 scaffolds, cranes, sets, lifts, and all other equipment. (Off-lot production crew: Be aware that most high
39 voltage power lines are not insulated.)

40 **Special Effects:**
41 All crew members involved with the use of smoke and fog effects should report any unsafe conditions
42 immediately. Interior use of smoke and fog effects will require periodic ventilation of the area, and
43 respirators will be available. Non-essential cast and crew should not be present. School rooms near
44 the set will be vacated and classes moved to another location.
45 Cell phones, radios, and other electronic equipment must not be used during filming of the scenes
46 with explosive devices or other pyrotechnic materials. Only authorized personnel are allowed in the
47 pyrotechnics area.
48 If you are involved in special effects, know the contingency plans and emergency procedures, including

49 hand signs or signals to stop work, primary and alternate escape routes, and the location of fire
50 suppression equipment.

Stunts:
52 Before filming each stunt, a safety meeting will be held and a dry run will be performed. Attendance is
53 mandatory. No performer shall participate in a stunt without prior training and consent.

Animals:
55 Only qualified trainers may work with the animals. A closed-set notice will be posted on the set where
56 animals are working. The trainer will provide any safety instructions to the cast and crew.
57 The use of snakes in several scenes will be the responsibility of a snake handler in possession of the
58 required special permit from the State of California Wildlife Protection Department. Proper clothing
59 protection and barriers will be provided. One day prior to use, the Producer will notify a nearby medical
60 facility so that anti-venom is available.
61 (American Humane Association guidelines on the treatment of animals during film-making will be
62 followed at all times.)

Personal Health:
64 If you feel ill, report this immediately.
65 If you are prescribed medication that may reduce your alertness or work performance, advise your
66 supervisor.
67 The use of alcohol and controlled substances is strictly forbidden.

Safety Training:
69 Every 10 days during production, there will be a short Tool Box Talk on safety. Attendance is
70 compulsory, and you must sign the sign-in sheet.

---

1. What is the purpose of this memo?
   A. to welcome the production crew to Galaxy Pictures
   B. to announce today's safety and emergency plan meetings
   C. to describe past safety incidents and emergencies
   D. to remind the crew about recent safety and emergency training

2. Based on the memo, which statement about the movie production is correct?
   A. Filming will occur at a nearby hospital.
   B. The actors' costumes will include Personal Protective Equipment.
   C. Filming will occur on the set and at another location.
   D. Someone from the Wildlife Protection Department will be present during filming.

3. What are *trafficked areas* as the term is used in Line 16?
   A. areas with lots of cars
   B. areas where people are walking
   C. sections of the lot that look like a street
   D. off-lot locations

4. What is the meaning of *dry run* as the term is used in Line 52?
   A. a safety meeting about a stunt
   B. a stunt that doesn't involve water
   C. a stunt in which no performer participates
   D. a rehearsal for a stunt before it is filmed

5. What will child actors do when smoke and fog special effects are being filmed?
   A. They'll have a school vacation.
   B. They'll watch the special effects at a safe location.
   C. They'll have classes elsewhere.
   D. They won't be present that day.

6. Which word in the memo DOESN'T have the same meaning as *compulsory* as the term is used in Line 70?
   A. forbidden
   B. required
   C. mandatory
   D. obligatory

DEMONSTRATING A PROCEDURE

Using YouTube, WikiHow, or another source, search online for a demonstration of how to do a procedure or operate equipment related to communication and the arts. Write out the instructions. Then prepare a media presentation. Make screenshots of the steps or video-record your demonstration. Present the procedure to the class.
Suggestions: how to use a boom mic; how to build a set; how to use a digital camera; how to make videos with a smartphone; how to design clothes; how to sculpt; how to record a song

Technology Innovations in the Creative Arts

1   Technological advances in recent years have had a major impact on many aspects of life and work, such as communication, commerce, health care, and transportation. The creative arts and related areas of work have also felt the effects of technology, which has changed processes, made work easier and faster, and opened up new and continually evolving possibilities.

Publishing

2   The starting point of creating a piece of writing used to be putting pen or pencil to paper. However, with the development of computers and word processing software, that process for most people now begins with keystrokes on a computer keyboard with text appearing on a screen. Whether in an office setting or at a publishing company, staff members use desktop publishing software to do the editing, formatting, and layout of text and graphics needed to produce finished copy—a final version of a document that is ready for print production. They collaborate with graphic designers to incorporate photos and other graphic elements into documents. Software also makes it easy to experiment with different formatting styles and document designs to achieve the desired look.

3   Documents may also be published in electronic format and offered to readers over the Internet or on websites. Placing materials on the Internet, as an alternative to producing paper copies, greatly expands their availability. Another popular format for publishers to offer books and other print media to customers is through downloads from the Internet to portable electronic reading tablets.

4   As for the writer, new laptop computers have added other modes of input such as touch pads, sketching tools, and handwriting on the screen. Voice recognition technology is also improving, allowing writers to get their words into print by speaking them into voice dictation software.

Graphic Design

5   The biggest technological development in graphic design has been computer graphics software. It is used by illustrators to create graphic

designs and images, and by graphic designers to work with and manipulate drawings, photographs, and other graphic images in electronic format. Graphic designers use typography, color, design themes, and layout to achieve appealing, creative, and sometimes eye-catching effects.   Whether creating logos, advertisements, brochures, or documents, graphic designers use software to work with various types of graphic elements to prepare projects for production.

6   Graphic designers play an important role in the publishing and advertising industries, as well as in electronic media. They contribute to achieving an attractive appearance in print materials such as books, magazines, catalogs, and reports. Modern advertising produced for traditional print media and the Internet relies heavily on computer-based graphic design to communicate a visual message. Product labeling and packaging are also the work of graphic designers.

7   Website design has a strong graphic component, and graphic designers work closely with web designers to create websites that have visual appeal and a consistent style. They have to conceptualize and design the appearance and function of web pages not only for computer browsers but also for mobile devices such as tablets and mobile phones. Graphic design is also an integral part of mobile app development.

Print Journalism

8   Advances in technology have produced significant changes in the way news is reported and published. Computers, tablets, mobile phones, digital recording devices, and digital cameras are standard equipment for the reporters and photojournalists who gather the news. Journalists e-mail their stories to editors who review and edit them. Page designers for a newspaper or magazine take these articles along with materials from the art department and advertising department and decide on the content to include in the newspaper or magazine edition they are creating. They plan pages and pass them on to the pre-press or layout department, where desktop publishers, graphic designers, and editors use desktop publishing software to assemble the content and lay out pages on computers, preparing them for publication.

9   The most profound impact of the digital age on journalism is the move of newspapers from traditional print editions to the production of online versions, or web editions. Digital documents and materials from editors and layout staff are sent to the web development department, where digital writers and editors produce versions of the publication that are designed for web pages and mobile devices such as tablets and mobile phones. This trend has had a significant effect on distribution and sales. As publications became available online, many people stopped buying newspapers and magazines. With drastic drops in subscription levels, newspaper companies have lost money and have been forced to reduce their staffing. Many companies have struggled to survive, and in fact some now only publish online.

Television and Radio Broadcasting

10   Television is based on technology, from the cameras that capture images, to the systems that broadcast them, to the devices that receive and display them. Recent advances in technology have led to changes in the equipment, processes, and systems that produce and deliver television broadcasts to the viewing public. Examples are the changeover to digital broadcasting, which is an improved system of transmitting electronic

television signals, and the high-definition television system now in common use that produces images with higher resolution, resulting in a clearer and more detailed picture.

11   In the television studio, broadcast technicians and sound engineers produce live broadcasts or record segments and edit them into a broadcast presentation. The video is then sent to equipment that prepares it for broadcast through various systems. For traditional broadcasts, electronic signals are sent to transmitters that produce radio waves that are picked up by antennas attached to television sets. Cable TV delivers broadcasts directly to television sets either as electrical signals through coaxial cables or as light pulses through fiber optic cables. With satellite TV, signals are sent to communications satellites orbiting above the Earth and are transmitted back down to home satellite dishes that are connected to customers' television sets. Internet TV involves the digital distribution of broadcast television through video streaming technology.

12   Another recent innovation in television is augmented reality. This technology allows special visual effects to be added to or superimposed onto real images. Common examples are the arrows and other graphics that are added to live weather broadcasts, and lines and scores added to sports broadcasts. Another technology is virtual advertising through digital replacement of ads, such as those on panels surrounding sports fields that can be changed to relate to specific audiences.

13   There have been many developments in the television set display systems that viewers use to watch broadcasts. The standard television set now uses LCD (liquid-crystal-display) technology. A new system, OLED (organic light-emitting diode), has been developed that has many advantages over LCD screens, and it may become the new standard system in the future. Display resolution is also improving, with HD (high-definition) and UHD (ultra-high-definition) TV screens providing very sharp, clear pictures. Smart TVs that have a built-in Internet connection and interactive features are becoming popular.

14   There have also been advances in radio broadcast technology. One is the high-definition digital radio system, which produces higher sound quality. Another is satellite radio, where broadcasts are sent to satellites and transmitted to Earth, reaching a large geographical area. Broadcasting radio on the Internet is called webcasting and involves streaming audio. Podcasting offers stored digital audio files that listeners download from websites and play on computers, mobile phones, or other devices.

Music Production

15   Technology plays a big role in music production. In recording studios, sound technicians carefully set up microphones in the right locations and adjust recording levels. The recording engineer uses a mixing board to control and manage the sound input from the performance to achieve the best sound quality and balance.

16   Two recent innovations have had a great impact on the music industry. One is computer software for digital music production, which allows anyone to produce music without a studio, without technicians, and even without musicians! Synthesizers can be used to produce sounds electronically, including imitating musical instruments. Everything can be created and put together on a computer using this software.

17   The other major innovation is the Internet. Until recently, the public purchased music from recording companies that signed up musical artists and recorded and sold their performances. Now artists have ways to produce their own music and release

it to the public on the Internet through websites and music streaming services, not just through old media formats such as albums and CDs. This new development gives exposure to many more artists than before and allows the public to hear a greater variety of music. At the same time, it diminishes the power of recording companies to create and profit from musical celebrities.

Movie Production

18   Technology has always been behind the scenes in movie-making, from the sophisticated camera, sound, and lighting equipment used in the filming or recording of a movie, to the machines used in editing and producing it. As anyone who watches movies knows, technology is often "in your face" in the form of computer-generated imagery used to depict special effects, simulations of reality, and fantasy scenes. Images are created with 3-D (three-dimensional) computer-generated graphics, and motion is achieved through computer animation. One method of computer animation is motion capture, a process in which the natural movements of a live actor are recorded to a computer and applied to an animated figure to create realistic movement. Advances in computer technology have made these processes easier and cheaper over time.

19   A major changeover is underway in cinematography, from the original film-based process using photography to digital electronics.

Digital movies have several advantages over film: Editing and adding digital effects is easier, they are easily distributed, they are easy to reproduce and store, and overall costs are lower. Movie theaters are now using digital projectors to show movies.

20 In recent years, 3-D movies have been regaining popularity. This technology normally involves a stereoscopic process using a special camera system that records a scene from two perspectives, and is usually not computer generated. Viewers in theaters wear special glasses that enable them to see images that seem to stand out from the screen. Advancements in technology are expected to bring improvements to 3-D systems for movies and also for television.

Theater

21 New technologies are being used in theater productions in various ways. Digital video projections onto stage sets serve not only as backdrops but as integrated elements of the performance. In digital theater, productions might incorporate video, computer-created effects, 3-D animation, and even virtual reality into performances. Video designers who use computer software to achieve special visual effects are part of the production team in some modern theater companies.

Architecture

22 Technology is an integral part of architecture, from design to construction. Computer-aided design (CAD) and computer-aided architectural design (CAAD) software programs are used by architects and draftspersons to create architectural drawings of buildings and other constructions based on the architect's preliminary planning and design. CAAD systems allow for depictions of designs through 3-D renderings. Building information modeling (BIM) is a new computer technology used in building development that allows for more sophisticated pre-visualization of structures. The system creates a comprehensive 3-D model of a building and can communicate the detailed information it contains about the overall structure and its components. Other methods for visualizing building projects are virtual reality (VR) tools used to give tours within VR building models and augmented reality depictions of a building design placed into a real-life setting. With the new systems, structures with shapes and designs previously thought unbuildable are being constructed.

3-D printing in the construction industry

23 In many parts of the world, a computer-controlled 3-D printing process is being used to construct buildings. Thin layers of wet concrete are laid down through a long tube according to a programmed building design. The layers build up one on top of another to form walls of any shape and design. An entire house can be built in days. Other innovations include using robots to do repetitive or dangerous construction work, and using drones—unmanned aerial vehicles—to help with construction in areas that are difficult to reach.

Visual Arts

24 Technology is influencing the visual arts in many ways. Although many artists continue to use traditional media and materials to produce

drawings and paintings, some are using computers, imaging software, and other modern technology as tools to create a diverse range of artworks. These new developments have prompted debate among artists as well as the viewing public on the role and importance of traditional skills versus technological abilities.

25 In contemporary art, artists are increasingly using technology itself as art, such as programmed lighting systems that produce visual effects, and images generated from data on atmospheric conditions translated into shapes and colors. Sometimes artists' work involves interaction with viewers. Visitors in a gallery move through laser lights and create visual effects, or move their hands on interactive panels to create light patterns, or manipulate displays on video screens through interactive animation.

26 The future of technology in art, and technology as art, is limited only by our imaginations.

DID YOU UNDERSTAND?

1. What is desktop publishing software used for?

2. What are some examples of materials graphic designers help produce?

3. What major impact has the Internet had on journalism?

4. What are some of the different ways television is delivered to viewers?

5. What is augmented reality?

6. What are smart TVs?

7. How does podcasting work?

8. What two innovations have had a significant effect on the music industry?

9. What are some examples of new technologies in movie-making?

10. What is a video backdrop in a theater production?

11. How are computer technologies used in architectural design?

12. In the last sentence, what is meant by "technology in art, and technology as art"?

WHAT'S YOUR EXPERIENCE?

1. From what sources do you get your news—printed newspapers and magazines, online sites, radio, or TV?

2. Do you or does your family get a newspaper delivered to your home? Do you have a subscription to an online edition of a newspaper? If you do, why?

3. How do you get television at your house?

4. Do you listen to podcasts? If you do, what do you like to listen to?

5. Do you buy music? If you do, how do you buy it?

WHAT'S YOUR OPINION?

1. Do you think newspapers are important? Why?

2. What do you think about music that is produced electronically instead of by musicians playing instruments? Does it make a difference to you?

3. What do you think of computer-generated special effects in movies?

4. Do you think traditional artistic skills will decline in society as computer technology advances?

READING COMPREHENSION

1. Creating and arranging electronic images is commonly done using _____.
   A. word processing software
   B. desktop publishing software
   C. computer graphics software
   D. sketching tools

2. Sales of newspapers and magazines have been adversely affected by _____.
   A. technological innovations in news reporting
   B. innovations in desktop publishing
   C. reductions in newspaper staffing
   D. the switch to web editions of publications

3. Options for transmission of television broadcasts are described in _____.
   A. Paragraph 10
   B. Paragraph 11
   C. Paragraph 12
   D. Paragraph 13

4. Which of the following innovations has had the greatest impact on the distribution of music?
   A. the use of computer software for digital music production
   B. the use of synthesizers to produce electronic sounds
   C. music streaming services
   D. albums and CDs

5. Which of the following is an example of what the author refers to as *in your face* movie technology?
   A. computer-generated imagery
   B. sophisticated camera, sound, and lighting equipment
   C. digital projectors
   D. digital electronic cinematography

6. Which of the following would provide an architect with the LEAST amount of information about what a building structure would actually look like?
   A. CAD
   B. CAAD
   C. BIM
   D. VR

7. Lighting systems that produce visual effects are an example of the use of _____.
   A. traditional media
   B. imaging software
   C. technology as art
   D. interactive animation

8. According to the reading, voice recognition technology is useful in the area of _____.
   A. theater
   B. television
   C. publishing
   D. music production

9. In which of the following areas does the use of technology provide the consumer different options for accessing the same product?
   A. Graphic design
   B. Theater
   C. Movie production
   D. Print journalism

10. What point does the author make about technology and the creative arts?
    A. Technology has brought restrictions as well as advances to the creative arts.
    B. Technology has not only facilitated work processes but has influenced the creative arts.
    C. Technology has made work in the creative arts both challenging and rewarding.
    D. Technology has enabled the creative arts to have a more positive impact on society.

ACADEMIC VOCABULARY

1. Producing digital versions of books greatly _____ their availability to the public.
   A. demands
   B. expands
   C. implements
   D. releases

2. There have been many improvements to voice recognition _____ in recent years.
   A. technology
   B. analysis
   C. perception
   D. communication

3. The transition of newspapers from print to online editions has had a major _____ on journalism.
   A. circumstance
   B. consequence
   C. outcome
   D. impact

4. Digital television is able to produce clear images with extremely high _____.
   A. implementation
   B. capacity
   C. resolution
   D. concentration

5. Technicians and sound engineers _____ recorded segments for broadcast presentation.
   A. edit
   B. contain
   C. decide
   D. involve

6. Advertising content can be modified to relate to the needs and interests of _____ audiences.
   A. approximate
   B. precise
   C. specific
   D. virtual

7. Sound technicians in recording studios set up microphones and _____ recording levels.
   A. acquire
   B. adjust
   C. justify
   D. construct

8. Recording artists are now able to produce their own music and _____ it to the public on the Internet.
   A. allow
   B. assign
   C. release
   D. transport

9. Special 3-D glasses _____ viewers in theaters to see three-dimensional images on the screen.
   A. enhance
   B. enforce
   C. ensure
   D. enable

10. Some theater productions _____ video and computer-assisted effects into stage performances.
    A. apply
    B. incorporate
    C. depict
    D. generate

11. A variety of software programs are used by architects to _____ realistic drawings of buildings.
    A. undergo
    B. conduct
    C. specify
    D. create

12. The use of robots and drones in the construction industry is a recent _____.
    A. outcome
    B. innovation
    C. tradition
    D. visualization

13. With the aid of modern technological tools, artists have the ability to produce a _____ range of artistic works.
    A. diverse
    B. dominant
    C. fundamental
    D. contemporary

14. These days there is a strong graphic _____ in website design.
    A. exhibition
    B. concept
    C. component
    D. implement

UNIT 17 LISTENING

PART A

Practice: A B C   3. A B C
     1. A B C   4. A B C
     2. A B C   5. A B C

PART B

Practice: A B C   3. A B C
     1. A B C   4. A B C
     2. A B C   5. A B C

Look at pages 258–259 of the core text. Write the correct words to complete the description.

attaching	climbers	hard hat	lineperson	pulling	technician
backfilling	climbing	hooking	lines	set	trench
bucket	dig	installers	modem	shovel	trencher
cell tower	dropping	laying down	programming	smoke	utility

Telecommunications workers are busy today. A telecommunications ___lineperson___ [1] has just drilled a hole for a _____ [2] pole and another is helping him _____ [3] the pole in place. A line installer wearing a lineman _____ [4], lineman belt, and pole _____ [5] is _____ [6] a utility pole. Another has been raised by a _____ [7] truck to the top of a utility pole where he is _____ [8] a cable to a strain suspension insulator. Many of the linepersons are working on a _____ [9]. One is using a ride-on _____ [10] to _____ [11] the trench, another is _____ [12] cable from a cable spool, another is _____ [13] conduit, and another is _____ [14] the trench using a long handle _____ [15]. In addition, a cell tower climber is working on a _____ [16]. In someone's home, phone company _____ [17] are wiring a telephone socket outlet, installing a residential _____ [18], and testing phone _____ [19]. A cable company installer is _____ [20] coaxial cable down a wall and another is _____ [21] a cable remote. Security installers are installing a _____ [22] detector and _____ [23] up an alarm control box. Outside, a telecommunications _____ [24] is working on a CMTS relay junction pedestal.

analyst	coding	handset	lines	outlet	receiver	software
attaching	creating	installers	offering	pulling	replying	typing
call center	customer	installing	office	reading	screwing	

Satellite TV _____ [25] are _____ [26] a satellite TV system at a company. One is _____ [27] a satellite disk mounting arm and connecting a feedhorn to the dish. Another is programming the satellite _____ [28]. A telecommunications technician is connecting a phone to a wall _____ [29]. There are several PBX installers doing different tasks. They're _____ [30] in phone features, attaching a _____ [31] to a speaker phone, _____ [32] on a PBX trunk where phone _____ [33] will be attached, and customizing PBX _____ [34]. At the central relay _____ [35], a voice communication _____ [36] is testing a line for a phone company installer, and a central office technician is _____ [37] out a switch. At the 611 _____ [38], a 611 customer service assistant is _____ [39] a customer service case number for a mobile phone _____ [40]. Another is _____ [41] to a customer's online question. At the 711 call center, a 711 relay client is _____ [42] in a message on a TTY device and the 711 communication assistant is _____ [43] it. At the telecommunications sales center, a telecommunications sales associate is _____ [44] an upgrade to a customer.

Using the O*NET Career Exploration Tools at mynextmove.org, search for information about one of the jobs in Unit 18. Write the information in the job profile below. Then prepare and give a presentation about the job.

Job Zone 2 (some job preparation)
611 customer service assistant, 711 communication assistant, 711 relay operator, customer service assistant, fiber optic cable installer, line installer, telecommunications lineperson, telecommunications sales associate, TTY/TDD 711 relay operator/711 communication assistant

Job Zone 3 (medium job preparation)
cable (company) installer, cell tower climber, central office technician, PBX installer, phone company installer, satellite TV installer, security/fire alarm installer, telecommunications installer, telecommunications technician, voice communication analyst

Job name: _____

What does a person do in this job?

_____

_____

_____

_____

What tools and equipment does a person use in this job?

_____

What skills and abilities are important?

_____

_____

What technology might a person use in this job?

_____

What kind of person will be interested in this work?

_____

What level of education, job training, and experience is required?

_____

_____

What is the job outlook?   What is the average salary?

_____   _____

A Cable Company Executive

1 I'm Audre Reed, an executive with the HomeNet Cable Company. My position is Vice President for Community Sales. In this role, I manage our company's program to provide low-cost Internet service to eligible low-income customers.

2 Through a government program, we're able to offer qualified customers a 10 mbps (megabits per second) connection for just $9.95 a month. An in-home WiFi setup is included, which allows multiple devices in the home to be used without wired connections. Customers can also buy an inexpensive desktop computer or laptop for just $149.99.

3 In addition to the connectivity and the equipment, qualified customers have access to our online education website, which offers tutorials for learning how to use email and social networking sites, how to research information on the World Wide Web, how to protect your privacy online, and other topics.

4 Several categories of people are permitted to participate in the program:

- Families that have a child who qualifies for the National School Lunch Program;
- Families or individuals that receive housing assistance through federal programs;
- Students who receive Pell Grants for college and who are enrolled in 2-year community colleges in certain states; and
- Seniors age 62 and older who receive public assistance and live in certain metropolitan areas.

5 You might say I attained this position by accident—literally. I started with the company many years ago as a residential installer. Then after a fall off a ladder on the job—fortunately, not too serious—I decided my years as an installer were over. I enjoyed working at the company and the contact with customers, so they offered me a position as a sales associate. By my second year in that role, I had the highest sales and was the top performer nationwide. One year later, when the company started offering the basic level of service to low-income customers, I was tapped to head up the program and promoted to my current position. In this information age, Internet connectivity is as important as electricity and clean water. I'm glad to play a role in making this available to our customers regardless of income.

---

1. Which term in the article DOESN'T refer to the customers who can participate in the program that is described?
A. eligible
B. qualified
C. attained
D. permitted

2. What is the meaning of *top performer* as used in paragraph 5?
A. busiest
B. most popular
C. highest paid
D. most successful

3. What best describes the person's attitude toward the accident that happened on the job?
A. It was a serious injury.
B. It led to her new successful role.
C. She didn't enjoy working as an installer anyway.
D. She was sorry to leave her installer position.

4. How does paragraph 5 contribute to the article?
A. It describes the person's career pathway.
B. It describes many different positions at the company.
C. It provides details about the person's job.
D. It provides information about Internet services for low-income customers

CLASSROOM VISITOR

Invite an employee of a cable TV, satellite TV, or Internet service provider to visit your class—an installer, a sales associate, a customer service assistant, or other worker. Ask about the types of jobs available in the person's company, the training required for different jobs, the working conditions, the opportunities for advancement, and how jobs in this industry are expected to change in the future. (Or, use job search websites on the Internet to find out what kind of positions in the telecommunications industry are available in your area.)

From the Telegraph to Fiber Optics:
A Short History of Telecommunications

1   Throughout human history, people have devised ways of communicating across long distances. In early times, fire and smoke signals transmitted alerts, networks of fire beacons relayed warnings, and drumbeats conveyed meaning. Later, tall structures were built with movable arms that could form visual signals representing letters to spell words. Such systems had very limited capabilities.

2   Modern telecommunications began in the 1830s with the invention of communication systems powered by electricity. The prefix *tele* is derived from a Greek word meaning at a distance, and is a component of the words *tele*communications— communicating at a distance; *tele*graph—writing at a distance; *tele*phone—sound across distance; and television—sight across distance. As systems of telecommunication have evolved and improved, reaching farther and wider and moving faster, they have influenced society and even shaped history itself.

The Telegraph

3   The first successful telecommunication system was the telegraph, a system that sent messages letter by letter over wires. After earlier experimentation by European scientists, British and American inventors developed workable electric telegraph systems in 1837. The telegraph developed by American Samuel Morse and other collaborators became the standard system, and its use spread to countries around the world.

4   The telegraph system used a basic electrical circuit, made up of a copper wire and a battery, that would be opened and closed. An operator pushed down a key that completed the circuit and sent an electrical signal to a receiver at the other end of the wire. A code of long and short signals was created to represent letters that together would spell words. The signals received were at first marked on a paper tape; later operators just had to listen to the clicks of the receiver. Skilled operators could quickly send and transcribe messages, which were called telegrams. Later improvements included a

Morse Code

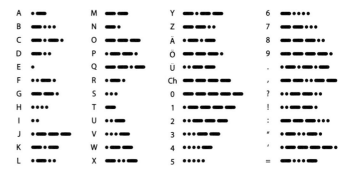

The Morse code system of transmitting information is named for Samuel F.B. Morse, inventor of the telegraph.

printing telegraph that could print out messages typographically.

5   Cities were soon connected by telegraph wires, and in 1861 a telegraph line reaching across the United States from coast to coast was completed. In 1866, a cable of copper telegraph wires was laid under the Atlantic Ocean from Ireland to Newfoundland, Canada that established fast communication between Europe and North America. Messages that had taken 12 days to send by ship could now be transmitted in just a few hours. In the decades that followed, cables were laid under oceans and across continents, and the world became electronically connected. These accomplishments were celebrated by the public as momentous history-making events.

Alexander Graham Bell at the opening of the long-distance line from New York to Chicago in 1892.

The Telephone

6   After the success of the telegraph, inventors in several European countries and in the United States worked on developing a system to send voice over wires using electricity. In 1876, the Scottish-born scientist and inventor Alexander Graham Bell, who had emigrated to the United States, designed the first practical telephone, and transmitted a spoken message to his assistant in another room. Later that year he made the first long-distance telephone call, across a distance of ten miles.

7   The device consisted of two parts, a mouthpiece and a receiver, connected by a wire. Speaking into the mouthpiece produced vibrations that induced electric currents. These currents passed through the wire to an electromagnet in the receiver that caused vibrations, producing sound for the listener to hear.

8   Soon another major advance took place–– the invention of the telephone exchange, or switchboard, which allowed phone lines to be connected to each other. As a result, telephone lines were strung from poles crisscrossing communities and connecting cities across the United States, and the public switched network was formed. Telephone communications was on its way to becoming the important industry it still is today.

9   Early wireless mobile phone services were developed for use in cars in the late 1940s. However, it wasn't until the 1980s when advances in wireless technology resulted in the establishment

of cell towers that were able to receive and relay phone signals to other mobile (or cell) phones. The first hand-held phones were large and heavy, but with continual technological advances in electronics, mobile phones have decreased in size and increased in capability, to where they are now more like small, hand-held computers. Mobile phones have become the primary means for common informal communication, including not only voice but SMS (short message service) text messaging.

Wireless Telegraphy

10   In the late 19th century, inventors were experimenting with newly discovered electromagnetic waves, or radio waves. Building on their work, a young Italian inventor, Guglielmo Marconi, developed a system to transmit radio waves through the air. He took his invention to England, and in 1897 showed that it could transmit Morse code signals over long distances. Also called radiotelegraphy, it became a useful way of communicating with ships at sea. Marconi's invention prepared the way for the next innovation— the radio.

Radio

11   Many inventors worked on ways to transmit sound and voices using radio waves. The Canadian-born inventor Reginald Fessenden developed new devices and systems to send audio over electromagnetic radio waves. In 1906, he made the first public broadcast in the new communication

medium called radio. Technical challenges prevented wider use of radio until the development of vacuum tubes around 1914. The potential for military use of radio in World War I also spurred development. After the war, many local radio stations were set up and began broadcasting—sending out signals that transmitted their programs. With the large-scale manufacture and sale of radio receivers in the 1920s, radio audiences grew, and broadcasts of news, music, drama, comedy shows, and other entertainment became very popular.

12 Following the invention of transistors (small electronic devices that replaced bulky and delicate vacuum tubes), production of portable transistor radios began in the 1950s. They became extremely popular and changed people's listening habits. Portable listening devices have continued to improve over the years. Recent developments in radio broadcast technology include high-definition digital radio, which produces higher sound quality; satellite radio, where broadcasts are sent to satellites and transmitted back to Earth; and radio programming transmitted over the Internet.

13 A special use of radio technology for voice communication is the two-way radio. A Canadian inventor created a portable radio signaling system in 1937. A special model called a "walkie-talkie" was developed for the U.S. military and used effectively in World War II. Two-way radios are still used in police and public safety work and other situations where a private channel is needed that can provide immediate communication to individuals or groups. This type of radio technology is also used in wireless PA (public address) systems to broadcast announcements over loudspeakers.

Television

14 Radio transmitted sound through the air. The next challenge was to send images. In the 1920s, European and American inventors were experimenting with systems that converted images into electrical signals and transmitted them through the air using radio waves. The systems used cathode rays (streams of electrons in vacuum tubes) to convert images in cameras into electronic signals for transmission and to create black-and-

white images in receivers. Elements of the various inventions were combined in later systems, and by the late 1940s, television sets were being mass-produced and television broadcasting became widespread. Within a short time, television sets became common fixtures in homes, and TV programming, including news and entertainment shows, became an important and influential means of communication on a wide scale.

15 Advances in the 1960s made broadcasting in color possible. The next major technological development, in the 2000s, was digital television, which processes audio and video signals in a different way and transmits higher quality pictures (HDTV—high definition TV). About the same time, manufacturers of television sets changed from cathode-ray picture tubes to flat panels, now most commonly using liquid-crystal display (LCD) technology. Broadcast technology has also evolved over time from the original system of sending signals over the air to antennas at individual homes. Other options now include cable television, which delivers signals through cables that connect to television sets; satellite TV, in which signals are transmitted first to satellites and then back down to satellite dish receivers; and webcasting of television programming delivered through video streaming on the Internet, often directly to "smart TVs."

The Teleprinter

16 The teleprinter, or teletypewriter, evolved from earlier machines that attempted to transmit written messages, such as the printing telegraph. Teleprinter operators typed messages on an alphabetic keyboard, and the text was sent to a connected teleprinter, where the message was

automatically typed out. Like the telegraph, teleprinters used a transmission system that involved opening and closing an electrical circuit, but the coding was done internally in the machine.

17 To move beyond point-to-point transmissions, networks of teleprinters called Telex systems (from "telegraph exchange") were established through which customers could deliver messages to any other teleprinter in the system. Telex service began in Europe and in the late 1940s spread around the world. It became the most common way for governments and businesses to send text-based messages long distances, and was in use up until the Internet era.

Fax

18 Various types of machines were invented in the 19th century that attempted to transmit print and pictures through wires over long distances. Fax (from the word facsimile) machines were improved over time, and by the 1960s a technology was developed that allowed documents to be sent over telephone lines. In the sending function, a scanner scans a printed page line-by-line, reading the black marks. The machine transmits this information to the receiving fax machine, which recreates the same patterns of black print on a piece of paper, producing an exact copy of the document that was sent.

19 Modern technology that involves scanning documents and e-mailing them over the Internet has been replacing faxing for many purposes. However, faxes are often still used where security is important, such as in personal health care and legal communications, because fax transmissions are more difficult to intercept than e-mails. Faxes can now conveniently be sent using computers and mobile phone apps instead of from traditional fax machines.

The Internet

20 The Internet has brought about major changes in communications systems. E-mail, an electronic mail system, was developed in early computer networks and came into wide use in the 1980s. It has surpassed physical mailing as a method of sending letters, documents, and other forms of text, and has replaced telexes. New methods of electronic communication are continuously being devised. Social media websites and mobile phone apps offer messaging services, and are widely used for communicating informally with other people anywhere in the world. Radio, television, movies, and videos are now commonly transmitted over the Internet to computers and mobile devices. Websites on the World Wide Web are now the most common way for organizations and businesses to disseminate information, and they comprise a huge repository of data that is available for public access.

21 A recently developed method of transmitting voice communications called Voice over Internet Protocol (VoIP), or IP telephony, delivers electronic signals to telephones over the Internet rather than through the standard public switched network of telephone lines. VoIP is cheaper to use and can carry both voice and data over the same network. Internationally, most private branch exchange (PBX) systems that connect a business or organization's internal telephones to the outside public switched network are increasingly changing over to VoIP. The growing use of VoIP for voice communication services is presenting a challenge to traditional telephone companies.

THE PHOTOPHONE

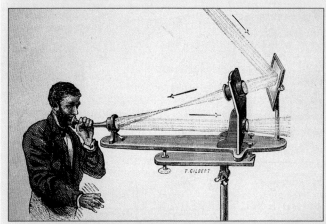

Alexander Graham Bell is famous for inventing the telephone. But he was most proud of another device he and his assistant invented—the photophone. In 1880, with this simple device, they transmitted human voice on a beam of sunlight between two buildings in Washington, D.C. It was the first long-distance wireless voice communication, and a precursor to the fiber-optic communications of 100 years later.

An Interconnected World

22   The first transoceanic electronic communications were made possible by undersea cables that carried telegraph signals across the Atlantic. By 1903 cables had circled the Earth, creating the first global communications network. The first transatlantic telephone cable was laid in 1956, but the copper wires of early cables had a small carrying capacity. In modern optical fiber cables, developed in the 1980s, light signals carry large flows of data communications traffic through glass fibers efficiently and at high speeds. By the early 2000s, a transcontinental and intercontinental network of high-capacity optical fiber cable had been completed.

23   In 1962, the first in a series of direct relay communications satellites was launched. They were used in making intercontinental long-distance telephone connections. Over the following years, many nations placed satellites in orbit to improve communications in remote areas of their countries. Satellites are also used for television, Internet data transmissions, and GPS (the global positioning system).

24   From the depths of the oceans to the upper reaches of the skies, the world is connected by communications networks that are able to transmit information instantaneously . . . anywhere, anytime. Will the limitless capability of telecommunications bring to society a new level of knowledge and understanding or a massive information overload?

DID YOU UNDERSTAND?

1. A telephone is an instrument that transmits sound across distance. What is the name of an instrument that is used to see objects that are far away, such as the moon? (Hint: It contains the word *scope*, meaning *view*.)

2. What was the first successful telecommunications system?

3. How were telegraph and telephone messages sent across oceans?

4. What is a telephone exchange?

5. What is another term for text messaging?

6. What is broadcasting?

7. How did early television systems work?

8. What are some examples of ways television programming is delivered to viewers?

9. How were formal written communications and documents sent electronically over long distances before the Internet and e-mail?

10. What advantage do optical fiber cables have over copper wires?

WHAT'S YOUR EXPERIENCE?

1. How do you most often communicate with other people at a distance—by e-mail, by phone calls, by text messaging, through social media sites, or in some other way?

2. What telephone service do you have at home? Do you have a home phone (a land line), or only a mobile phone? If you have both, how do you use each one?

3. If you have a television at home, how do you receive television programs—by antenna, cable TV, Internet, or some other way?

READING COMPREHENSION

1. Electronic connection throughout the world was first made possible when _____.
   A. the telegraph was invented
   B. telegraph messages were able to be typed out typographically
   C. wire cables were laid across continents and under oceans
   D. telegraph lines were set up to connect cities

2. Which of the following enabled people to communicate with each other wirelessly?
   A. the invention of the switchboard
   B. the establishment of cell towers
   C. the use of electromagnets
   D. the establishment of a public switched network

3. Which paragraph describes how the decrease in size of a product resulted in an increase in sales?
   A. Paragraph 10
   B. Paragraph 11
   C. Paragraph 12
   D. Paragraph 13

4. What is the meaning of the word *process* based on its use in paragraph 15?
   A. handle
   B. protect
   C. change
   D. provide

5. Webcasting of television programs was made possible through _____.
   A. signals sent to television antennas
   B. video streaming on the Internet
   C. cables connected to television sets
   D. satellite dishes

6. The goal for teleprinters to "move beyond" point-to-point transmissions was to enable _____.
   A. direct message delivery
   B. fast message delivery
   C. automatic message delivery
   D. message delivery to multiple teleprinters

7. According to the reading, what is an advantage of faxing compared to scanning and e-mailing important documents?
   A. Fax communication is faster than e-mail communication.
   B. Fax machines are able to depict both printed text and images.
   C. Faxed documents are less likely to be intercepted than scanned documents.
   D. Faxing can be done by using either mobile apps or fax machines.

8. Which paragraph describes a recent innovation that can save consumers money?
   A. Paragraph 20
   B. Paragraph 21
   C. Paragraph 22
   D. Paragraph 23

9. Which of the following has made communication accessible in every part of the world?
   A. communications satellites
   B. transoceanic cables
   C. fiber optic cables
   D. intercontinental cable connections

10. In what way was Alexander Graham Bell's photophone a *precursor* of contemporary fiber-optic communication?
    A. It was not a complex device.
    B. It used fibers for transmission.
    C. It transmitted voices across a distance.
    D. It used light to transmit voices.

ACADEMIC VOCABULARY

1. Early communication systems had very limited _____.
   A. relations
   B. approaches
   C. capabilities
   D. circumstances

2. Telecommunication systems have significantly _____ over the centuries.
   A. evolved
   B. induced
   C. proceeded
   D. emerged

3. Alexander Graham Bell _____ the first practical telephone.
   A. functioned
   B. designed
   C. revealed
   D. initiated

4. An early telephone device _____ of a mouthpiece and receiver, connected by a wire.
   A. contained
   B. comprised
   C. conceived
   D. consisted

5. Inventors in the 19th century searched for ways to _____ sound and voices.
   A. obtain
   B. transmit
   C. promote
   D. release

6. The prefix *tele* is _____ from a Greek word meaning *at a distance*.
   A. detected
   B. initiated
   C. interpreted
   D. derived

7. Scientists saw a great _____ for the use of radio in the military.
   A. dimension
   B. indication
   C. potential
   D. inclination

8. A system was developed to _____ images in cameras into electronic signals.
   A. convert
   B. create
   C. operate
   D. produce

9. Teleprinters use a transmission system that _____ the opening and closing of an electrical circuit.
   A. involves
   B. evolves
   C. connects
   D. provides

10. At the time, the invention of the switchboard was a _____ advance in communication.
    A. challenging
    B. mature
    C. major
    D. predominant

11. By the late 1940s, television broadcasting had become _____.
    A. experimental
    B. automatic
    C. fundamental
    D. widespread

12. The introduction of digital television was a major _____ development.
    A. typographical
    B. technological
    C. ideological
    D. theoretical

13. Mobile phones have become the _____ means of information communication.
    A. primary
    B. accurate
    C. equivalent
    D. original

14. New _____ of electronic communication are continuously being devised.
    A. symbols
    B. limitations
    C. methods
    D. structures

UNIT 18 LISTENING

PART A			
Practice: A B C		3. A B C	
1. A B C		4. A B C	
2. A B C		5. A B C	

PART B			
Practice: A B C		3. A B C	
1. A B C		4. A B C	
2. A B C		5. A B C	

Look at pages 272–273 of the core text. Write the correct words to complete the description.

adapter	bundling	entering	punching	scanning	specialist	training
attaching	cables	hard	reviewing	schematic	technical	virus
box	drive	loading	router	security	text	

This company is upgrading its technology! A network engineer is _____reviewing_____ [1] a LAN

_____ [2] with the computer administrator. Computer service technicians are doing many tasks.

They're _____ [3] and banding CAT cables, fishing CAT6 _____ [4] through walls,

adding _____ [5] drives to a RAID, _____ [6] down a patch panel, attaching a wireless

_____ [7] to a modem, and installing an internal network _____ [8]. Computer

installers are also doing a variety of tasks. They're connecting a computer to a data floor _____ [9],

connecting an external _____ [10] to a computer, and _____ [11] a monitor with a DVI

cable. A _____ [12] support specialist is _____ [13] software. An information systems

security _____ [14] is installing _____ [15] detection and network _____ [16]

software. One technical support specialist is _____ [17] an employee on new software. Another is

_____ [18] a document. A date entry keyer is _____ [19] data. An information

processing worker is capturing _____ [20] in an OCR program.

answering	designing	helping	recommending	screen	studio	tester
chat	develop	measuring	repair	software	technicians	UI artists
code	disk	order	repairing	storyboards	test	writing
composing	help	programmers	room			

At a computer repair and support center, customer support specialists are _____ [21] customers.

One is running a diagnostic _____ [22], another is writing up a repair _____ [23],

and another is _____ [24] the proper cable to a customer. At the help desk, one of the

_____ [25] desk technicians is _____ [26] technical support questions while the other

is having a live _____ [27] session with a customer. In the computer _____ [28] lab,

computer repair _____ [29] are doing many things. They're changing a hard _____ [30],

adding RAM, replacing a touch _____ [31] digitizer on a tablet, and _____ [32] voltage on

a motherboard. In the data recovery _____ [33], a data recovery specialist is _____ [34]

a hard disk drive. In a programming department, computer _____ [35] are writing programming

source _____ [36] and developing debugging _____ [37]. At a digital development

_____ [38], game designers are _____ [39] video games, _____ [40] are

designing video game graphics, and video game music composers are _____ [41] music. A mobile

app developer is using framework software to _____ [42] apps and a mobile app designer is creating

game _____ [43]. Apps and games are also being tested. One game _____ [44] is

testing a video game and another is _____ [45] a defect report.

CAREER RESEARCH

Using the O*NET Career Exploration Tools at mynextmove.org, search for information about one of the jobs in Unit 19. Write the information in the job profile below. Then prepare and give a presentation about the job.

Job Zone 2 (some job preparation)
customer support specialist, data entry keyer

Job Zone 3 (medium job preparation)
computer installer, computer repair technician, computer service technician, help desk technician, technical support specialist, UI (user interface) artist, video game music composer

Job Zone 4 (high job preparation)
computer programmer, computer/network administrator, data recovery specialist, game designer, game developer, game producer, game tester, information processing worker, information systems security specialist, mobile app designer, mobile app developer, network engineer, systems analyst

Job name: _____

What does a person do in this job?

_____

_____

_____

What tools and equipment does a person use in this job?

_____

What skills and abilities are important?

_____

_____

What technology might a person use in this job?

_____

What kind of person will be interested in this work?

_____

What level of education, job training, and experience is required?

_____

_____

What is the job outlook?   What is the average salary?

_____   _____

Read the memo from the IT Department and answer the questions.

1 **TO:** All Staff
2 **FROM:** Sofia Yelchin, Chief Technology Officer
3 **SUBJECT:** Malware and Ransomware Protection

4 In light of yesterday's attempted (but unsuccessful) ransomware attack on our computer systems,
5 please review these reminders about cybersecurity at the company:

6 Make sure all operating systems, software, and Web browsers on your computer are current. When
7 we recommend that you install a software or security update, do so immediately. After installing an
8 update, restart your computer to make sure the update is installed correctly.

9 Check carefully before opening attachments or clicking links in e-mails. If you are uncertain about
10 the authenticity of an e-mail, check with the sender. If you can't verify that an attachment or e-mail is
11 legitimate, it may be a scam produced by a hacker. Delete it. Also, avoid clicking buttons or links in
12 pop-up windows.

13 Make sure Web pages that you access are safe. Look for https (not http) in the Web address. The "s"
14 stands for secure.

15 Use strong passwords that contain at least eight characters, uppercase and lowercase letters,
16 numbers, and symbols (!, @, etc.). Change passwords frequently. Don't use the same password for
17 multiple accounts.

18 Don't log into your work e-mail account from public WiFi sites. Make sure your device is set so it will
19 not automatically log into any wireless network it detects. For remote logins, only use the company's
20 special secure WiFi network with encryption.

21 Never leave your office computer or laptop unattended without shutting it down or putting it to sleep.
22 (Turning on a device and waking up from sleep mode must require a secure password.)

23 Back up all files on the company server. Don't store sensitive information on your laptop or mobile
24 device (e.g., phone, tablet) or on storage media (e.g., CDs, DVDs, memory sticks).

25 Our computers are well-protected against malware that infects files, steals passwords and data, and
26 spies on computer activity including online browsing. Our network is also protected from worms that
27 spread infections from one device to another. However, as we experienced yesterday, ransomware
28 is a growing problem. Many companies and public agencies have been denied access to their data
29 by attackers who encrypt the data and demand a payment to restore it. We prevent these attacks
30 by continually updating our operating systems and antivirus software. If you receive a ransomware
31 message, notify the IT department immediately. (Backing up all files will reduce the damage if a future
32 attack is successful.)

1. What is the reason for this memo?
A. A worm infected the company's computer network.
B. Employees need to install a new security update.
C. The company just prevented an attack on its data.
D. All staff need to back up files immediately.

2. In Line 11, what is the meaning of the term *hacker*?
A. an employee who allowed an attack on the company's system
B. the source of a computer scam or attack
C. a creator of antivirus software
D. an IT department administrator

3. According to the memo, which password is strong?
A. CluDt4!
B. R2D2SWF$
C. 1@2b3C4d
D. icu&ucme2

4. Based on the memo, what aspect of cybersecurity is the writer most concerned about?
A. attacks denying access to data
B. e-mail scams
C. pop-up windows
D. weak passwords and unattended devices

DEMONSTRATING A PROCEDURE

Using YouTube, WikiHow, or another source, search online for a demonstration of how to use technology. Write out the instructions. Then prepare a media presentation. Make screenshots of the steps or video-record your demonstration. Present the procedure to the class.

Suggestions: how to set up a _____ (computer, tablet, smart speaker, etc.); how to block pop-up messages on a smartphone; how to create a website

Coding, Cables, and Computers:
The Growing InfoTech Sector

1   Since the computer revolution of the 1980s and the application of computer technology to every part of the economy, information technology (infotech, or IT) has become one of the fastest-growing job sectors. Professionals and technicians are in demand for their expertise in *hardware* (computers and related devices and equipment) and *software* (the programming that allows computers to perform functions).

Working in IT

2   There are employment opportunities in IT for job-seekers at all levels, and career paths are open for those with the right skills and the motivation to learn and advance. IT can be a rewarding career, with high salaries for the most skilled workers, especially those with university degrees in computer-related fields. Jobs in high demand include cyber security analysts, who protect computer systems from attacks; web developers, who design and program web pages; and computer systems analysts, whose job is to assess companies' operations and design computer systems to help them meet their needs. Mobile app development is another high-growth area. Several million mobile apps are currently in existence and thousands are being created every day, but there is still a market for more, and a need for qualified developers.

3   Most large businesses and organizations employ their own IT staff to take care of their hardware and software needs. Some IT specialists work for companies that sell IT services to customers. The current trend toward *cloud computing*, in which computer-related services such as software and storage space are accessed over the Internet instead of from a company's own computer systems, has led some companies to rent IT services from vendors rather than building up their own onsite IT resources and staff. In any case, opportunities in IT are growing overall.

Computer Systems and Networking

4   Computer systems are an integral part of modern business. A company's computers, printers,

servers, and other equipment are interconnected in a network, or LAN (local area network), that plays a key role in the company's day-to-day operations, communications, and information storage. There are various functions involved in setting up and maintaining computer systems and networks. These functions are carried out by individuals in many different IT positions—whether they are the in-house staff of a company's IT department or employees of a computer services company.

NETWORK ENGINEERS AND ADMINISTRATORS

5   Careful planning goes into designing networks in an effective way. In doing this work, network engineers coordinate with network and computer systems administrators who assess the technology needs of the organization and individual staff members and supervise installation and maintenance of computer systems. The administrators also manage e-mail, data storage, and telecommunications networks, and often supervise support technicians.

COMPUTER INSTALLERS AND COMPUTER SERVICE TECHNICIANS

6   Computer installers do the work of setting up and connecting computers and other equipment, running cables, and hooking up workstations. Computer service technicians install or change internal components on computers and servers, maintain printers and other equipment, and load software.

TECHNICAL SUPPORT SPECIALISTS

7   Tech support is an important function of IT departments.   Tech support specialists help maintain the smooth operation of computer networks.   They troubleshoot problems with networks and help individual computer users with difficulties, either in person, over the phone, or by messaging through computer. Companies that sell software programs usually employ tech support specialists to assist customers who need help in using their products.

Information Systems

8   An information system focuses on how information is used in business processes.   It is both a work system and a data system. Modern businesses and organizations use information systems to create, collect, organize, store, process, and distribute information within their network to carry out their work. Company administrative data, or information pertaining to the work of the company, is entered and stored in an information system, which must be protected from computer viruses and other types of attack.

SYSTEMS ANALYSTS

9   Systems analysts design information systems that help businesses and organizations operate more effectively. They assess and analyze clients' needs and devise a plan for using information technology to solve business problems. Systems analysts may work with IT vendors to identify the right hardware and software to use in the information system. They provide instructions for programmers to use in building the system, including flowcharts and diagrams.

DATA ENTRY AND INFORMATION PROCESSING WORKERS

10   Many organizations use database and spreadsheet software to store and process data. Entering data into a computer is often a laborious and time-consuming process done by data entry keyers, although some data entry can be automated. Information processing staff access the data to extract information that is needed.   For example, customer information entered in a database can be accessed to produce a list of customers who share certain characteristics.

INFORMATION SYSTEMS SECURITY SPECIALISTS

11   Systems security specialists are responsible for guarding an organization's data and communications systems against threats from viruses and malware—software designed to harm or invade computers. This is usually done by installing antivirus software on the network, keeping it up-to-date with the latest versions, and dealing with junk e-mail, spam, and other types of suspicious activity. Security specialists also need to watch out for hacking—attempts to break into a computer system to steal information or cause trouble.

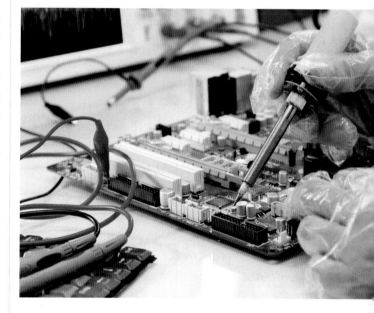

Computer Repair and Support

12   With computers used so widely in the world of work and by private individuals, computer repair and support has become a major area of employment. This type of work involves diagnosing and repairing computers and related equipment, and guiding computer users remotely on how to resolve equipment or software problems. Large organizations and businesses often have their own IT departments and staff that perform these functions.   Companies that sell IT services to businesses and to the public also employ computer repair and support technicians. Large tech retailers have a staff of IT specialists in customer service roles, and may offer repair services as well.

Customer Support Specialists and Help Desk Technicians

13 Customer support specialists work with customers to identify problems they are having with their computers and other devices, and process requests for technician services. Help desk technicians offer technical assistance to computer users over the phone, often providing step-by-step instructions to arrive at fixes for whatever type of problem users or their computers are experiencing.

Computer Repair Technicians

14 Computer repair technicians work with many kinds of hardware, including computers, laptops, servers, and peripherals such as printers, scanners, and external hard drives. They troubleshoot and fix computer malfunctions, and can also address software issues that may be causing problems.

Data Recovery Specialists

15 When a computer has malfunctioned, or if files have been accidentally deleted, it can be difficult to recover data from the computer's memory. Data recovery specialists use special software and other techniques to try to recover data that can no longer be accessed in the usual way.

Software Development and Computer Programming

16 More than half of IT jobs are in software development and computer programming. One type of software development is the creation of computer applications designed to perform particular functions—for example, custom software to meet a client's specific needs, or commercial software products, including mobile apps and games. Another type of software development is the creation or modification of system software, the operating systems for computers and networks. Programming provides the instructions, written in code, for computers to carry out tasks, and is one part of the software development process. Programming is also involved in the development and maintenance of operating instructions for computer systems and information systems.

Software Developers

17 Software developers create computer applications that allow computer users to perform specific tasks. When working for a client with a specific need or problem, for example, processing information or automating a task, the process involves working with the client to do an initial analysis and gather relevant information. The developer then devises a solution, codes the software, and tests it. The developer might work alone or as part of a team. Software developers may also write operating system software, the instructions that control how devices operate, or software that controls networks.

Computer Programmers

18 Computer programmers write the instructions, or code, for software that computers follow to perform functions. They work with designs from software developers and engineers and write code in a variety of computer languages, such as Java and C#. They also test and debug (find and fix problems in) computer programs. Programmers work with systems analysts to do the programming required

for developing information systems and computer systems.

MOBILE APP DESIGNERS AND DEVELOPERS

19 Mobile apps are specially designed software programs that operate on mobile phones, tablets, and other mobile devices. Designers come up with the concept for the app and formulate a development plan. Developing these applications presents special challenges, such as dealing with a variety of screen sizes and hardware types. Planning the user interface (UI)—how the user operates and controls the application on the device—is an essential part of the design process. Testing and troubleshooting are other important development functions.

VIDEO GAME DESIGNERS AND DEVELOPERS

20 Game design is a special and complex type of software development project. There are many aspects to it, and there are several different developer roles, including lead designer, mechanics designer, environmental designer, UI artist, music composer, and tester.

Qualifications and Careers

21 The future of the information technology job market is bright. Opportunities are available at all levels, and it is common for IT workers to improve their skills and move up. Those who specialize in hardware (such as computer repair) and software (such as programming) usually follow different career paths. As in most fields of work, higher level jobs require higher levels of education, but it is also good to have experience working with computers and using different kinds of software programs.

22 One path into IT work is through gaining experience in entry-level jobs. Data entry work has no special educational requirements. Workers can be easily trained on-the-job in using common software to key in most types of data. With additional training, these workers can learn how to process data, for example, to access information in spreadsheets and produce reports from databases.

23 Computer installers and assistant computer technicians are entry level jobs that can give people practical experience working with computers. With one or two years of study in a college or technical school to get an associate's degree or a certificate in electronics and computer technology, it is possible to acquire the knowledge and skills related to computer hardware and common software to qualify for work as a computer service and repair technician or customer support specialist. With further training and experience in various types of computer software, it is possible to qualify for positions such as tech support specialist, help desk technician, or data recovery specialist.

24 Most higher-level IT jobs require a bachelor's degree in a computer-related field. To work at larger companies or to receive higher pay, it is also helpful to have several years of experience working with information systems. Computer network engineers need to have at least a bachelor's degree in computer science, information systems, or information engineering. With experience, and sometimes a master's degree, they can advance to become computer and information systems

managers. Network administrators and systems analysts usually have a degree in computer or information science. Information security specialists also need a degree in computer science or programming, as well as certification in systems security.

25   Software developers usually have a bachelor's degree in computer science or software engineering, along with strong programming skills. Most computer programmers have a bachelor's degree in computer science or a related field. Knowledge of several different programming languages is helpful. With experience, it is possible for programmers to advance to become software developers. Mobile app developers also generally have a degree, and it is advantageous for them to be familiar with the most common mobile app programming languages. College-level study and strong programming skills are required for working in video game design, as well as creativity, problem-solving skills, teamwork, and experience in gaming. Web designers often only need an associate's degree, as well as proficiency in web languages such as HTML and JavaScript.

26   As information technology continues to evolve, it is important for all IT workers to keep up-to-date on the latest developments in their field. They need to be constantly learning through professional development seminars, continuing education classes, online courses, and other education opportunities, so they can keep their skills sharp for their current jobs as well as to prepare for new job opportunities in the future.

DID YOU UNDERSTAND?

1. What do the terms *hardware* and *software* refer to?

2. What does *cloud computing* refer to?

3. What is a local area network?

4. Who designs computer networks?

5. When computer users have difficulty in using software programs, who do they usually call?

6. What do systems analysts do?

7. What are two types of software that are used to store and process data?

8. What are three types of threats that systems security specialists need to guard against?

9. What are some examples of peripherals?

10. What is the user interface?

11. What kind of basic experience is important for anyone seeking a job in IT?

12. What are some examples of entry-level IT jobs?

WHAT'S YOUR EXPERIENCE?

1. How do you most often communicate with other people at a distance—by e-mail, by phone calls, by text messaging, through social media sites, or in some other way?

2. What telephone service do you have at home? Do you have a home phone (a land line), or only a mobile phone? If you have both, how do you use each one?

3. If you have a television at home, how do you receive television programs—by antenna, cable TV, Internet, or some other way?

READING COMPREHENSION

1. According to the reading, what background and experience would be required for the highest-paid IT positions?
   A. extensive knowledge of computer devices and equipment
   B. expertise in software
   C. a university degree in a field related to computers
   D. experience in mobile app development

2. Network engineers _____.
   A. protect computer systems from attacks
   B. design and program web pages
   C. develop mobile applications
   D. design computer systems for organizations

3. In general, individual computer users probably have the most direct contact with _____.
   A. tech support specialists
   B. network engineers
   C. computer installers
   D. network administrators

4. Which of the following statements is true?
   A. A company's LAN is often shared by different businesses.
   B. Outside service companies are sometimes hired to set up a company's computer system.
   C. Support technicians are usually in charge of a company's telecommunications network.
   D. Computer installers make decisions on the kind of equipment companies should acquire.

5. In paragraph 10, what does it mean to "access" data in an information system?
   A. to search for information in the system
   B. to put information into the system
   C. to change or remove information from the system
   D. to get or see or use information stored in the system

6. Which of the following computer specialists would deal with issues involving hacking and computer malware?
   A. information processing workers
   B. information systems security specialists
   C. systems analysts
   D. computer support specialists

7. When computer repair technicians *troubleshoot*, they _____.
   A. replace something that has been causing trouble
   B. complete a repair
   C. attempt to discover the source of a problem
   D. identify equipment that malfunctions

8. Retrieval of lost data is discussed in _____.
   A. Paragraph 12
   B. Paragraph 13
   C. Paragraph 14
   D. Paragraph 15

9. Which of the following positions requires the LEAST amount of professional training?
   A. computer installer
   B. computer repair technician
   C. help desk technician
   D. customer support specialist

10. The main reason the author advises IT workers to keep up to date is that _____.
    A. there are many opportunities for professional development
    B. the number of jobs will increase in the future
    C. the field is constantly changing
    D. there are many benefits offered by continuing education classes

ACADEMIC LESSON / LISTENING

ACADEMIC VOCABULARY

1. Information technology has become one of the fastest-growing job _____ of the US economy.
   A. sections
   B. sectors
   C. occupations
   D. opportunities

2. The company is looking for an individual with _____ in all aspects of computer technology.
   A. concentration
   B. availability
   C. expertise
   D. awareness

3. There are numerous opportunities for individuals with the _____ to learn new skills.
   A. demonstration
   B. mechanism
   C. cooperation
   D. motivation

4. Web developers _____ and program web pages.
   A. design
   B. network
   C. implement
   D. process

5. There is no question that computer systems are an _____ part of today's business.
   A. informative
   B. integral
   C. ultimate
   D. overall

6. Network engineers must _____ with computer systems administrators.
   A. coordinate
   B. accommodate
   C. regulate
   D. initiate

7. Service technicians install internal _____ on computers.
   A. mechanics
   B. compartments
   C. components
   D. reinforcements

8. Systems analysts need to _____ a client's needs and devise an appropriate plan for solving problems.
   A. assure
   B. select
   C. reveal
   D. analyze

9. The data must be accessed before information can be _____.
   A. extracted
   B. operated
   C. achieved
   D. devised

10. The staff will work hard to _____ any equipment and software-related problems.
    A. generate
    B. conclude
    C. resolve
    D. reinforce

11. Data entry work does not have any special educational _____.
    A. requirements
    B. acknowledgements
    C. capacities
    D. demonstrations

12. Operating _____ must be carefully followed.
    A. establishments
    B. authorities
    C. circumstances
    D. instructions

13. It can be difficult to _____ data from a computer's memory.
    A. contact
    B. recover
    C. undertake
    D. contribute

14. Once a concept has been approved, it is necessary to _____ a development plan.
    A. decide
    B. accumulate
    C. formulate
    D. involve

UNIT 19 LISTENING

PART A
Practice: A B C
1. A B C
2. A B C
3. A B C
4. A B C
5. A B C

PART B
Practice: A B C
1. A B C
2. A B C
3. A B C
4. A B C
5. A B C

Look at pages 288–289 of the core text. Write the correct words to complete the description.

assemblers	debris	inspecting	quality	technicians
assembly	digging	operator	screwing	testing
attaching	electrician	push	suctioning	tightening
boom	hooking	putting down	tank	wind

These workers are helping the world "go green"! To produce _____wind_____ ¹ energy, wind

turbine _____ ² are _____ ³ tower bolts, a tractor trailer truck driver is

_____ ⁴ a cable to a tower section, and a _____ ⁵ crane operator is guiding a

rotor blade _____ ⁶ into a nacelle. For solar energy, solar photovoltaic _____ ⁷

are assembling photovoltaic cells on a backsheet and _____ ⁸ control specialists are

_____ ⁹ the cells. A solar installation technician is _____ ¹⁰ in roof mounts and

an _____ ¹¹ is wiring an inverter. Geothermal energy is heat produced from the Earth. To access

this energy, geothermal installers are doing several different tasks. One is _____ ¹² surface

casings and rings, another is _____ ¹³ a header trench, and several are working together to

_____ ¹⁴ a pipe down a drill hole. In addition, a geothermal technician is _____ ¹⁵

up a geothermal heat pump. For conversion energy, a waste oil reclamation truck _____ ¹⁶ is

_____ ¹⁷ out used oil and another is hooking up a hose to a rendering _____ ¹⁸.

In addition, a conversion technician is removing _____ ¹⁹ from a filtration system and chemical

technicians are _____ ²⁰ feedstock.

blowing	converting	dumpster	holes	planting	setting
camera	disposing	filling	image	replacing	test
changing	drilling	hanging	installing	reviewing	weather

To achieve energy efficiency, several energy auditors are at this home. One is taking an _____ ²¹

of an attic with a thermal imaging infrared _____ ²², another is doing a smoke stick

_____ ²³, and another is _____ ²⁴ up a blower door test unit. An energy auditor is

also _____ ²⁵ an energy audit with the homeowner. An insulation specialist is _____ ²⁶

in loose fill insulation. Another is installing _____ ²⁷ stripping on an exterior door. Appliance

installers are _____ ²⁸ an old refrigerator with an energy-efficient one.

At a downtown building, window installers are _____ ²⁹ energy-efficient windows, door installers

are _____ ³⁰ a new door, and an electrician is _____ ³¹ incandescent light bulbs to

CFL light bulbs. Foam insulation installers are also working in this building. One is _____ ³² a hole

through brick grout, another is _____ ³³ a wall with insulation through a drilled hole, and another

is covering _____ ³⁴ with aluminum foil tape. A traffic light installer is _____ ³⁵ a

traffic light to solar LED. A conservation technician is _____ ³⁶ a tree and a construction worker is

_____ ³⁷ of old materials in a recycling _____ ³⁸.

(continued)

CAREER VOCABULARY

Look at pages 290–291 of the core text. Write the correct words to complete the description.

baler	driver	inspecting	planting	reading	sorting
baling	dumping	laborers	pollution	recovery	tagging
collecting	environmental	loading	produce	recyclables	test
conservation	foresters	output	quality	samples	

At a materials _____ [39] facility (an MRF), a recyclable collections _____ [40] is _____ [41] recyclables and MRF workers are pushing _____ [42] onto a belt. MRF sorters are _____ [43] through recyclables and an MRF technician is _____ [44] cardboard in a vertical _____ [45]. On a tree farm, _____ [46] are _____ [47] saplings and _____ [48] technicians are examining them. On a farm, farm _____ [49] are filling crates with _____ [50] and then _____ [51] the crates for delivery to sites where CSA members purchase the produce. At a _____ [52] location, _____ [53] technicians are laying out a boom, _____ [54] water samples, retrieving habitat _____ [55], and _____ [56] birds. At an air _____ [57] monitoring site, an air _____ [58] specialist is taking an air quality _____ [59]. An environmental installation technician is checking particle _____ [60] of a cyclone particle collector, and a dust collection specialist is _____ [61] a baghouse for leaks.

attaching	bolting	connecting	donor	gauges	installers	operator	stenciling
batteries	brainstorming	customers	driver	hoisting	installing	painting	switchgrass
biorefinery	charging	delivering	farm	industrial	operating	positioning	vehicle

Workers at an electric _____ [62] plant are doing a variety of tasks. An assembly line worker is _____ [63] the underbody battery on a chassis. Another is installing a _____ [64] system inlet. An assembly line hoist operator is _____ [65] an engine from a _____ [66] car. An EV technician is installing _____ [67]. Another is wiring _____ [68] together. An EV mechanic is _____ [69] a DC controller to an electric motor. On a street in the community, a light rail _____ [70] is _____ [71] a light rail vehicle. There are many light rail workers. One is _____ [72] a rail to a concrete tie. Another is _____ [73] catenary wire to a power pole. There are also many road construction workers. One is _____ [74] road lines, another is _____ [75] a bollard on the street, and another is _____ [76] a logo on a bike path. Two charging station _____ [77] are installing a charging station for electric vehicles. At a switchgrass _____ [78], agricultural equipment operators are baling _____ [79]. A flatbed truck driver is _____ [80] the switchgrass to a _____ [81], where it will be converted to ethanol. An ethanol transport _____ [82] is arriving at an ethanol station where _____ [83] will purchase the ethanol. It's essential to plan for the future! A group of _____ [84] designers and engineers are _____ [85] ideas for the cars of tomorrow.

Using the O*NET Career Exploration Tools at mynextmove.org, search for information about one of the jobs in Unit 20. Write the information in the job profile below. Then prepare and give a presentation about the job.

Job Zone 1 (little or no job preparation)
farm worker/laborer, MRF sorter, restaurant worker

Job Zone 2 (some job preparation)
agricultural equipment operator, assembly line hoist operator, assembly line worker, biorefinery production operator, bricklayer, construction worker, conversion technician, door installer, dust collection specialist, ethanol transport driver, flatbed truck driver, foam insulation installer, geothermal installer, geothermal technician, insulation installer, insulation specialist, light rail operator, light rail worker, mixing truck operator, MRF technician, MRF worker, pump technician, recyclable collections driver, restaurant manager, road construction worker, solar photovoltaic assembler, tractor-trailer truck driver, waste oil reclamation truck driver, window installer

Job Zone 3 (medium job preparation)
appliance installer, boom crane operator, charging station installer, chemical technician, conservation technician, crane operator, electrician, energy auditor, EV mechanic, EV technician, forester, handyman, industrial designer, quality control specialist, residential wind energy installer, solar installation technician, traffic signal installer, wind turbine technician

Job Zone 4 (high job preparation)
air pollution specialist, assistant engineer, CSA organizer, design assistant, engineer, environmental installation technician, environmental technician, farm manager, urban forester

Job name: _____

What does a person do in this job?

_____

_____

_____

What tools and equipment does a person use in this job?

_____

What skills and abilities are important?

_____

What technology might a person use in this job?

_____

What kind of person will be interested in this work?

_____

What level of education, job training, and experience is required?

_____

What is the job outlook?   What is the average salary?

_____   _____

A CSA(Community-Supported Agriculture) Coordinator

1   I'm Jenny Kwon—coordinator of the Downtown Farm CSA, a community-supported agriculture program that serves our inner-city residents. Our downtown neighborhoods are known as food deserts. There isn't a single major supermarket in the area and most residents don't have cars, so they rely on small walking-distance grocery stores to purchase food. Given the limited space in these stores and the smaller volume of business, they stock more canned and packaged items rather than fresh produce.

2   Our CSA solves this problem by enabling residents to receive high quality fresh vegetables that are grown on nearby farms. For a very low fee, residents sign up to be CSA shareholders. Each share entitles them to receive a weekly basket of produce at one of our pick-up locations during our region's growing season, June through November. The basket usually includes up to ten types of vegetables that will feed a family of three. Half-shares are also available.

3   Unlike many CSAs, we don't ask shareholders to pay for an entire season of produce ahead of time. They can pay the fee in monthly installments. We also accept food stamps now that we have free wireless EBT (Electronic Benefits Transfer) equipment provided by the government. And we have a sliding scale for shareholders at low income levels.

4   This is an excellent arrangement for everyone involved. Small farmers have guaranteed customers for their produce, which can be delivered fresh to our CSA pick-up locations (often on the same day it is picked on the farm), and our shareholders have easy access to fresh produce. An added benefit is that our farmers use natural growing practices without harmful chemicals, so the food isn't just fresher, it's healthier.

5   Shareholders aren't just customers. As members, they run the CSA and have responsibilities to volunteer to participate in the work. They can help at the distribution sites, sign up new members at local events, or lead our education programs. These include popular workshops on cooking, gardening, and nutrition. In the summer, we also have a wonderful program that enables our ShareKids—children of our members—to spend a few days helping on some of the farms that supply our produce.

---

1. What does *sliding scale* in paragraph 3 refer to?
A. equipment for weighing vegetables
B. wireless EBT equipment
C. monthly installments
D. different fees for different members

2. Select the paragraphs that describe the health benefits of CSA produce.
A. Paragraphs 1 and 3
B. Paragraphs 2 and 4
C. Paragraphs 1 and 5
D. Paragraphs 3 and 5

3. How does paragraph 4 contribute to the article?
A. It describes the problem.
B. It gives details about CSA shares.
C. It explains the benefits for shareholders and farmers.
D. It describes CSA members' responsibilities.

4. Which statement would this person likely agree with?
A. Grocery stores downtown should be larger.
B. Everyone deserves access to healthy produce.
C. If more downtown residents had cars, they would drive to major supermarkets.
D. CSAs shouldn't rely on volunteers.

Energy, the Environment, and Emerging Employment Opportunities

1 Climate change, air pollution, deforestation, decreasing fresh water resources, rising sea levels, extreme weather events—these are all signs of an environment and a planet under stress. The nations of the world have recognized the problem, and there is a growing emphasis on conservation of resources, clean energy generation, and sustainability. Governments are committed to working to meet the needs of their populations and develop their economies in a sustainable way, with wise and efficient use of resources and care for the environment we live in.

2 A new *green economy* is developing, and it involves many sectors, including energy, building construction, transportation, waste management, land and water management, and air quality, as well as human well-being and social equity. New technologies are playing a role in meeting the challenges. Businesses are being created and employment opportunities are growing, including jobs that did not even exist a few years ago!

Energy

3 When traditional fossil fuels such as petroleum and coal are burned, they release gases and other substances that pollute the air. The search for alternative sources of energy has headed in many directions. The goal has been to find or develop renewable energy sources—sources that naturally replenish themselves or are not consumed. For generating electricity, the main renewable sources currently being developed are solar energy, wind energy, and geothermal energy. Hydroelectric power—electricity generated from flowing water— is also an important renewable energy source, although it can have significant environmental impact. There are also alternative liquid fuels that can be used to power engines.

SOLAR ENERGY

4 Since the beginning of the 21st century, continuing technological advances and expanding manufacturing capabilities have contributed to a dramatic increase in the use of solar energy.

Electricity can be produced on a large scale in arrays of solar panels—called solar farms—that are connected to existing regional power grids. Solar panels can also be placed on or near buildings to provide power for specific structures. As photovoltaic cells have become cheaper to produce and the cost of solar installations has decreased, the solar energy industry has boomed.

WIND ENERGY

5 Huge wind turbines are being used around the world to generate electricity for regional power systems. Turbines are often grouped into large wind farms at locations that receive regular strong winds. Small wind turbines of various designs can be installed on individual buildings to help meet electric power needs.

GEOTHERMAL ENERGY

6 At many locations around the world, heated water and steam from deep in the Earth are brought to the surface and used as energy sources to heat buildings and to generate electricity. Geothermal energy is an important clean, renewable power source for many countries.

7 Another type of geothermal system makes use of the natural temperature of the Earth to heat and cool homes and buildings. It uses a heat pump that is connected to a long loop of pipes placed under the ground outside a building. In cold weather, the heat pump pushes water from the cold building

out to the pipes. The water is warmed by the heat in the ground and circulates back, where the heat is used to warm the inside air. In hot weather, the interior warmth is transferred through the pipes to the ground outside, and cooler water returns and is used to cool the building.

Biofuels

8   Biofuels are derived from plant materials. The most widely produced biofuel is ethanol, made from corn, sugarcane, switchgrass, and other crops. Used cooking oil, or waste vegetable oil, can be converted into a type of biofuel. Biofuels are used in many parts of the world, primarily in vehicles as an alternative to petroleum-based fuels.

Conservation

9   Conserving energy makes good sense for several reasons: It lowers energy users' expenses, saves natural resources, and reduces pollution. Governments in many areas have established programs to promote energy conservation in homes and other buildings. Construction companies follow guidelines to build structures that are environmentally friendly, and businesses are providing services to homeowners to improve energy efficiency.

The Environment

10   Support for environmentalism and conservation has strengthened as the extent of pollution and environmental degradation has become more and more obvious. There are growing concerns about poor air quality, contamination of soil and water by industrial facilities, the exploitation of natural resources, and waste disposal in trash dumps, landfills, and oceans, as well as the loss of natural forests and habitats for animal life. Governments and civil society organizations are making efforts to remedy some of these serious problems.

Waste Management and Recycling

11   It is essential to manage waste disposal as efficiently as possible to avoid contaminating the environment. The three main principles of waste management are reduce, reuse, and recycle: Reduce the amount of waste material discarded, reuse material that is still useful, and recycle or convert waste material into new products. What remains is either incinerated or placed in landfills or trash dumps. Most major cities have recycling programs that collect paper, glass, plastic, and cans. Some cities also collect and compost garden waste such as grass clippings and leaves, and some communities have started food waste collection programs.

Farming and Forests

12   Growing environmental concerns have led to a movement for sustainable agriculture, which uses resources and farming practices in a way that maintains the quality of the natural environment. Organic farming has also increased due to consumer demand for organic food. A system called Community Supported Agriculture (CSA) has become popular in recent years. In this model, members subscribe to buy the products of a local farm they would like to support.

13   Forests contribute to the green economy by supplying wood, a renewable biological resource. Trees play an important role in the global ecosystem by taking in carbon dioxide, producing oxygen, preventing erosion, and protecting biodiversity. Sustainable forest management is vital to the health of the planet.

Environmental Remediation

14   The release of hazardous waste and chemicals from sites such as energy plants, mining operations, paper mills, and industrial plants can cause severe damage to ecosystems and can endanger public health. Environmental remediation

involves cleaning up land or water that has been contaminated by these pollutants. Restoration of these areas may also be part of clean-up projects.

AIR POLLUTION

15 Economic development is often accompanied by increased industrialization, more vehicles on the road, and air that is gray and unhealthy. Even with emissions controls on vehicles, factories, and power plants, air pollution can often rise to dangerous levels. Air quality monitoring, pollution control equipment, and regulatory measures are small ways of trying to stay on top of this serious problem.

Transportation

16 Auto manufacturers are responding to consumer desires and governmental demands for increased fuel economy and lower emission levels by producing hybrid and all-electric vehicles. Cities are also making efforts to get commuters out of their cars and into alternative modes of transportation, particularly light rail systems. Some cities are building bike lanes along city streets and are encouraging residents to commute to work by bicycle.

ELECTRIC VEHICLES

17 Hybrid vehicles, which have both a gasoline engine and an electric motor, use much less gasoline than conventional cars. The car's battery charges while the gasoline engine is in use. In "plug-in" hybrids, the battery can also be charged by connecting to household electricity. All-electric vehicles run on electricity only and produce no emissions, but the range they can travel is limited. However, a growing network of charging stations is making it more practical for them to travel long distances. All-electric vehicles may eventually replace gasoline-powered vehicles. Another approach to improving fuel economy is to convert regular gasoline-powered vehicles to electric power.

LIGHT RAIL

18 Urban light rail systems are typically powered through overhead electrical wires, and sometimes they can make use of existing railroad tracks. They travel at lower speeds than regular passenger trains, but run on a more frequent schedule. Light rail trains usually operate at street level, making stops throughout the city and connecting with a network of buses that carry passengers closer to their final destinations. City transit systems are trying to improve their efficiency and attract commuters who normally drive to work.

BICYCLING

19 Many cities are promoting the idea of commuting by bicycle, and some employers have established "bike to work" programs. Biking advocacy groups work with city planners to identify practical routes for biking into the city center and other areas. Many cities have shown that bike lanes can be safely integrated into traffic systems. Bike-share programs, in which users pay a small fee to use public bicycles, are becoming increasingly popular in cities around the world.

Working in the Green Economy

JOBS IN ENERGY

20   One of the fastest growing sectors in the green economy is renewable energy, especially solar. Solar installations are being set up for commercial power generation and for office buildings and homes, as well as for smaller-scale uses such as powering traffic signal lights at intersections. Many state governments offer financial incentives to homeowners to make energy efficiency improvements, including rebates for installing solar panels.

21   There is high demand for solar installation technicians, who set up and maintain solar panel systems on roofs and other structures under the guidance of installation managers. They learn this work through on-the-job training or by taking courses at a technical school.

22   Jobs in solar photovoltaic manufacturing companies range from assemblers, who assemble parts to make solar panels, to a variety of technicians with different roles in the manufacturing process, including supporting production processes, operating machinery, and monitoring equipment, including robots. Technician jobs usually require an associate's degree in a technical field or equivalent work experience.

23   Businesses specializing in energy efficiency modifications to homes employ various kinds of technicians. Energy auditors use equipment to see how air-tight the building's living spaces are. Improvements to buildings may include installing energy-efficient windows, attic and wall insulation, and efficient heating and air conditioning systems. Insulation specialists seal gaps around doors, windows, and walls. Most workers have had some experience in building maintenance or construction and learn the specific skills they need through college courses, training programs, or on-the-job training.

24   With the growing focus on wind energy, there are many job opportunities for wind turbine technicians. Most wind turbines are large, heavy machines, and the technicians who service and maintain them need special training from technical schools. They also receive training from the manufacturers of the equipment they work on. Certification in electrical safety and tower climbing is also useful.

25   Most jobs in biofuel production require only a high school education. Biofuel processing technicians operate machines and monitor production processes, along with collecting and testing samples. Production managers and supervisors usually have a bachelor's degree, and need to understand technical details about the materials and processes involved, including computerized systems.

JOBS RELATED TO THE ENVIRONMENT

26   Most jobs in waste management and recycling are for workers who do the physical work of collecting, sorting, and transporting waste materials and recyclables. They may use equipment such as forklifts to move materials. For some of these jobs, a high school diploma may not be required.

Recycling program coordinators and managers usually have had some college education.

27 Agricultural work can be physically demanding, and safety training is important. Workers learn on the job and build skills with experience. Managers of organic farms need to learn effective organic growing practices, as farms must comply with certification requirements. Business skills are also important for managers who operate farming businesses and buy supplies and sell products. There is a growing need for precision agriculture technicians, who collect information about farm fields and use Global Positioning Systems (GPS), geographic information systems (GIS), and computer mapping systems. These jobs may require a university degree.

28 Implementing sustainable forestry requires many types of workers. Cultivators and loggers grow and harvest trees. Scientists who manage and monitor forest conditions include conservation scientists, environmental scientists, soil and plant scientists, and wildlife biologists. They have at least a bachelor's degree in their field. Technicians assist the scientists in each of these areas. Technician jobs usually require an associate's degree and relevant experience.

29 Controlling pollution and cleaning up contaminants are important functions in keeping the environment safe and healthy. Companies that produce waste materials that can pollute the air, land, and water employ workers, such as environmental specialists and air quality engineers, who monitor and maintain systems that measure and control the output of contaminants. Technician jobs require a bachelor's degree, and engineers need a degree in environmental sciences or engineering. There are also positions such as air pollution analysts who work in agencies that monitor pollution levels.

30 Companies and government agencies that work in environmental remediation employ workers to deal with the effects of environmental damage resulting from the release of contaminants. There are many types of jobs involved in this work, including hazardous material removal workers, soil and water sampling and remediation technicians, environmental and conservation scientists and specialists, chemists and chemical technicians, and other scientists such as hydrologists and microbiologists. Scientific positions may require graduate degrees.

Jobs in Transportation

31 Over the last century, cars have been a big contributor to local air pollution, especially in the world's large cities. Governments have been building mass transit systems such as light rails as an alternative. Construction companies contracted by government transportation agencies employ a variety of workers in building such systems. Jobs include construction workers, project managers, civil engineers, and rail and transit engineers. Rail system technicians, vehicle maintenance technicians, and systems supervisors are employed in operating and maintaining the systems.

32　Two current developments in the auto industry will soon have a profound impact not only on the environment but on the economy and society as well. These changes are the movement toward electric vehicles and driverless, or self-driving, cars. Auto manufacturers will be switching more assembly lines from producing gasoline-powered vehicles to electrically-powered vehicles, but they may not require more workers. There will be many new jobs in the future, however, for technicians to convert gasoline-powered vehicles to electric power. The changeover to driverless cars will mean a reduction in jobs for commercial truck drivers and taxi drivers. Whether enough jobs will be created in the economy of the future for these millions of workers remains to be seen.

33　It is an exciting time to be working in the green economy. The world has recognized that we must take care of our planet and our people, and governments and businesses are responding. By working in green jobs, people can not only contribute to the health of the environment, but also pursue a career in a rewarding field of work.

DID YOU UNDERSTAND?

1. What sectors are included in the green economy?

2. What are some examples of renewable energy sources?

3. What are solar farms and wind farms?

4. What is biofuel?

5. What are some of the benefits of conserving energy?

6. What are the three main principles of waste management?

7. How do forests contribute to the health of the environment?

8. What is the main difference between hybrid vehicles and electric vehicles?

9. What is one way that governments have been encouraging homeowners to make energy efficiency improvements?

10. How do most workers in the solar installation business learn their jobs?

11. What are some of jobs in the green economy that may not require a high school education?

12. What are some examples of scientific positions in environmental remediation work?

WHAT'S YOUR EXPERIENCE?

1. Have you ever experienced severe air pollution or seen polluted water? If you have, where and when?

2. Have you noticed solar panels anywhere in your city? If you have, where, and what were they used for?

3. What do you and your family do to conserve energy and water at home?

4. How much attention do you pay to recycling when you throw things away?

5. How do you travel to work? Do you drive? Take public transportation? Ride a bike? Walk? Why?

WHAT DO YOU THINK?

1. There is a controversy about biofuels, as agricultural land and water that could be used to produce food is instead used to produce fuel. What do you think about this issue?

2. Would you pay more for a product—for example, paper towels—that contains recycled material than for a similar product that contains all new material? Why, or why not?

3. A process called *fracking* that pumps chemicals into the ground has increased natural gas production and created many jobs. However, it may be contaminating groundwater and causing harm to the environment. How would you balance the economic benefit with the risk to the environment?

4. Do you think technological advances such as the use of robots in factories or the use of driverless cars should go ahead even if they will cause a lot of people to lose their jobs?

READING COMPREHENSION

1. What do solar, wind, and geothermal energy have in common?
   A. They make use of heat pumps.
   B. They produce liquid forms of energy.
   C. They can be used to generate electricity.
   D. They are often grouped in "farms."

2. When items are *recycled*, they are _____.
   A. converted into new materials
   B. discarded and destroyed
   C. crushed and incinerated
   D. composted into biodegradable elements

3. Which paragraph warns about the dangers of industrial waste?
   A. Paragraph 11
   B. Paragraph 12
   C. Paragraph 13
   D. Paragraph 14

4. In view of the overall theme of the reading, which of the following can be inferred about the main purpose of encouraging biking in urban areas?
   A. It is to promote a love of the environment.
   B. It is to popularize this effective form of exercise.
   C. It is to discourage people from driving to work.
   D. It is to reduce degradation of city streets by cars.

5. In paragraph 20, a synonym for *rebates* is _____.
   A. repairs
   B. refunds
   C. rewards
   D. instructions

6. Which of the following areas of employment requires the least amount of education for the majority of jobs?
   A. biofuel production
   B. solar energy
   C. home energy
   D. wind energy

7. Which of the following technician jobs needs the highest level of education?
   A. solar installation technician
   B. wind turbine technician
   C. agricultural technician
   D. chemical technician

8. According to the reading, which of these work areas requires knowledge of satellite-based positioning systems?
   A. waste management
   B. agriculture
   C. environmental remediation
   D. forestry

9. According to the reading, which equipment manufacturers offer training on the use of their products?
   A. solar photovoltaic manufacturing companies
   B. manufacturers of heating and air conditioning systems
   C. wind turbine manufacturers
   D. biofuel processing machine manufacturers

10. Which of the following does the author predict will happen?
    A. The need for truck and taxi drivers will be eliminated.
    B. Employment at auto manufacturers will increase.
    C. There will be jobs for everyone in the new green economy.
    D. Jobs that do not exist today will be created.

ACADEMIC VOCABULARY

1. Most countries are _____ to establishing environmentally sensitive policies.
   A. concerned
   B. committed
   C. submitted
   D. acknowledged

2. Fossil fuels _____ gases that pollute the air.
   A. export
   B. project
   C. dispose
   D. release

3. Hydroelectric power produces energy that is _____ from flowing water.
   A. generated
   B. transformed
   C. initiated
   D. enabled

4. Geothermal energy is a clean renewable _____ of energy.
   A. material
   B. output
   C. force
   D. source

5. Many programs have been established to _____ energy conservation.
   A. recycle
   B. promote
   C. project
   D. transport

6. There is great concern about the _____ of natural resources.
   A. facilitation
   B. manipulation
   C. exploitation
   D. intervention

7. Cleaning up polluted water is an important part of _____ remediation.
   A. chemical
   B. economical
   C. mechanical
   D. environmental

8. Hybrid vehicles use less gasoline than _____ cars.
   A. commercial
   B. conventional
   C. individual
   D. manual

9. Cities are working on ways to _____ bicycle lanes into urban traffic systems.
   A. integrate
   B. coordinate
   C. construct
   D. replace

10. Jobs for technicians require an associate's degree or _____ work experience.
    A. functional
    B. approximate
    C. equivalent
    D. potential

11. Air pollution _____ monitor pollution levels.
    A. facilitators
    B. practitioners
    C. assemblers
    D. analysts

12. Most governments have _____ programs to promote energy conservation.
    A. participated
    B. established
    C. responded
    D. released

13. Workers in green jobs are _____ to the health of the environment.
    A. contributing
    B. achieving
    C. providing
    D. promoting

14. Everyone should be aware of the _____ of conserving energy.
    A. welfare
    B. credits
    C. benefits
    D. attention

UNIT 20 LISTENING

PART A

Practice: A B C   3. A B C
1. A B C   4. A B C
2. A B C   5. A B C

PART B

Practice: A B C   3. A B C
1. A B C   4. A B C
2. A B C   5. A B C

PART C: MY CAREER JOURNEY

The **CareerView** *ToolSite* at pearsoneltusa.com/careerview provides downloadable resources for lessons in this section.

BUILDING A CAREER PATHWAY: LADDERS AND LATTICES

Climbing a ladder is a common metaphor for a person's career journey, but in the 21st-century world of work it has become outdated in many employment sectors. The traditional career ladder concept suggests that there is a single path for advancing in a career and moving upward in an organization, with established steps—the rungs of the ladder—to move from one position to the next. But ladders are narrow. Following a narrow path can limit a person's career opportunities and prevent an employee from learning about the overall work of an organization. And if an employee gets stuck on a rung of a ladder because people above are not moving up (or out), the employee's *upward mobility* can be restricted.

A more current and useful concept is the *career lattice*. It's broader, and it offers opportunities for career advancement that may be vertical, lateral (sideways), or diagonal. As a result, there can be more opportunities along a person's career path, and an employee who moves to different positions can develop a wider perspective about an organization.

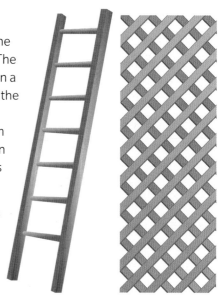

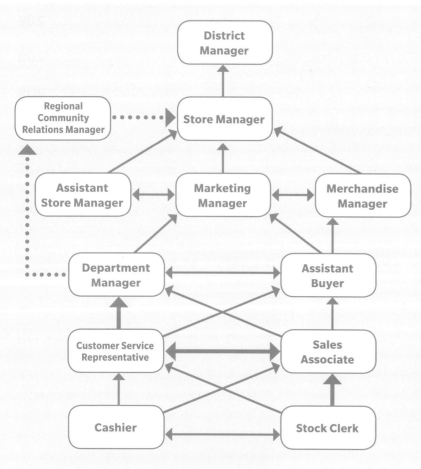

The career pathway of Isabella Rojas, the retail community relations manager featured on page 20, is a good example of a career lattice. Isabella started as a stock clerk at one of her company's department stores. Then she moved up to a position as a sales associate. She made a lateral move to a job as a customer service representative. It wasn't a promotion and it didn't involve a pay raise, but she enjoyed helping customers and she wanted a broader view of the operation of the store. She eventually became the manager of her department. Then she was promoted to a management role in one of the company's regional offices. Isabella's goal is to be a district manager someday at the company's headquarters. She knows that in order to do that, she'll need to have some years of experience managing one of the company's stores. She's planning to apply as soon as a position opens up. As you can see from her career lattice diagram, she isn't following the normal route to the top, but she's confident she'll get there.

CAREER JOURNEY TASK

Go to www.careeronestop.org* and enter the search term *sample career ladders/lattices*. You will find a link to career pathway diagrams for the following employment sectors: Retail, Construction, Hospitality, Information Technology, Long-term Health Care, Advanced Manufacturing, Energy, and Financial Services. Notice how the diagrams show many occupations and the multiple ways a worker can advance in a career. Then make your own career lattice (not a ladder!) for an employment sector. List all the key job titles, even if certain occupations don't interest you, so that you have a complete picture of opportunities in that sector.

* CareerOneStop is sponsored by the US Department of Labor/Employment and Training Administration (USDOL/ETA).

EDUCATION, TRAINING, AND CREDENTIALS

There are many options for continuing your education and preparing for the jobs along your career pathway.

High School Equivalency (HSE): For students who have not completed high school, it is possible to study for and take a test to earn a High School Equivalency diploma. Different states recognize different tests, and some states also have alternative diploma programs. It's important to know which test is the correct one for your location. (Important: If you have education and training from another country but don't have a diploma, you may not need an HSE diploma to continue your education at a higher level. Be sure to ask your school's career counselor if it is needed.)

Adult Basic Education (ABE): If you are enrolled in an English program, it may be part of an ABE program that is partially funded by the US Department of Education. In addition to English courses, ABE programs offer basic skills instruction in reading, writing, and mathematics, and HSE preparation.

Certificate programs and other short-term training programs: Community colleges, technical and vocational schools (sometimes called trade schools), and other institutions offer short programs (usually less than two years) that can lead to certification to meet job requirements related to certain occupations and the use of tools, technology, safety procedures, and other skills.

Internships: Short-term jobs that offer work experience—often without a salary—can be a valuable way to learn skills on-the-job and to become familiar with a workplace setting.

Apprenticeship programs: Apprenticeships offer a way to get hands-on work experience while earning a salary. They are becoming more common in many employment sectors, including construction, health care, and manufacturing. Employers, professional associations, and labor unions usually sponsor these programs, which can be one to six years in length. The US Department of Labor offers information on more than 150,000 employers that offer apprenticeship programs in more than 1,000 occupations, at www.dol.gov/apprenticeship.

Certifications: Certifications are credentials that prove that a worker has specialized knowledge or skills for a particular occupation or employment sector. The credentials are usually earned by taking a test, and many education programs offer classes to help students prepare. It's important to know what certifications are required for occupations you are considering. Some may be required in order to apply for a job, and others may be required as you plan to advance along your career pathway.

Licenses: Many occupations in health care, cosmetology, and other employment sectors require workers to have a license. Each state has its own licensing procedures, so it's important to know what is required where you plan to work.

Colleges: Community colleges usually offer two years of coursework leading to an Associate degree, and many allow students to attend part-time so that they are able to work while they are enrolled. Four-year colleges offer a Bachelor's degree, and full-time enrollment is more common.

Graduate Schools: Students who have completed college can enroll in graduate schools to earn Master's and Doctoral degrees for advanced studies in medicine, law, science, and other subjects.

Online Education: Many education institutions offer online courses. Some are free, and some are part of certification or degree programs and charge a fee.

UpSkilling: Many companies that employ entry-level workers now offer tuition assistance as a benefit to help employees continue their education. Some of these programs are partnerships with online colleges. Use the search term *UpSkilling* to learn more.

Buyer beware: Make sure you know a trade or technical school's reputation before enrolling. Some schools may give inaccurate information about student graduation rates, job placements, or salaries in order to encourage students to apply. Some schools offer student loans with very high interest rates, and some have closed in recent years due to financial problems.

CAREER JOURNEY TASK

Go back to www.careeronestop.org* and enter the search term *sample career ladders/lattices*. Look again at some of the career pathway diagrams. You will see that the job titles and many arrows are highlighted. When you click on the job titles, you will see a job description and the education, training, and work experience required. When you click on the arrows, you will see the *critical development experiences* that are required to move from one job to the other.

Now look at the career lattice you created. Plan a pathway you might follow to advance in a career. On a separate sheet of paper, list the job titles from lowest to highest. For each job, list the education, training, and work experience required. (You can find this Job Zone information at mynextmove.org.) Then write the name of a school or other institution where you can study and prepare for the job. The careeronestop.org website's *Find Training* menu will take you to this information. Share your information with other students in pairs, in small groups, or as a class.

PLANNING A JOB SEARCH

There are many ways to do a job search. You probably won't use all of them, but it will be helpful to know all the resources that are available to you.

Online job boards: Websites such as monster.com, indeed.com, careerbuilder.com, and simplyhired.com provide job boards with lots of listings. These sites are popular, but the amount of information they offer can be overwhelming and time-consuming to explore. Another option is to use the *Find a Job* search tool at careeronestop.org.

CLASS SURVEY

How have you, the students in your class, and everyone's family members and friends found their current and previous jobs? Do a class survey and make a chart. List all the job-finding strategies and the number of times they were used. Which strategies were the most effective? Discuss as a class.

Help Wanted ads: Before the Internet, the Help Wanted sections of newspapers usually had the most job listings. They are still a valuable source of information.

School career and placement services: Your school may have a career and placement office with counselors or career navigators who can offer advice about your job search. Make sure you know how to use the resources that are available.

Local workforce and employment agencies: Government-funded job centers throughout the country offer career counseling, job search assistance, and training. You can access this network and other government agencies through careeronestop.org. Private employment agencies also provide job placement services.

Job fairs: Employers exhibit at job fairs to provide information to potential applicants about job openings. These events are excellent opportunities to get information and to gain experience talking about yourself and your career objective.

Networking (IRL): A large percentage of jobs are found by *word-of-mouth* through information from family members, friends, neighbors, and other people we know. In Real Life Networking (not online!) offers the opportunity for face-to-face communication about a job search with people we meet at job fairs and other events.

Networking (Social media): *Facebook*, *Twitter*, and *LinkedIn* can be useful tools for learning about job openings and for letting people know about your job search. See page 208 for advice about using social media.

Employer websites: The websites of companies and institutions have useful descriptions about the work they do, and they often include information about job openings and requirements. Some websites provide an initial online job application or a *Contact Us* button or e-mail address to request information about available positions.

Informational interviews: Meeting with someone at a worksite to get advice about working in an occupation—but not actually applying or interviewing for a job—can be an excellent way to learn about the work and future job opportunities. A good way to set up this kind of meeting is to ask if anyone in your network has a *contact*—a person who would be useful to talk to.

The careeronestop.org website's *Job Search* menu provides links to valuable information about these job search strategies, including the best ways to use job fairs and informational interviews, and tips for creating effective elevator speeches.

1. Do Internet research using search terms such as *best job search sites* or *Top 10 job search sites*. Gather information about the usefulness of the job boards on these sites. Which employment sectors do they focus on? Share your information with the class.

2. Bring to class a copy of your local newspaper that offers the largest Help Wanted section. (This will often be the Sunday edition.) Describe the kinds of jobs that are listed, the information that is provided, and the different ways applicants need to respond to the ads.

3. What career and placement services are available through your school, through local offices of government workforce agencies, and through private employment agencies? Gather information and share as a class.

4. Do job fairs occur in your area? Who sponsors them? Which employers attend them? Invite a job fair organizer to visit your class and discuss the best ways to use these events as part of a job search.

5. What questions should you ask at an informational interview? Use the careeronestop.org *Job Search* menu to find this information. Make a list of questions and share as a class.

WORK EXPERIENCE, EDUCATION HISTORY, AND REFERENCES

Fill in the chart with information you will include in job applications and resumes, including three references—people who know you well and who would give a good recommendation about you to a potential employer.

WORK EXPERIENCE (List most recent first)		
Dates Worked	Employer/Company Name	Position

EDUCATION				
High School (Name, Location):			Date of Graduation:	
College/School	Location	Field of Study	Degree/Certification	Date of Completion

REFERENCES (Name, Description)
1.
2.
3.

YOUR ELEVATOR SPEECH

If you're a job applicant, you need an *elevator speech*—a short statement describing who you are, your career goal, and your skills. It should also include your *value proposition*—something special about your work experience, background, interests, or personality that would be valuable to an employer. The speech should be 30 seconds to one minute in length. (Don't go to a job fair without one!) Create a first draft of an elevator speech. Show it to other students and your teacher, and ask for advice about how to improve it. Then revise it, write a final version, and practice it often.

USING SOCIAL MEDIA

Most employers will use the Google search engine to find information on the Internet about a job applicant. You should search your name as well in order to check your reputation online. The search results can determine your *personal branding*—the impression you make with a potential employer.

Also, take a close look at your Facebook, Twitter, or other social media presence. Check for any information or photos that may be damaging to your reputation. You can also use these social media networks in a positive way to let people know about your job search.

LinkedIn is an excellent service for creating a professional online presence, learning about job openings, and even applying for positions. You can use LinkedIn to search for general information about an employment sector or for specific information about a company or institution that interests you. The information about LinkedIn members includes their connections to other members, so the service can be a good networking tool for a job search. You can also join LinkedIn groups related to your employment sector.

CAREER JOURNEY TASKS

1. Google yourself to check your reputation on the Internet. Enter your name "in quotes" for a basic search and review at least one or two pages of results. (90% of users won't search past the first page, but an employer might.) Also enter your name in Google Images to check for photos. If you find something damaging that you posted yourself, remove it at its source. If someone else posted it, you'll need to ask the website or person to remove it, but this may be difficult. Look at the negative information only once so that you don't add to the frequency of clicks on that page. (Companies exist that will improve the search results for positive information that appears about you, but their services can be expensive and the damaging information will probably just move farther down the search listings rather than be removed.)

2. Check your social media profile and history on sites such as Facebook and Twitter. Look for any harmful or embarrassing posts or photos (such as drinking irresponsibly) and delete them. Check your privacy settings to make sure that friends don't add content to your social media accounts that might be damaging to your reputation.

3. Use your Facebook, Twitter, or other social media account as a way to let your friends and contacts know about your job search. And consider adding more posts and photos that create a favorable impression about you and your *personal brand.*

4. Join the professional online networking site LinkedIn. Sign up for a free account, learn how to use the service, and create a profile that can serve as an online version of a resume and a networking tool to explore job opportunities. (Your elevator speech can be a good starting point for creating your profile.) Join LinkedIn's *Job Openings, Job Leads, and Job Connections* group for information about positions available, including internships.

JOB APPLICATIONS

Although paper job applications still exist if you walk into some fast-food restaurants and other worksites, more and more job applications are now online. To become familiar with the career information and job application procedures that exist on the Internet, you can use as a search term the name of a major company plus the word *careers* or *jobs.* You will probably find a link to the company's careers page and information about job opportunities.

Applicants beware! Some websites and e-mails may look like authentic company sites or messages but are actually fraudulent. They may include company logos and look official, but they are actually created by scammers who collect personal information for identity theft or even request payment of processing fees for fake job applications. Check to make sure a company's web address includes an "s" in "https," which stands for *secure,* and don't respond to or click anywhere in an e-mail you didn't expect that looks like a job offer from a company.

1. Find the careers or jobs section of a major company's website. Use as a search term the company's name plus the word *careers* or *jobs*. Explore the kinds of information provided, which often includes job opportunities in various work locations and departments, job requirements, employee benefits, and job application forms for completion online. If you can do so without registering with the company, start a job application to get experience completing one online. (But don't submit it if you aren't seeking the position!) As a class, discuss the different company websites that students explored.

2. On the careeronestop.org website's *Job Search* menu, select *Resumes and applications*, and then select *Job applications* and *Online applications*. Review and summarize the information, and share as a class.

RESUMES

There are excellent *resume builders* available—software and online tools that offer *templates* to help you create professional-looking resumes to use when applying for jobs. Your school's career office may have a special arrangement with a company that has a resume product, or you can find many excellent free resume builders online.

Creating resumes electronically using templates is better than typing them into plain word processing software. The reason is that most resumes these days are submitted via e-mail, company websites, or online job boards rather than through regular mail. Resumes therefore need correct formatting to appear properly on a screen and when printed out.

The best resume templates provide simple formatting that looks well-organized and not too fancy. Information is presented clearly with easy-to-read headers, sub-heads, dates of employment, and other information. Short bulleted lines are used to present key information instead of long paragraphs.

The Google Docs resume templates are especially useful because they are free, the files can be saved in multiple file formats, and they can be saved to the *cloud*, and therefore, accessed from anywhere.

1. On the careeronestop.org website's Job Search menu, select *Resumes and applications*, and then select *Resumes, Cover letters*, and *Cover letter sample*. Review and summarize the information, and share as a class.

2. Do this activity with a group of five or more students: On the careeronestop.org website, when you click on *Job Search*, don't select the pull-down menu. Instead, look at the right side of the screen to find the *Job Tools* section and click on *Resume Guide*. This will take you to a valuable set of web pages about creating a great resume, including effective strategies and step-by-step writing instructions. Have each student in the group read and summarize the information on one or more of the web pages. Then as a group, do a presentation for the class.

3. Use your school's resume builder, a Google Docs resume template, or another template to create your own resume. You can refer to the information you wrote on page 207 about your work experience, education history, and references. Also write a cover letter that you can adapt when you are ready to send in your resume to apply for a job. The *Cover letter sample* at careeronestop.org is a good model.

PREPARING FOR INTERVIEWS

There are different types of job interviews, and you may experience more than one.

After submitting a resume, you may be expecting a call to set up a time for an interview, but that call might actually be the first step in the interview process—a *screening interview*. Employers use this type of interview to narrow down an applicant pool in order to devote time and energy only to the strongest candidates. Screening interviews often occur as phone conversations, but they also happen in person. Therefore, as soon as you have applied for a position, be prepared to answer some of the most important interview questions—even in a phone call.

A *selection interview* includes questions that involve more detail about your qualifications and how you would handle situations at work. You shouldn't talk about everything that's in your resume. That's too much information, and the interviewer has probably read it. Instead, you should plan to highlight key parts of your education or previous work experience that tie directly to the qualifications listed for the job. You may be asked to give examples of your skills and personal qualities, including being a fast learner, a team player, and a leader. Questions may also be designed to see how you deal with problems, resolve conflicts, or handle ethical dilemmas. The interviewer will be making judgements about your confidence in yourself and whether your attitudes and behavior will be a good fit at the workplace. A selection interview usually happens in person. However, some selection interviews now occur as video communication via Skype or other telecommunication services.

A *follow-up interview* could involve a meeting with employees who might be your co-workers, or an informal lunch or coffee shop meeting that will help the employer see how you handle social situations. While these meetings may not feel like interviews, they can be very important in helping the employer evaluate how you would fit in with the rest of the workforce.

CAREER JOURNEY TASKS

1. On the careeronestop.org website's *Job Search* menu, select *Interview and negotiate,* and then select *Interview tips*. Read the information. Then discuss as a class your answers to these questions:

   How should you dress for an interview?

   When should you arrive?

   What should you bring to the interview?

   What *shouldn't* you bring?

   How can you display confidence during the interview?

   How can you make a positive impression at the end of the interview?

   What should you do within a day after the interview?

2. There are hundreds of helpful (and often entertaining) videos available about how to prepare for a job interview. Videos about how to answer difficult interview questions are especially useful. Use these search terms and others to find videos with job interview tips: *tell me about yourself, job interview tips, ace a job interview, difficult job interview questions*. Write down the best advice in the videos and share as a class.

   Also, have a class video festival: Save links to your favorite videos of job interview tips. Play the videos for the class and discuss the advice.

Tell Me About Yourself

One of the most challenging interview questions is one of the shortest: "Tell me about yourself." Your answer shouldn't be a life story or autobiography. You should focus on why you were motivated to enter your occupation; key highlights about your education, training, and experience; and your future ambitions. If you want to share something about your background, your journey to a new country, or other information that helps you stand out as a special and interesting applicant, it may be useful. But make it brief, and try to connect it to what you share about your career pathway.

Create a first draft of an answer to the question, "Tell me about yourself." (Your elevator speech can be a good starting point.) Your answer should be about five or six sentences so you can say it in about one minute. Show your first draft to other students and your teacher, and ask for advice about how to improve it. Then revise your answer, write a final version, and practice it often.

Preparing Your Interview Answers

Review your answers to the questions in Part A about your vocational personality type (pages 3–4) and your personal qualities (pages 8–9). These answers will help you decide how to respond to many of the common interview questions. Write complete answers to Questions 2–15 on a separate sheet. (You've already written your answer to Question 1.) Practice your answers so you are well-prepared for an interview. (The first eight questions commonly occur in phone screening interviews. All the questions occur in selection interviews.)

1. Tell me about yourself.

2. Why are you interested in this position?

3. Why should we hire you? (Why do you consider yourself qualified for this position?)

4. Why are you leaving your current job? / What is the reason you left your previous job?

5. How would you describe your work style?

6. What do you consider some of your greatest strengths?

7. How do other people describe you?

8. What are your long-term goals? Where do you see yourself in five years?

9. What is a weakness or fault that you need to work on?

10. Our workplace is constantly changing. Everyone here is learning new things to keep up. Do you consider yourself a fast learner? Can you give me an example?

11. Teamwork is very important here. Can you give me an example that illustrates how you work well with people?

12. We encourage employees to take initiative and play leadership roles here. Can you give me an example of your leadership skills?

13. We have a very diverse workforce and we serve customers/clients from many different backgrounds. Can you give me an example of how you work well with diversity?

14. Tell me about a time when you faced a major challenge and overcame it, or when you experienced a major problem and solved it.

15. Tell me about a time when you helped to resolve a conflict.

16. Integrity is an important quality that we look for in the people we hire. Can you give me an example of an ethical dilemma that you faced and how you handled it?

(Suggestion: When you give your answers, don't ask questions. You will probably have an opportunity to ask questions toward the end of the interview, but first allow the interviewer to get through the questions that she or he needs to ask.)

Preparing Your Interview Questions

Your answers to an interviewer's questions are important, but the questions you *ask* the interviewer are very important, too. Asking a question about something you learned during your research is a good way to demonstrate your interest in the company or institution. It's okay to write down some of these questions on an index card or notepad that you bring to the interview. This will show that you're well-prepared. (Don't ask too many questions. Four or five should be sufficient, and there may not be time to ask all of them.) Some good questions might include:

What are the most important responsibilities of the position?

What qualities are you looking for in the best candidate for this position?

What is a typical day like for a person in the position?

How does the position fit into the organization?

What are the opportunities for more responsibility and advancement for someone who does well in this position?

How would my performance be evaluated?

Who would I be working with?

Who would be my supervisor?

What kind of ongoing training is provided?

What will the next step be in your hiring process?

When will you be making a decision about filling this position?

Also, if there is sufficient time, you might ask the interviewer about her or his work at the company—for example, how long the person has worked there, or why it's a good place to work. If you seem genuinely interested in the interviewer's own role at the company, you can make a good impression as someone who is friendly and who cares about other people.

(Important: A first interview isn't the right time to ask about salary, holidays, vacation time, health insurance, and other benefits. These are usually discussed in a final interview or after a job offer has been made.)

CAREER JOURNEY TASKS

1. Prepare for an actual job interview, or imagine that you have applied for a job and are getting ready for an interview. Follow these steps:

   a. Find the job description for the position you are applying for.

   b. Research the employer on the Internet. Check the employer's website and Facebook page and look for news items. Learn about the employer's work, the products or services it provides, and who the customers or clients are.

   c. Practice your answers to the interview questions on page 211.

   d. Practice questions that you will ask the interviewer.

   e. Do a mock interview. Have another student interview you for the job. Give the student the job description and some background information about the company or institution so the student knows what kinds of questions to ask. (Have an Interview Day in your class! Everyone should dress up for the mock interviews and practice being job applicants and interviewers.)

2. Write a thank-you note or e-mail to the person who interviewed you in the mock interview. Express appreciation for the person's time, reinforce your interest in the position, and very briefly restate your key skills and qualifications. You can also add some important information if you forgot to mention it in the interview. Finally, if the person promised to get in touch with you by a certain date, mention that date and say you look forward to hearing from the person. For a sample thank-you note, go to the careeronestop.org website's *Job Search* menu, select *Interview and negotiate*, and then select *Thank-you notes*.

SKILLS BOOK / PART A

Page 4 PERSONALITY EXPRESSIONS

1. e
2. d
3. b
4. f
5. a
6. c

Page 7 TEST YOUR VOCATIONAL PERSONALITY KNOWLEDGE

1. B
2. D
3. A
4. C

Pages 8–9 YOUR PERSONAL QUALITIES

1. c
2. e
3. d
4. a
5. b
6. k
7. i
8. g
9. h
10. j
11. f
12. o
13. p
14. l
15. n
16. m

Page 9 PERSONALITY EXPRESSIONS

1. e
2. d
3. a
4. c
5. b

Page 11 JOB ZONES

1. 4
   2
   3
   1
   5
2. 4
   3
   5
   2
   1

SKILLS BOOK / PART B

UNIT 1

Page 17 CAREER VOCABULARY

1. associate
2. department
3. information
4. assisting
5. display case
6. stock
7. carton
8. hand truck
9. warehouse
10. shelves
11. merchandise
12. workers
13. stocking
14. ladder
15. support
16. pallet
17. trucker
18. manager
19. signing
20. delivery
21. operator
22. unpacked
23. shipping carton
24. rack
25. scanning
26. inventory
27. cashiers
28. checkout
29. till
30. scanner
31. processing
32. checked
33. swipe
34. security
35. receipt
36. bags
37. cart
38. customer service
39. representative
40. return
41. clothing
42. inventory
43. unit
44. manager
45. setting up
46. sale sign
47. straightening
48. table

Page 19 ON-THE-JOB INSTRUCTIONS

1. C
2. B
3. D
4. A

Page 20 CIVICS CONNECTION PROFILE

1. D
2. B
3. C
4. A

Page 21 DID YOU UNDERSTAND?

1. Retail businesses sell goods and services to customers.
2. Big box retailers are companies that sell many different kinds of products and operate a network of large stores.
3. In online shopping, customers make purchases from Internet websites.
4. E-tailers don't have to maintain store buildings, a large supply of merchandise, and a large staff.
5. Apps from traditional retail companies, apps from online retailers, and apps that list coupons and discounts
6. Businesses pay websites, search engines, and social media sites to show their ads.
7. They collect information about their customers by following their purchases on company websites, on credit cards, and with store club cards.
8. They use information to determine what kinds of products consumers like, so they can send them targeted ads.
9. Sales associates, cashiers, stock clerks, customer service representatives, managers, security personnel, warehouse workers, distribution managers, drivers
10. Cashiers, warehouse workers, and delivery drivers
11. There will be fewer jobs in stores, but more jobs in online sales.
12. Computer skills, information technology, software development, data management, computer and IT technicians, math skills, mobile marketing, computer programming, web development

Page 24 READING COMPREHENSION

1. A	5. D	9. B
2. B	6. C	10. A
3. C	7. C	
4. C	8. A	

Page 25 ACADEMIC VOCABULARY

1. B	6. A	11. C
2. D	7. C	12. A
3. A	8. D	13. D
4. D	9. B	14. B
5. B	10. A	

Page 25 UNIT 1 LISTENING

PART A:	PART B:
Practice: C	*Practice:* B
1. B	1. C
2. A	2. A
3. B	3. B
4. B	4. C
5. C	5. B

UNIT 2

Page 27 CAREER VOCABULARY

1. manager	25. order
2. delivery	26. calling
3. receiving	27. line
4. dietician	28. grilling
5. supervisor	29. tongs
6. workers	30. frying
7. weighing	31. basket
8. scale	32. cooking
9. cutting	33. replenishing
10. board	34. taking
11. boiling	35. serving
12. broiling	36. greeting
13. roasting	37. reservations
14. oven	38. resolving
15. counters	39. grill
16. service	40. short-order
17. tasting	41. manager
18. spoon	42. checking
19. pastry	43. steam table
20. icing bag	44. dishing out
21. decorate	45. scoop
22. rack	46. checking out
23. baking	47. attendant
24. mitt	

Page 29 ON-THE-JOB INSTRUCTIONS

1. A	3. D
2. C	4. B

Page 32 DID YOU UNDERSTAND?

1. The culinary arts refer to preparing, cooking, and presenting food.
2. Culinary specialists can work as cooks, research chefs, and food scientists.
3. Food scientists usually work for companies that process and produce food in large quantities.
4. Food scientists study microbiology to understand how microorganisms cause food to spoil and cause food poisoning.
5. They might want to find substitutes for elements such as fat and sugar because in large quantities they may not be healthy.
6. Nutrition and dietetics examine the nutritional value of food and how what we eat affects our body and our health.
7. A healthy diet contributes to proper growth, maintaining strength, and avoiding illness.
8. The typical American diet contains a lot of fried foods, meat, sugary drinks, and processed food products, and lacks sufficient fresh fruits and vegetables.
9. They can buy food products from local farms, and they can reduce waste.
10. It is an area of science that analyzes human reactions to products through the senses.

Page 33 READING COMPREHENSION

1. C	5. B	9. C
2. B	6. A	10. A
3. C	7. B	
4. D	8. D	

Page 34 ACADEMIC VOCABULARY

1. B	6. C	11. C
2. C	7. B	12. B
3. A	8. D	13. A
4. D	9. A	14. D
5. A	10. B	

Page 34 UNIT 2 LISTENING

PART A:	PART B:
Practice: A	*Practice:* B
1. B	1. C
2. C	2. B
3. A	3. C
4. B	4. A
5. C	5. B

UNIT 3

Page 35 CAREER VOCABULARY

1. office	27. cherry
2. trimmer	28. light bulbs
3. pruner	29. washer
4. prune	30. scaffold
5. handler	31. safety
6. respirator	32. squeegee
7. mechanic	33. custodians
8. maintaining	34. cleaning
9. equipment	35. cleaner
10. landscape	36. extractor
11. spreader	37. shampoo
12. fertilize	38. carpeted
13. mowing	39. mopping
14. lawnmower	40. wiping
15. trimming	41. removing
16. shovel	42. vacuum
17. shrubbery	43. polishing
18. edges	44. broom
19. edger	45. step ladder
20. supervisor	46. changing
21. sod	47. lights
22. maintenance	48. repairs
23. picking	49. filters
24. stick	50. boiler
25. walkways	51. moving
26. power	52. storage

Page 37 ON-THE-JOB INSTRUCTIONS

1. C
2. D
3. A
4. B

Page 40 DID YOU UNDERSTAND?

1. The world's population is growing, and poor countries are developing their economies.
2. Commercial and residential buildings use 40% of the world's energy.
3. The main goal of green retrofitting is to reduce the amount of energy that a building uses.
4. Increasing the efficiency of equipment and systems in the building that use energy, and decreasing heat loss and heat transfer
5. New systems use less energy to deliver the same amount of heat as older systems that use more gas or electricity.
6. New bulbs use 10% to 25% of the amount of electricity that older bulbs use.
7. Sensors placed throughout the building transmit information to the control system.
8. If there is more sunlight in a room, then less artificial lighting is needed and energy can be conserved.
9. Losing heat in cold weather requires the system to produce more heat. Heat transfer in the summer requires more air conditioning.
10. Two sources of renewable energy are solar power and wind power. They are clean and do not consume resources.
11. Low-flow water fixtures, improved flush valves, and flow control systems that use sensors
12. It only waters plants when they need water.

Page 41 READING COMPREHENSION

1. C
2. B
3. A
4. B
5. D
6. C
7. D
8. A
9. B
10. A

Page 42 ACADEMIC VOCABULARY

1. B
2. C
3. A
4. D
5. B
6. A
7. B
8. D
9. C
10. A
11. B
12. D
13. C
14. A

Page 42 UNIT 3 LISTENING

PART A:
Practice: A
1. B
2. C
3. C
4. B
5. A

PART B:
Practice: C
1. A
2. B
3. A
4. C
5. B

ANSWER KEY

UNIT 4

Page 43 CAREER VOCABULARY

1. manager
2. client
3. counter
4. salon
5. stylists
6. stations
7. smocks
8. capes
9. shears
10. cut
11. hair
12. consulting
13. selecting
14. color
15. sample
16. comb
17. hairpiece
18. shampooist
19. shampooing
20. area
21. towels
22. bin
23. colorist
24. apron
25. applying
26. standing
27. dryer
28. nail
29. stations
30. massaging
31. pushing back
32. artist
33. brush
34. apron
35. bib
36. makeup
37. mirror
38. applying
39. blending
40. pedicurist
41. stool
42. polish
43. chair
44. spa
45. esthetician
46. plucked
47. cleansing
48. massage
49. therapist

Page 45 CIVICS CONNECTION PROFILE

1. C
2. A
3. C
4. D

Page 48 DID YOU UNDERSTAND?

1. Hair styling, application of cosmetics, skin care, and manicures
2. They are created in scientific laboratories by cosmetic chemists.
3. They study materials and chemicals, how they interact with each other, and their effect on the human body.
4. Cosmetics do not cause health problems for most people. Some salon products can be harmful, especially after long or regular exposure.
5. Formaldehyde is a dangerous chemical used in many hair treatment products. It is sometimes used as an ingredient in nail polish.
6. It gets into the nose and lungs and can irritate the eyes, throat, and skin. It can cause breathing difficulties, chest pain, headaches, and cancer.
7. OSHA is the U.S. Department of Labor Occupational Safety and Health Administration.
8. They can read the label on the bottle or box, or look at the safety data sheet.
9. Formaldehyde, toluene, dibutyl phthalate, and ethyl acetate
10. Ventilation can pull dangerous vapors out of the work area.
11. They should wear long-sleeved shirts and gloves. They should wash their hands after working on clients and before they eat or drink. They should not eat or drink in work areas and should keep their food and drinks covered. They should close chemical bottles tightly and dispose of used chemicals safely.
12. They can read government information sheets about working safely in nail salons.

Page 49 READING COMPREHENSION

1. B
2. C
3. C
4. D
5. B
6. A
7. C
8. D
9. B
10. A

Page 50 ACADEMIC VOCABULARY

1. C
2. D
3. A
4. B
5. C
6. A
7. B
8. D
9. B
10. A
11. C
12. D
13. B
14. D

Page 50 UNIT 4 LISTENING

PART A:
Practice: C
1. B
2. A
3. B
4. A
5. C

PART B:
Practice: B
1. C
2. A
3. B
4. B
5. A

UNIT 5

Page 51 CAREER VOCABULARY

1. receiving
2. unloading
3. distribution
4. rack
5. move
6. assemblers
7. assembly
8. grinding
9. sealing
10. fabrication
11. welder
12. welding
13. fabricator
14. bending
15. paint
16. robot
17. pinstripe
18. attaching
19. moving
20. machine
21. tightening
22. supervisor
23. assistant
24. parts
25. floor
26. quality
27. inspector
28. imperfections
29. tester
30. packing
31. shipping
32. hoist
33. crates
34. conveyor
35. assembly
36. engineer
37. drawings
38. electronics
39. clean
40. wires
41. soldering
42. assemblers
43. production
44. attaching
45. snapping
46. samplers
47. checkpoint
48. testing
49. defective
50. packers
51. trays
52. manual
53. box
54. carton
55. department

Page 53 ON-THE-JOB INSTRUCTIONS

1. D
2. D
3. B
4. C

Page 56 DID YOU UNDERSTAND?

1. Before the Industrial Revolution, products were made by hand. Later they were made using machines.
2. Horses, water, and steam engines
3. It changed how people worked and where they lived. Many people went to live in cities and work in factories.
4. At first most of the work was done by women working for a contractor at home. Later the work was done in sweatshops and factories.
5. Millions of new immigrants worked in the factories.
6. The two biggest developments of the Second Industrial Revolution were electrification and the production line.
7. The third industrial revolution (the Digital Revolution) is a change from mechanical technology to electronic technology.
8. The computer, the Internet, and cellular phones
9. Automation involves the automatic control of machinery, systems, and operations in manufacturing and other areas of production.
10. Automation reduces the need for human workers.
11. Current uses include welding, painting, and handling materials in automobile manufacturing. In industries such as steel production and plastics, robots do jobs that are dangerous for humans. Future uses include household, agricultural, and medical robots.
12. Skills in using technology and computers

Page 57 READING COMPREHENSION

1. C
2. D
3. B
4. A
5. B
6. C
7. D
8. A
9. D
10. B

Page 58 ACADEMIC VOCABULARY

1. B
2. A
3. C
4. D
5. B
6. C
7. A
8. B
9. D
10. A
11. C
12. B
13. A
14. D

Page 58 UNIT 5 LISTENING

PART A:
Practice: B
1. C
2. A
3. B
4. A
5. C

PART B:
Practice: B
1. A
2. C
3. B
4. A
5. B

ANSWER KEY

UNIT 6

Page 59 CAREER VOCABULARY

1. roofers
2. stapling
3. attaching
4. installers
5. cutting
6. caulking
7. buttering
8. setting
9. duct
10. helpers
11. square
12. mark
13. measuring
14. shimming
15. glazier
16. installing
17. blockmason
18. mixing
19. positioning
20. cutting
21. soldering
22. tightening
23. wiring
24. testing
25. contractor
26. plastering
27. taper
28. taping
29. installers
30. scoring
31. screwing
32. charging
33. sawing
34. saw
35. sheathing
36. stapling
37. tile
38. grouting
39. installers
40. laying
41. flooring
42. roller
43. brush
44. trim
45. spray gun
46. spray paint
47. hanging
48. installing

Page 61 CIVICS CONNECTION PROFILE

1. C
2. B
3. D
4. C

Page 64 DID YOU UNDERSTAND?

1. A green home has a low impact on the environment.
2. The focus of sustainable architecture is on energy and ecological conservation in building design.
3. The most important aspect of a green home is its energy efficiency.
4. The location, size, and natural features of the property need to be considered in the design of the home and its landscaping.
5. A smaller house is more energy-efficient than a larger one.
6. In a passive solar design system, windows, walls, and floors collect warmth from the sun, and it is distributed to heat the home.
7. Windows should be placed on the sides of the house that receive morning and early afternoon sun.
8. Insulation keeps heat in during the cold season and cold air in during the hot season.
9. Insulation made from recycled newspaper, sheep's wool, and shredded denim; nonsynthetic and nontoxic paints, finishes, and glues; wood products for kitchen cabinets that do not contain air contaminants; bamboo and wood flooring
10. A geothermal heat pump is a heating and cooling system that makes use of the natural temperature of the earth.
11. Less electricity from outside sources would be needed.
12. In integrated design, the architect collaborates with specialists in different areas of sustainable building design.

Page 65 READING COMPREHENSION

1. B
2. B
3. A
4. D
5. A
6. B
7. D
8. C
9. B
10. C

Page 66 ACADEMIC VOCABULARY

1. B
2. D
3. C
4. A
5. D
6. B
7. B
8. A
9. C
10. D
11. B
12. C
13. D
14. B

Page 66 UNIT 6 LISTENING

PART A:
Practice: A
1. C
2. A
3. B
4. A
5. C

PART B:
Practice: C
1. C
2. C
3. B
4. C
5. A

UNIT 7

Page 67 CAREER VOCABULARY

1. fencing
2. foreman
3. dirt
4. dump
5. bulldozer
6. taking
7. stakes
8. cutting
9. hats
10. vests
11. installers
12. laying
13. backhoe
14. electrician
15. flatbed
16. jobsite
17. bill
18. officer
19. safety
20. flagger
21. cement
22. mixer
23. controlling
24. forms
25. installers
26. crane truck
27. hoisting
28. steelworker
29. signals
30. guide
31. releasing
32. truck
33. laying
34. out
35. driving
36. leveling
37. trowels
38. front-end
39. foundation
40. welder
41. shield
42. torch
43. basket
44. picker
45. technician
46. roofers
47. pouring
48. bucket
49. mopping
50. rolling out
51. securing
52. plumber
53. cutting
54. pipefitter
55. bending
56. manager
57. construction
58. erecting
59. pipe
60. glazier
61. cutter
62. tile
63. blockmason
64. leveling
65. welding
66. laborers
67. walkway
68. driving
69. spreading
70. laying
71. dumping
72. installer
73. clipping
74. trimming
75. channel
76. electrician
77. cable
78. ceiling
79. panels
80. plasterer
81. sanding
82. spacing
83. applying
84. brickmasons
85. laying
86. contractor
87. automatic
88. apprentice
89. panes
90. finisher
91. cutting
92. smoothing
93. stonemason
94. wall

Page 70 ON-THE-JOB INSTRUCTIONS

1. C
2. B
3. C
4. D

Page 74 DID YOU UNDERSTAND?

1. The green building movement began as a response to concern about the impact of buildings on the environment.
2. LEED stands for Leadership in Energy and Environmental Design.
3. They must meet the program's high standards for design, construction, operation, and maintenance.
4. Platinum level
5. Providing areas for separating recyclable materials
6. To design for flexibility of the building and ease of future adaptation
7. Improved indoor air quality
8. In at least 90% of individual occupant spaces, allow for individual adjustment of lighting.
9. Using a strategy that is not specified by the program
10. Architectural engineering, mechanical, electrical, and plumbing systems, and structural engineering
11. A structural engineer can help decrease material use, identify local material sources, and design rainwater runoff systems.
12. They must pass the LEED accreditation exam.

Page 75 READING COMPREHENSION

1. D
2. B
3. C
4. A
5. D
6. C
7. B
8. C
9. C
10. A

Page 76 ACADEMIC VOCABULARY

1. B
2. C
3. A
4. D
5. B
6. A
7. B
8. C
9. B
10. D
11. C
12. A
13. D
14. C

Page 76 UNIT 7 LISTENING

PART A:
Practice: A
1. C
2. A
3. B
4. A
5. B

PART B:
Practice: A
1. B
2. A
3. A
4. C
5. C

ANSWER KEY

UNIT 8

Page 77 CAREER VOCABULARY

1. service
2. advisor
3. work order
4. waiting
5. diagnosing
6. bay
7. scanner
8. analyzer
9. charging
10. exchanging
11. exchange
12. system
13. balance
14. mounting
15. tuning up
16. brake
17. pad
18. technicians
19. undercarriage
20. auto lift
21. muffler
22. suspension
23. absorber
24. lube
25. draining
26. oil
27. leaks
28. driver
29. lowering
30. tow truck
31. frame
32. straighten
33. removal
34. windshield
35. tint film
36. filling
37. filler
38. sanding
39. sander
40. grinding
41. grinder
42. hammer
43. smooth
44. sunroof
45. roof
46. upholsterer
47. stapler
48. seat
49. mixing
50. spray gun

Page 79 CIVICS CONNECTION PROFILE

1. A
2. C
3. D
4. B

Page 82 DID YOU UNDERSTAND?

1. The introduction of electronic technology
2. Engine operation, passenger safety, and fuel economy
3. The engine control unit or engine management system controls engine functions.
4. Protecting passengers on the inside of the vehicle, designing the car structure so it can withstand the force of a collision, and preventing accidents
5. Human error causes most car accidents.
6. A blind spot is an area at the side and rear of the vehicle that cannot be seen in the car's mirrors.
7. The system monitors the driver's steering, the position and movement of the vehicle in the lane, and the driver's face and eyes.
8. Another name for a self-driving car is autonomous vehicle.
9. Consumers want to buy fuel-efficient cars when the price of gas is high, and they don't care about fuel efficiency when the price of gas is low.
10. They have a limited driving range.
11. A hybrid vehicle has an electric motor and a gasoline engine.
12. High-tech dashboards contain displays of vehicle systems and incorporate other functions, including audio, communications, entertainment, and maps. Some can connect with apps on mobile phones.

Page 83 READING COMPREHENSION

1. B
2. C
3. D
4. A
5. D
6. C
7. B
8. A
9. A
10. B

Page 84 ACADEMIC VOCABULARY

1. B
2. D
3. A
4. C
5. B
6. C
7. A
8. D
9. B
10. D
11. C
12. A
13. C
14. B

Page 84 UNIT 8 LISTENING

PART A:
Practice: B
1. A
2. C
3. A
4. A
5. B

PART B:
Practice: B
1. C
2. B
3. A
4. C
5. B

UNIT 9

Page 85 CAREER VOCABULARY

1. nursing
2. taking
3. checking
4. changing
5. bed
6. medication
7. ventilator
8. oxygen
9. dietetic
10. certified
11. orderly
12. gloves
13. sanitizing
14. measuring
15. discussing
16. monitor
17. ambulance
18. emergency
19. transporting
20. gurney
21. entrance
22. surgical
23. setting up
24. surgeon
25. transport
26. wheelchair
27. therapist
28. perform
29. ball
30. weights
31. aide
32. belt
33. prepares
34. reports
35. status
36. evaluate
37. nurse
38. vital
39. homemaker
40. sanitize
41. walker
42. shops
43. organizes
44. activities
45. safety
46. raised
47. portable
48. ramp

Page 87 ON-THE-JOB INSTRUCTIONS

1. B
2. A
3. C
4. D

Page 90 DID YOU UNDERSTAND?

1. The person wearing it does not have to be connected to a machine.
2. Doctors need to remove a tissue sample and conduct a biopsy to determine the presence of cancer.
3. By comparing photos of suspicious spots to a data bank of cancerous moles
4. Data from the patient is compared to information in a data bank.
5. Nanobots are tiny robots. They can be used inside the body to deliver drugs to a targeted area.
6. Immunotherapy uses the body's immune system to target and destroy cancer cells.
7. Gene editing can prevent disease by correcting genetic mutations or defects that cause certain diseases.
8. A prosthetic limb is an artificial arm or leg.
9. A surgeon in another location uses a robotic surgical assistant to do the operation.
10. Ultraviolet light inactivates bacteria and kills pathogens.
11. Scientists create tissue and organs in a laboratory using a patient's own stem cells.
12. Surgical glue holds incisions together.

Page 91 READING COMPREHENSION

1. B
2. C
3. D
4. A
5. C
6. D
7. B
8. C
9. A
10. B

Page 92 ACADEMIC VOCABULARY

1. B
2. D
3. A
4. B
5. C
6. B
7. D
8. A
9. C
10. A
11. B
12. D
13. C
14. A

Page 92 UNIT 9 LISTENING

PART A:
Practice: A
1. B
2. C
3. B
4. A
5. C

PART B:
Practice: B
1. B
2. A
3. C
4. A
5. B

UNIT 10

Page 93 CAREER VOCABULARY

1. receptionist	28. assisting
2. checking in	29. lab
3. scheduling	30. making
4. retrieving	31. imaging
5. transcriptionist	32. radiology
6. transcriber	33. radiologist
7. transcribing	34. reading
8. coder	35. injecting
9. coding	36. preparing
10. diagnoses	37. MRI
11. clinical	38. phlebotomy
12. measuring	39. phlebotomists
13. escorting	40. drawing
14. collecting	41. analyzed
15. blood	42. optometry
16. record	43. dilating
17. taking	44. optometrist
18. giving	45. optical
19. suturing	46. grinding
20. needle	47. display
21. technician	48. optician
22. assistant	49. adjusting
23. assisting	50. pharmacy
24. dental	51. pharmacist
25. hygienist	52. filling
26. cleaning	53. giving
27. taking	

Page 95 CIVICS CONNECTION PROFILE

1. D	3. A
2. C	4. C

Page 98 DID YOU UNDERSTAND?

1. Health informatics is a field in health care that involves storing patients' health-care information electronically and making it accessible to health-care providers for the purpose of improving collaboration, efficiency, cost-effectiveness, and results for patients.
2. It is important for health-care data to be stored in electronic format so that it can be shared in a data exchange system.
3. Interoperability means that different data systems can communicate with each other and exchange information.
4. They work for hospitals, large health-care organizations, nursing care facilities, dental practices, community clinics, public health offices, and insurance companies.
5. Most jobs in health informatics require skills in information technology, data management, computer systems, and in software related to these areas.
6. A medical transcriptionist listens to voice recordings made by doctors and other health-care workers and writes them as reports that can be entered in digital data banks.
7. Coding provides a standardized method of documenting health-care information and is an efficient way of analyzing and handling the massive amounts of health-care data being collected.
8. It is used in documenting health insurance claims, building databases, and maintaining patients' medical histories.
9. Nursing informatics specialist
10. The use of technology in health care settings

Page 99 READING COMPREHENSION

1. B	5. B	9. B
2. C	6. B	10. D
3. D	7. D	
4. C	8. C	

Page 100 ACADEMIC VOCABULARY

1. C	6. C	11. B
2. B	7. B	12. C
3. A	8. A	13. D
4. D	9. D	14. C
5. B	10. A	

Page 100 UNIT 10 LISTENING

PART A:	PART B:
Practice: B	*Practice:* C
1. A	1. A
2. B	2. B
3. A	3. C
4. B	4. B
5. A	5. A

UNIT 11

Page 101 CAREER VOCABULARY

1. operators
2. chasing
3. apprehending
4. frisking
5. handcuff
6. traffic
7. control
8. parking
9. ticketing
10. collecting
11. paramedic
12. victim
13. detective
14. witnesses
15. booking
16. fingerprinting
17. holding
18. interview
19. forensics
20. testing
21. firefighters
22. gear
23. directing
24. entering
25. rescuing
26. escorting
27. defending
28. corrections
29. searching
30. contraband
31. parole
32. parolee
33. probation
34. probationer
35. screeners
36. checking
37. luggage
38. images
39. confiscating
40. detectors
41. searches
42. guards
43. watching
44. badge
45. locker
46. asset
47. apprehending
48. watchman
49. patrolling

Page 103 ON-THE-JOB INSTRUCTIONS

1. B
2. D
3. A
4. C

Page 107 DID YOU UNDERSTAND?

1. Biometrics is the unique physical characteristics every individual possesses.
2. Fingerprints, facial features, eyes, voice, DNA, and behavior
3. Each person's fingerprints are unique––they are different from everyone else's fingerprints.
4. Numeric codes created from the fingerprints are stored in a data bank and compared.
5. A capacitance scanner
6. A faceprint is created by software that analyzes the shape and position of facial features and takes measurements such as the distance between a person's eyes.
7. The iris, the sclera, and the retina
8. Voice verification is used in the banking industry to identify customers on the phone.
9. Walking, speaking, gesturing, and standing
10. DNA is the unique genetic material in every living organism. Short Tandem Repeat sequences in the DNA are analyzed to measure the number of repeating units. This information can be used to identify a person.
11. A person's biometric information could be shared with other organizations. It could be used to identify people in a peaceful protest. It could be stolen and used to access someone's bank account.
12. Fingerprint technician, fingerprint examiner, biometric examiner, forensic analyst, biometric intelligence analyst, biometric engineer

Page 108 READING COMPREHENSION

1. D
2. C
3. A
4. C
5. B
6. D
7. B
8. C
9. A
10. D

Page 109 ACADEMIC VOCABULARY

1. B
2. C
3. A
4. D
5. B
6. C
7. A
8. C
9. D
10. A
11. C
12. D
13. B
14. A

Page 109 UNIT 11 LISTENING

PART A:
Practice: B
1. A
2. C
3. B
4. B
5. A

PART B:
Practice: B
1. B
2. C
3. C
4. B
5. A

ANSWER KEY

UNIT 12

Page 111 CAREER VOCABULARY

1. greeting
2. information
3. establish
4. explaining
5. auto loan
6. application
7. officer
8. standing
9. teller
10. windows
11. check
12. withdrawal
13. printer
14. counting
15. checking
16. handling
17. bag
18. reconciling
19. drive-through
20. vault
21. accessing
22. agency
23. obtaining
24. reviewing
25. center
26. selling
27. associates
28. processing
29. examiner
30. appraiser
31. damage
32. video
33. property
34. investigates
35. activating
36. handling
37. verifying
38. calling
39. collecting
40. tax
41. preparing
42. returns

Page 113 CIVICS CONNECTION PROFILE

1. C
2. D
3. A
4. B

Page 117 DID YOU UNDERSTAND?

1. Savings accounts and checking accounts
2. Borrowers pay interest on loans, and banks pay interest on savings accounts.
3. Fees and requirements are different at different banks.
4. Banks can charge a fee if the balance is too low. They can charge a penalty fee if the account does not have enough money to make a payment. They can charge a fee to use an ATM at another bank.
5. Money for a debit card purchase is withdrawn directly from the depositor's account. In a credit card purchase, the bank pays the seller and collects money from the card holder later.
6. A finance charge is interest on an unpaid amount of money.
7. The period of time that the borrower has to pay back the loan
8. Payday loans charge a very high fee. People who cannot pay back the loan may have to get another loan to repay the first one and will pay a lot of fees.
9. The borrower's job and income, and whether the person has other loans or bills; also, the person's credit score

10. In a fixed-rate mortgage the interest rate will not change. In an adjustable-rate mortgage the rate might increase, along with the borrower's monthly payment amount.
11. Compounding is a means of calculating interest not just on the principal amount of money in the account, but interest on previously earned interest.
12. An investment account makes money as the value of the investments increases.

Page 118 CAN YOU FIGURE IT OUT?

1. $3.00 x .03 = $0.09 back per gallon
   $3.00 - $0.09 = **$2.91 per gallon cost**
2. (a) Fee: $7,200 x .03 = **$216**
   (b) $7,200 ÷ 18 = **$400**
3. $4,400 – $220 = $4,180
   $4,180 x .28 = **$1,170.40**
4. Yes. Mortgage insurance is required if the down payment is less than 20% of the purchase price of the home. Their down payment is 18.2%.
   [$50,000 ÷ $275,000 = 0.182]
5. $469,482.60 – $250,000 = **$219,482.60**
6. $10,000 x .03 x 5 = **$1,500**

Page 119 READING COMPREHENSION

1. B
2. A
3. D
4. C
5. A
6. D
7. A
8. D
9. C
10. B

Page 120 ACADEMIC VOCABULARY

1. B
2. C
3. D
4. B
5. A
6. C
7. A
8. C
9. D
10. B
11. C
12. A
13. D
14. A

Page 120 UNIT 12 LISTENING

PART A:
Practice: A
1. B
2. A
3. C
4. B
5. A

PART B:
Practice: C
1. A
2. B
3. C
4. A
5. C

UNIT 13

Page 121 CAREER VOCABULARY

1. reception
2. client
3. receptionist
4. sign in
5. handling
6. switchboard
7. signing
8. delivery
9. setting up
10. conference
11. assigning
12. reviewing
13. applications
14. interviewing
15. applicant
16. accounting
17. receivable
18. payable
19. payroll
20. distributing
21. secretaries
22. composing
23. spreadsheets
24. answering
25. faxing
26. shorthand
27. marketing
28. preparing
29. materials
30. updating
31. website
32. sales
33. calling
34. clients
35. mailroom
36. sorting
37. weighing
38. scale
39. postage
40. copy
41. copiers
42. repair
43. fixing
44. filing
45. file
46. supplies
47. inventory
48. taking
49. lounge

Page 123 ON-THE-JOB INSTRUCTIONS

1. C
2. B
3. A
4. D

Page 126 DID YOU UNDERSTAND?

1. Cubicles
2. Telecommuting is working at home or another location away from a company office and connecting to the office over the Internet.
3. The open office design has an open floor plan with few walls and tables where employees sit side-by-side at computers.
4. There were fewer staff members working in the office. It was cheaper for businesses. Technology allowed flexible office planning. The staff did not like cubicles because they were isolating and not conducive to communication.
5. The open office design allows personal interaction and promotes information sharing and teamwork.
6. Factories and warehouses have large open spaces.
7. A co-working space is a location where people doing different jobs work side-by-side in a shared space.
8. They feel that close contact with people working in a wide variety of fields facilitates an exchange of information and ideas and fosters creativity.
9. Many workers find that noise and distractions keep them from focusing on their work. They also don't like the lack of privacy.
10. They think that having employees all present in the same location promotes face-to-face collaboration and a sense of connection among the staff.

Page 127 READING COMPREHENSION

1. B
2. C
3. B
4. D
5. A
6. A
7. C
8. D
9. C
10. B

Page 128 ACADEMIC VOCABULARY

1. B
2. C
3. A
4. D
5. B
6. A
7. C
8. D
9. B
10. D
11. C
12. C
13. A
14. B

Page 128 UNIT 13 LISTENING

PART A:
Practice: C
1. B
2. C
3. A
4. B
5. C

PART B:
Practice: B
1. C
2. A
3. B
4. C
5. C

UNIT 14

Page 129 CAREER VOCABULARY

1. sitter
2. feeding
3. handyman
4. install
5. technician
6. repairing
7. supplies
8. cleaning
9. cleaner
10. vacuuming
11. nanny
12. giving
13. snack
14. caregiver
15. exterminator
16. insecticide
17. locksmith
18. drill
19. lock
20. walker
21. installers
22. mounting
23. tutor
24. delivery
25. coordinator
26. aide
27. assisting
28. clerk
29. accepting
30. checking out
31. supervising
32. playground
33. assistant
34. shelving
35. handler
36. sorting
37. fitness
38. aerobics
39. leading
40. child-care
41. paralegal
42. research
43. courier
44. clinic
45. veterinarian
46. director
47. make
48. driver
49. tow

Page 131 CIVICS CONNECTION PROFILE

1. A
2. C
3. C
4. D

Page 135 DID YOU UNDERSTAND?

1. An app, or application, is a computer software program that lets the person using it perform certain functions.
2. The mobile app has to fit on the small screen of a mobile phone, and functions and commands need to be operated on a touch screen.
3. Mobile apps offer an easy and convenient way for customers to connect with companies and access their services.
4. Games, messaging, social media, and business apps
5. Geolocation identifies the exact location of the phone.
6. Apps may access users' personal information and sometimes their contacts, photos, and messaging history.
7. On-demand businesses help people find and connect with providers who offer services.
8. Customers rate the work that was done for them on a scale such as one to five stars (from poor to excellent). Other customers use the ratings to help them choose service providers.
9. An app from a home improvement store uses a phone's camera to measure furnishings or spaces in the home. (or) Customers buy food on an app and can watch a delivery person enter their houses and put the food into the refrigerator. (or) Apps for fitness training connect with wearable sensors that monitor physical exercise, collect information, and send signals that transmit feedback through vibration and earphones.
10. The Internet of things refers to objects such as medical devices and household appliances that can transmit data and communicate with computers and mobile devices.
11. The user interface is how the user interacts with the app and provides input to operate it.
12. An app developer's goal is to create a clear, logical, and well-organized design that makes the app easy to operate through commands and signals from the user.

Page 136 READING COMPREHENSION

1. A
2. B
3. C
4. D
5. D
6. C
7. D
8. A
9. C
10. B

Page 137 ACADEMIC VOCABULARY

1. C
2. A
3. B
4. B
5. D
6. C
7. A
8. C
9. D
10. B
11. C
12. A
13. D
14. B

Page 137 UNIT 14 LISTENING

PART A:
Practice: B
1. C
2. B
3. C
4. A
5. B

PART B:
Practice: B
1. C
2. A
3. B
4. B
5. C

UNIT 15

Page 139 CAREER VOCABULARY

1. temp	23. designer
2. specialists	24. studio
3. greets	25. training
4. floral	26. studio
5. designing	27. clothing
6. cobbler	28. esthetician
7. baker	29. shop
8. bakery	30. copy
9. proprietor	31. copies
10. newsstand	32. sporting
11. photographer	33. packaging
12. photography	34. repairer
13. day-care	35. service
14. supervising	36. distributor
15. cooked	37. operates
16. food truck	38. selling
17. helping	39. making
18. limo	40. serving
19. chauffeur	41. grooming
20. owner	42. vendor
21. caterer	43. owner
22. service	44. changing

Page 141 ON-THE-JOB INSTRUCTIONS

1. D
2. A
3. C
4. B

Page 146 DID YOU UNDERSTAND?

1. Some people like the idea of being their own boss. Some people feel motivated to build their own business around an idea or a passion or special skills they have. Some people think that they will be able to make money. They want to bring their dream to reality through their hard work.
2. Certain kinds of service providers, such as plumbers, handymen, and babysitters, as well as businesses that exist only online
3. 20%
4. Whether there is a need for what the business intends to sell or the service it plans to provide
5. A business plan includes a detailed description of the company and its products or services, a market analysis, the strategy for marketing and sales, and a financial analysis.
6. One-time expenses and monthly expenses
7. The number of units that must be sold to cover costs
8. Raising the selling price or lowering production costs or other expenses
9. Gross profit margin = (Revenue – Cost of goods sold) ÷ Revenue
10. Net profit margin = (Revenue – Total Expenses) ÷ Revenue

Page 146 CAN YOU FIGURE IT OUT?

1. Gross total revenue: $8,400 ÷ 0.80 = **$10,500**
   Profit: 20% x $10,500 = **$2,100**
2. Percent salary increase: **25%**
   ($3.00 is 25% of $12.00)
   New estimate of monthly salary expenses: $4,000 + (.25 x $4,000) = **$5,000**
3. Materials: $5.93 ÷ $10.49 = 0.565 = **56.5%**
   Labor: $4.56 ÷ $10.49 = 0.435 = **43.5%**
4. $5.93 – $0.72 = $5.21
       $5.21 + $4.56 = $9.77
   $39.95 – $9.77 = $30.18
   $30.18 – $29.46 = $0.72
   $0.72 ÷ $29.46 = 0.024 = **2.4%**

Page 147 READING COMPREHENSION

1. D	5. A	9. D
2. B	6. D	10. B
3. B	7. C	
4. A	8. C	

Page 148 ACADEMIC VOCABULARY

1. B	6. A	11. C
2. C	7. B	12. A
3. A	8. D	13. D
4. D	9. A	14. C
5. C	10. B	

Page 148 UNIT 15 LISTENING

PART A:	PART B:
Practice: B	*Practice:* B
1. C	1. B
2. C	2. A
3. B	3. B
4. A	4. C
5. A	5. C

UNIT 16

Page 149 CAREER VOCABULARY

1. agency
2. dropping off
3. skycap
4. wheelchair
5. ticket
6. checking
7. boarding pass
8. weighed
9. screener
10. check-in
11. boarding
12. serviceperson
13. food service
14. line service
15. handler
16. flight deck
17. directing
18. demonstrating
19. overhead
20. rental
21. counter
22. shuttle
23. recording
24. valet
25. doorman
26. entrance
27. checking in
28. reviewing
29. concierge
30. bellhop
31. attendant
32. maintenance
33. housekeeping
34. inspecting
35. housekeeper
36. function
37. wall
38. planner
39. coordinator
40. setting up
41. servers
42. observing
43. operating
44. leading

Page 151 ON-THE-JOB INSTRUCTIONS

1. B
2. C
3. A
4. D

Page 152 CIVICS CONNECTION PROFILE

1. B
2. C
3. D
4. A

Page 156 DID YOU UNDERSTAND?

1. Travel agencies have lost business in recent years because most people now make travel bookings by themselves on the Internet.
2. Prices of room options, pictures, descriptions of the hotel and its services, maps, and reviews
3. Property owners list their apartments or houses with the rental company, and travelers register with the company and search the company's website for rentals at their travel destinations.
4. Fewer travelers are staying in hotels.
5. New wing designs and advanced, lightweight materials such as carbon fiber are making airplanes more fuel-efficient. Also, jet engines are achieving greater fuel economy.
6. Biometric technology is being used at passenger check-in, baggage drops, immigration checkpoints, and boarding areas.
7. Beacons transmit signals to travelers' phone apps.
8. Maglev trains are raised up by a magnetic force and are propelled forward by a flow of electric current in the rails.
9. Ridesharing businesses
10. Guests at some hotels can use apps on their mobile phones to check in, manage their booking, enter their rooms, control the room temperature and lighting, and access hotel services and information.
11. They can use it to track where guests are and what facilities they use.
12. In marketing, to give potential guests virtual reality walking tours through hotels and their facilities; to help hotel guests view local neighborhoods and attractions to plan excursions

Page 157 READING COMPREHENSION

1. C
2. D
3. B
4. C
5. D
6. A
7. D
8. B
9. C
10. B

Page 158 ACADEMIC VOCABULARY

1. C
2. B
3. A
4. D
5. B
6. D
7. A
8. C
9. A
10. C
11. B
12. D
13. B
14. A

Page 158 UNIT 16 LISTENING

PART A:
Practice: C
1. A
2. B
3. C
4. B
5. A

PART B:
Practice: B
1. B
2. A
3. C
4. B
5. C

UNIT 17

Page 159 CAREER VOCABULARY

1. desktop
2. manuscript
3. illustrator
4. designer
5. technician
6. printing
7. binding
8. art
9. creative
10. creating
11. writing
12. presentation
13. reporter
14. photojournalist
15. assignment
16. stories
17. editing
18. columnist
19. producer
20. digital
21. studio
22. operator
23. news
24. desk
25. meteorologist
26. weather
27. production
28. giving
29. directing
30. switching
31. monitoring
32. field
33. report
34. camera
35. engineering
36. broadcaster
37. booth
38. technician
39. musicians
40. hooking up
41. vocal
42. recording
43. session
44. script
45. evaluating
46. casting
47. auditioning
48. soundstage
49. director
50. grip
51. dresser
52. gaffer
53. operator
54. operating
55. clapper
56. boom
57. cables
58. prop
59. cart
60. changes
61. updating
62. editor
63. software
64. mixer
65. mix
66. Foley
67. creating
68. carpenter
69. painter
70. scenery
71. lighting
72. gels
73. marking
74. tape
75. equipment
76. rehearsing
77. choreographer
78. routine
79. architectural
80. building
81. drafting
82. sculptor
83. sculpture
84. artist
85. artist's
86. glassblower
87. ceramic
88. pottery
89. fashion
90. pattern
91. photographer
92. photographs
93. selecting

Page 163 ON-THE-JOB INSTRUCTIONS

1. D
2. C
3. B
4. D
5. C
6. A

Page 168 DID YOU UNDERSTAND?

1. It is used to do the editing, formatting, and layout of text and graphics in producing documents for publication.
2. Logos, advertisements, brochures, documents, product labels, and packaging
3. Many people have stopped buying print editions of newspapers and magazines. As a result, many newspaper companies have lost money and have been forced to reduce their staffing.
4. Television is sent to antennas on TV sets, delivered through cables, transmitted by satellites, and distributed over the Internet.
5. Augmented reality is a technology in television that allows special visual effects to be added to or superimposed onto real images.
6. Smart TVs have a built-in Internet connection and interactive features.
7. Podcasting offers stored digital audio files that listeners download from websites and play on computers, mobile phones, or other devices.
8. Computer software for digital music production, and the Internet
9. Computer-generated imagery, 3-D graphics, computer animation, and motion capture
10. A video is projected at the back of a stage set to show images behind the actors.
11. Architects use computer-aided design software to create architectural drawings of buildings. Building information modeling allows for pre-visualization of structures and creates 3-D models.
12. *Technology in art* refers to how technology is used in making art. *Technology as art refers* to technology as part of the art itself.

Page 169 READING COMPREHENSION

1. C
2. D
3. B
4. C
5. A
6. A
7. C
8. C
9. D
10. B

Page 170 ACADEMIC VOCABULARY

1. B
2. A
3. D
4. C
5. A
6. C
7. B
8. C
9. D
10. B
11. D
12. B
13. A
14. C

Page 170 UNIT 17 LISTENING

PART A:
Practice: C
1. B
2. C
3. B
4. A
5. C

PART B:
Practice: C
1. A
2. B
3. B
4. A
5. C

UNIT 18

Page 171 CAREER VOCABULARY

1. lineperson
2. utility
3. set
4. hard hat
5. climbers
6. climbing
7. bucket
8. attaching
9. trench
10. trencher
11. dig
12. pulling
13. laying down
14. backfilling
15. shovel
16. cell tower
17. installers
18. modem
19. lines
20. dropping
21. programming
22. smoke
23. hooking
24. technician
25. installers
26. installing
27. attaching
28. receiver
29. outlet
30. coding
31. handset
32. screwing
33. lines
34. software
35. office
36. analyst
37. pulling
38. call center
39. creating
40. customer
41. replying
42. typing
43. reading
44. offering

Page 173 CIVICS CONNECTION PROFILE

1. C
2. D
3. B
4. A

Page 178 DID YOU UNDERSTAND?

1. A telescope
2. The telegraph
3. They were sent through undersea cables.
4. A telephone exchange is a switchboard that connects phone lines to each other.
5. SMS – short message service
6. Sending out signals that transmit programs
7. They converted images into electrical signals and transmitted them through the air using radio waves.
8. Television programming is sent through the air to antennas, through cables, by satellites, and through the Internet.
9. Written communications were sent by teleprinters through Telex systems. Documents were sent by fax.
10. Optical fiber cables can carry larger flows of data communications traffic at higher speeds.

Page 179 READING COMPREHENSION

1. C
2. B
3. C
4. A
5. B
6. D
7. C
8. B
9. A
10. D

Page 180 ACADEMIC VOCABULARY

1. C
2. A
3. B
4. D
5. B
6. D
7. C
8. A
9. A
10. C
11. D
12. B
13. A
14. C

Page 180 UNIT 18 LISTENING

PART A:
Practice: B
1. C
2. B
3. A
4. C
5. C

PART B:
Practice: A
1. B
2. B
3. A
4. C
5. C

UNIT 19

Page 181 CAREER VOCABULARY

1. reviewing
2. schematic
3. bundling
4. cables
5. hard
6. punching
7. router
8. adapter
9. box
10. drive
11. attaching
12. technical
13. loading
14. specialist
15. virus
16. security
17. training
18. scanning
19. entering
20. text
21. helping
22. test
23. order
24. recommending
25. help
26. answering
27. chat
28. repair
29. technicians
30. disk
31. screen
32. measuring
33. room
34. repairing
35. programmers
36. code
37. software
38. studio
39. designing
40. UI artists
41. composing
42. develop
43. storyboards
44. tester
45. writing

Page 183 ON-THE-JOB INSTRUCTIONS

1. C
2. B
3. C
4. A

Page 188 DID YOU UNDERSTAND?

1. Hardware refers to computers and related devices and equipment, and software refers to the programming that puts computers to work to perform functions.
2. With cloud computing, computer-related services such as software and storage space are accessed over the Internet rather than from a company's own computer systems.
3. A local area network (or LAN) is a system of interconnected computers, printers, servers, and other equipment.
4. Network engineers
5. They usually call tech support specialists.
6. Systems analysts design information systems that help businesses and organizations operate more effectively. They assess and analyze clients' needs and devise a plan for using information technology to solve business problems.
7. Databases and spreadsheets
8. Viruses, malware, and hacking
9. Printers, scanners, and external hard drives
10. The user interface is how the user operates and controls an application on a device.
11. Experience in working with computers and using different kinds of software programs
12. Data entry workers, computer installers, and assistant computer technicians

Page 189 READING COMPREHENSION

1. C
2. D
3. A
4. B
5. D
6. B
7. C
8. D
9. A
10. C

Page 190 ACADEMIC VOCABULARY

1. B
2. C
3. D
4. A
5. B
6. A
7. C
8. D
9. A
10. C
11. A
12. D
13. B
14. C

Page 190 UNIT 19 LISTENING

PART A:
Practice: B
1. C
2. B
3. B
4. C
5. A

PART B:
Practice: A
1. B
2. C
3. A
4. B
5. B

UNIT 20

Page 191 CAREER VOCABULARY

1. wind
2. technicians
3. tightening
4. attaching
5. boom
6. assembly
7. assemblers
8. quality
9. inspecting
10. screwing
11. electrician
12. putting down
13. digging
14. push
15. hooking
16. operator
17. suctioning
18. tank
19. debris
20. testing
21. image
22. camera
23. test
24. setting
25. reviewing
26. blowing
27. weather
28. replacing
29. installing
30. hanging
31. changing
32. drilling
33. filling
34. holes
35. converting
36. planting
37. disposing
38. dumpster
39. recovery
40. driver
41. dumping
42. recyclables
43. sorting
44. baling
45. baler
46. foresters
47. planting
48. conservation
49. laborers
50. produce
51. loading
52. test
53. environmental
54. collecting
55. samples
56. tagging
57. quality
58. pollution
59. reading
60. output
61. inspecting
62. vehicle
63. positioning
64. charging
65. hoisting
66. donor
67. gauges
68. batteries
69. connecting
70. operator
71. operating
72. bolting
73. attaching
74. painting
75. installing
76. stenciling
77. installers
78. farm
79. switchgrass
80. delivering
81. biorefinery
82. driver
83. customers
84. industrial
85. brainstorming

Page 194 CIVICS CONNECTION PROFILE

1. D
2. B
3. C
4. B

Page 200 DID YOU UNDERSTAND?

1. Energy, building construction, transportation, waste management, land and water management, air quality, human well-being, and social equity
2. Solar energy, wind energy, geothermal energy, and hydroelectric power
3. Solar farms and wind farms are large installations of solar panels and wind turbines that generate electricity.
4. Biofuel is a type of fuel that is derived from plant materials. Used cooking oil can also be converted into a type of biofuel.
5. Conservation lowers energy users' expenses, saves natural resources, and reduces pollution.
6. Reduce, reuse, and recycle
7. Trees play an important role in the global ecosystem by taking in carbon dioxide, producing oxygen, preventing erosion, and protecting biodiversity.
8. Hybrid vehicles have both a gasoline engine and an electric motor. Electric vehicles have only an electric motor.
9. They have offered financial incentives, such as rebates.
10. They learn through on-the-job training or by taking courses in technical schools.
11. Waste management and recycling workers, and agricultural workers
12. Environmental and conservation scientists and specialists, chemists and chemical technicians, hydrologists, and microbiologists

Page 201 READING COMPREHENSION

1. C
2. A
3. D
4. C
5. B
6. A
7. D
8. B
9. C
10. D

Page 202 ACADEMIC VOCABULARY

1. B
2. D
3. A
4. D
5. B
6. C
7. D
8. B
9. A
10. C
11. D
12. B
13. A
14. C

Page 202 UNIT 20 LISTENING

PART A:
Practice: B
1. A
2. B
3. A
4. C
5. C

PART B:
Practice: C
1. A
2. A
3. B
4. B
5. C